# Above the River
The Complete Poems

James Wright

With an Introduction
by Donald Hall

A Wesleyan University Press Edition

Farrar, Straus and Giroux
and
University Press of New England

Eighth printing, 2000

Library of Congress Cataloging-in-Publication Data
Wright, James Arlington.
    Above the river : the complete poems and selected prose / James Wright.
    I. Title.   II. Series.
    PS3573.R5358A63   1990   811'.54—dc20   89-16538 CIP

In memory of James Wright's parents,
Jessie and Dudley Wright

In honor of his sons,
Franz and Marshall

And you, with no shadow now, sleep and be;
deep peace to your bones . . .
  It is final now,
sleep your untroubled and true dream.

—*Antonio Machado,* Times Alone,
translated by Robert Bly, 1983

And still in my dreams I sway like one fainting strand
Of spiderweb, glittering and vanishing and frail
Above the river.

—*James Wright, "On a Phrase from*
Southern Ohio"

Contents

Saint Judas (1959)

Some Translations (from *Collected Poems*, 1971, and new translations)

The Branch Will Not Break (1963)

Shall We Gather at the River (1968)

New Poems (from *Collected Poems*, 1971)

Two Citizens (1973)

Selected Prose Pieces

To a Blossoming Pear Tree (1977)

This Journey (1982)

Acknowledgments

I wish to thank Roland Flint, Jonathan Galassi, and Roger Hecht for encouragement and good advice and Kay and Gibbons Ruark for help and criticism.

I also wish to thank Peter Stitt, who has given so much of himself in so many ways to James' work in general and to this book in particular.

Anne Wright

A Note on the Order of *Above the River*

When James Wright assembled his 1971 *Collected Poems*, he placed a group of translations after *Saint Judas*. Kevin Stein, in his book *James Wright: The Poetry of a Grown Man*, explains the order of this arrangement as a way to "neatly separate the formal poems of *The Green Wall* and *Saint Judas* from the experimental poems of *The Branch Will Not Break*" and later books.

Most of the translations were done after the publication of *Saint Judas*, in the days when James was a frequent visitor to Robert and Carol Bly's farm in Madison, Minnesota, and became as devoted as Robert to the work of Neruda, Lorca, Vallejo, and Jiménez, among others.

The selected translations in *Above the River* are placed as they were in *Collected Poems* and include later translations of Hesse and Katz.

After *Two Citizens*, James began to work on prose pieces and published a series of them in the 1976 chapbook *Moments of the Italian Summer*. Seven of these pieces appear in revised form in *To a Blossoming Pear Tree*. Another group of prose pieces, written in 1979, came out in *The Summers of James and Annie Wright* (1981). These two chapbooks were combined in the later publication *The Shape of Light*. The prose pieces in *Above the River* are placed after *Two Citizens*, the point in his career when he first wrote in this form.

The translations served as a bridge between formal and experimental poetry. The prose pieces served as a bridge also, one which led from the dark of Ohio to the light of Italy and France.

Anne Wright

Lament for a Maker

Donald Hall

I that in heill wes and gladnes,
Am trublit now with gret seiknes,
And feblit with infermite;
  Timor mortis conturbat me.

He hes done petuously devour,
The noble Chaucer, of makaris flour,
The Monk of Bery, and Gower, all thre;
  Timor mortis conturbat me.

He has Blind Hary and Sandy Traill
Slaine with his schour of mortall haill,
Quhilk Patrik Johnestoun myght nocht fle;
  Timor mortis conturbat me.

In Dumfermelyne he hes done roune
With Maister Robert Henrisoun;
Schir Johne the Ros enbrast hes he;
  Timor mortis conturbat me.

from William Dunbar,
"Lament for the Makaris"

It is a mystery, how poetry will thrive in an age or a country, then fade out only to appear elsewhere. Between Chaucer (dead in 1400) and Wyatt (born in 1503), poetry was sparse in England and copious north of the border in William Dunbar's Edinburgh. When he lamented the dead and dying poets, William Dunbar listed "The noble Chaucer, of poets the flower, / The Monk of Bury, and Gower, all three. / *Timor mortis conturbat me.*" (The Latin means "The fear of death confounds me.") Gower died just after Chaucer, and Lydgate in a Bury St. Edmunds monastery half a century later. Mostly, Dunbar mourns the Scots makers, naming twenty-five poets in twenty-five stanzas; of most of them, not a line survives. When Dunbar complains that "Good Master Walter Kennedy / At point of death lies verily. / Great ruth it were that it should be. / *Timor mortis conturbat me,*" he must speak of a dear friend, for "The Flyting and Dunbar and Kennedie" survives; a flyting is a poets' fight or slanging match. Dunbar also mourns the genius of his age and his country, author of *The Testament of Cresseid*, which is the great work between Chaucer and Shakespeare: "In Dunfermline he has whispered/ With Master Robert Henryson. . . ."

Dunbar's *Lament* is the universal elegy for the dead poets, and a poem I grew up with. James Wright loved it, and recited Dunbar's poem in my hearing half a dozen times, in what passed with us for a Scots accent. I remember his eyes flashing over the names: "Blind Harry," "Sandy Traill," "Sir Mungo Lockhart of the Lee." Jim died ten years ago, and many of his friends have lamented this maker; has any American poet been the subject of so many elegies?

He was born (Martins Ferry, Ohio) on 13 December 1927, and belonged like Dunbar to a numerous and varied generation of poets*—makers of James Wright's moment; and the poetic community of friends and rivals was central to his life and work. We were highly aware of each other. At Harvard College I argued poetry with Bly, Rich, Creeley, O'Hara, Ashbery, and Koch; at the same time Merwin and Kinnell read Yeats at Princeton: Louis Simpson returned from the war to the Columbia of Allen Ginsberg, where the young would soon include Hollander and Howard. Wright studied under John Crowe Ransom at Kenyon College, overlapping with Robert Mezey and the novelist E. L. Doctorow. Philip Whalen and Gary Snyder roomed together at Reed College. A little later, Iowa collected Philip Levine, Donald Justice, and W. D. Snodgrass. Never had so many American poets crowded into one decade to be born. Then in 1966 Frank O'Hara died of injuries suffered in an accident. Paul Blackburn died in 1971, Anne Sexton in 1974, L. E. Sissman in 1976, James Wright in 1980, Richard Hugo in 1982, and John Logan in 1987. *Timor mortis* . . .

* Also born in 1927 were John Ashbery, Galway Kinnell, and W. S. Merwin. Maybe 1926 was the annus mirabilis—Robert Bly, Robert Creeley, Allen Ginsberg, James Merrill, Frank O'Hara, A. R. Ammons, W. D. Snodgrass, David Wagoner, Paul Blackburn—unless it was 1923: Denise Levertov, James Dickey, Richard Hugo, James Schuyler, Anthony Hecht, Alan Dugan, John Logan, Louis Simpson. There was also 1924: John Haines, Jane Cooper, Edgar Bowers; 1925: Donald Justice, Gerald Stern, Caroline Kizer, Maxine Kumin, Philip Booth, Kenneth Koch; 1928: Philip Levine, Anne Sexton, L. E. Sissman, Peter Davison, me; 1929: Adrienne Rich, X. J. Kennedy, Ed Dorn, John Hollander, Richard Howard; 1930: Gary Snyder, Gregory Corso. In 1931 came Etheridge Knight, in 1932 Sylvia Plath—but as we stray outside the decade, our numbers diminish.

All lists are invidious. But if you make your own, it will remain numerous. My list is largely male and white. Robert Hayden and Gwendolyn Brooks belong with Jarrell, Lowell, Berryman, Stafford, and Nemerov in an earlier generation. Women become numerous among poets born after the war.

Why were so many poets born in the 1920s? This generation emerged blinking into the American Century—which endured from 1945 to 1963—almost the first literary generation in American history for whom Europe was no issue. (James Wright's love for Italy and France implied no diffidence about American poetry. His love was the northerner's discovery of sun and flesh; he burrowed in the sweet meat of the Italian pear.) This generation grew up alienated adolescents in mill towns and suburbs, in California, on the great plains, in factory cities, and in Palm Beach. Like all generations of American artists, it was largely middle class—but these childhoods endured the Depression. In Wheeling, West Virginia, across the river from Ohio, James Wright's father, Dudley, worked in the Hazel-Atlas Glass factory all his life, laid off during bad times. Although Jim admired and praised his father—who never surrendered to adversity—the family lived through hardships, enduring the 1930s under threat of poverty in a succession of rented houses. Jim's whole life was compelled by his necessity to leave the blighted valley, to escape his father's fate, never to work at Hazel-Atlas Glass. In his poems, Martins Ferry and its sibling valley towns blacken with Satanic mills along the river and under the green hill.

When he graduated from high school and joined the Army at eighteen, he planned to evade the factories by means of the G.I. bill and a college education. Once he wrote me about his army paydays in Japan: "I was paid $120. on the first day of each month. And I remember walking, every single time, from the end of the payline to the Fort post office, two blocks away, and writing a money order for exactly $110 . . . sending it home to Ohio for banking. . . . At the time I thought of nothing but the Ohio Valley (i.e., death, real death to the soul) on the one side and life (escape to my own life . . .) on the other." For no one more than James Wright was literature so much the choice of life over death: Thomas Hardy and Beethoven on the one hand; on the other hand Martins Ferry and Hazel-Atlas Glass. "Life" was *art*, poetry as paradise or at least as refuge—for the free and natural expression of feeling, for delight in the wit and sensuousness of words, and for sensitivity or receptivity to the world's pleasures. At the same time, most important for James Wright, poetry expressed and enacted compassion over the world's suffering.

He was fifteen when he started to write his poems. Words in the mouth must have pleased him always; when you heard Jim tell a story, or say a poem, you felt his joy in the words. There was also for Jim the desire to make in art an alternative and improved universe. If he reviled his Ohio, he understood that Ohio made him—and Ohio remained his material. We choose exile as a vantage point; from exile we look back on the rejected, rejecting place—to make our poems out of it *and* against it. Wright's poems, alternatives to Ohio, are populated with people who never left the valley—factory workers and fullbacks, executed murderers, drunks, and down-and-outs. If some of his *maudits* derive from other milieux—from the Pacific Northwest, from Minneapolis, from New York—they live the life Jim intended to abandon by leaving the Ohio valley. Withdrawing from his desolate internal Ohio, he observed and preserved. He is like Yeats's musician in "Lapus Lazuli," privileged to observe the "tragic scene" and to make, with the skill of his "accomplished fingers," "mournful melodies."

The "mournful" began early on the fifty-two-year journey. In 1943, when he turned sixteen, Jim lost a year of high school to a nervous breakdown. There would be more breakdowns—but he struggled against wreckage (the branch did not break) and graduated from high school. When he mustered out of the Army in 1947, he entered Kenyon College—the most literary enclave in the state of Ohio, with its poet Ransom, its tradition of writer-students, and *The Kenyon Review*, which was the journal of its literary moment. Older than his classmates, he would graduate at twenty-three in January of 1952. Attending Kenyon, Jim must have felt at home for the first time in his life—among teachers like Charles Coffin and Philip Timberlake as well as Ransom; and with literary and even writerly friends among the undergraduates. At the same time, he must have felt the scholarship boy's guilt, living for the first time among people largely middle class. It could not have been easy, and his G.I. bill ran out after his junior year. Jim used his brain to keep himself at Kenyon and later to study abroad and to send himself to graduate school. When he made Phi Beta Kappa as a junior, Kenyon gave him a full scholarship for his senior year.

As an undergraduate poet, Wright wrote poems with fierce patience and dedicated haste. The undergraduate magazine *Hika* published many; then, when Wright was a senior, John Crowe Ransom printed two poems in *The Kenyon Review*: "Lonely" and "Father." The latter may be found in this volume, a strong and tender poem, which is also curious: In its dreaminess, it resembles the poetry that Wright wrote fifteen or twenty years later—and not the narrative and reasonable iambic with which "Father" surrounded itself at the time; so often, in a poet's life, today's anomaly foreshadows tomorrow's invention.

A month after graduation Jim married his high-school sweetheart, Liberty Kardules, who had become a nurse, and taught for a few months at a school in Texas. The next year they spent in Austria, Wright with a Fulbright grant to study at the University of Vienna; he worked on the poems of Georg Trakl and the stories of Theodor Storm—both of whom he translated, both of whom contributed portions to his mature work. In the same year, Liberty gave birth to their first child, Franz.

Jim and I became acquainted in the autumn of 1954 and we were friends until he died. Although our friendship was crucial to us, each of us had closer friends among our generation. There were times when we became irritated with each other, and on the whole we had bad luck in getting together, mostly connecting by letter. Like any friendship among artists, ours was partly based on rivalry. I became aware of "James Wright" as early as 1952. When I was a senior at college, an undergraduate literary magazine called *Coraddi* (from the Women's College of North Carolina; now the University of North Carolina at Greensboro) solicited work for an issue devoted to undergraduate writing everywhere. They printed a poem I sent them, and a year later mailed me the 1952 issue, which included James Wright from Kenyon College, with a poem called "Oenone to Paris . . ." It was a sonnet, pretty nifty, referring to

> Some buttons made of artificial gold,
> These ordinary pumps, and rarely sheer
> Stockings to celebrate the turning year.
> I need an aspirin. My eyes are old.

Soon, I began to see other Wright poems in visible places. I looked at work in other magazines with an acquisitive eye because I became poetry editor for the upstarting *Paris Review*, which wanted to be the magazine of a generation. One day in the autumn of 1954, I solicited poetry from James Wright and our friendship started. Jim's answering letter (with poems) came from Seattle, 2 December 1954. ("Dear Mr. Hall, Thank you very much for your extremely kind letter.") I knew of the University of Washington because Theodore Roethke taught there. By this time in the history of the American academy, poets had begun to make their livings as teachers—but they did not yet spend their lives teaching only Line Breaks 101. When Roethke taught his famous class in writing he brought old poetry into it—whereby he filled the cistern as much as he emptied it. Deciding to support himself as a teacher, Jim pursued a conventional Ph.D. in English and wrote a thesis about Charles Dickens. In his academic career, by preference, Jim taught literature rather than creative writing.

The older poet resembled the younger. Roethke came from a background more prosperous than Wright's (Otto Roethke owned a greenhouse) but from the mill town of Saginaw in Michigan; Ann Arbor had been Roethke's Kenyon. Both men were provincial, literary, and shy; both relied on comic routines to get them through social situations; both enjoyed sports, and when Jim took his Ph.D., Roethke's graduation present was a ticket to the world heavyweight championship bout of 1957 between Floyd Patterson and Pete Rademacher in Seattle. Jim and Ted attended the bout together (Jim described that fight for me, round by round, a dozen times.) And both men drank too much. Roethke was manic-depressive, delusional—a thought disorder, not merely a mood disorder—and was several times hospitalized. If James was delusional, I do not know it, but like most poets he suffered from a bipolar mood disorder. Some alcoholics start from bipolarity; they drink to relieve depression (and become more depressed) or in mania drink in order to calm down (and induce depression). In the letters we wrote to each other—sometimes multipage single-spaced letters like manic monologues—the bravado about drink was continuous.

Our letters talked *poetry* more than drink, of course. We talked about old poets—we both loved E. A. Robinson; not many did—and we talked of our friends and contemporaries. We worked over each other's things. Poets of our generation worked together, not institutionally, in workshops, but privately, as friends and rivals. I don't believe that we merely conspired at mutual promotion; we acted as if we shared a common endeavor. Competition between artists can be fierce but benign, dedicated to the art rather than to the artist, as when older athletes (sometimes) help younger ones who will succeed them. I remember a trivial gesture that may stand for the serious generosity of many people. About the time my first book came out, Jim planned to submit *The Green Wall* to the Yale Younger Poets competition. I was visiting my parents' house outside New Haven. Jim wanted me to see the manuscript—and so I offered to deliver the book to Yale University Press when I had read it. I handed his prizewinner to the receptionist.

Over the years, Jim's letters were full of Robert Bly, John Logan, Theodore Roethke, Galway Kinnell, Carolyn Kizer, Anne Sexton, Jean Valentine, Jane Cooper, Bill Merwin, Vassar Miller, Dick Hugo, and . . . In our letters we talked prosody, enthralled by iambic; most of the old poetry we loved was metrical. But we were so saturated with iambic that later we needed to jettison both meter and rhyme—virtually all of us did—in favor of other tunes and musics. In *The Green Wall* Jim shows a joyous skill in rhyme, line breaks, and caesura. His learning comes not from workshops but from love of Pope, Keats, Dunbar, Robinson, Hardy, Herrick, Marvell, and company. While he takes pleasure in being champion of the socially unacceptable, as in "A Gesture by a Lady with an Assumed Name," in the same words and without contradiction, he takes pleasure in rhyme and metrical inversion:

> Whether or not, how could she love so many,
> Then turn away to die as though for none?
> I saw the last offer a child a penny
> To creep outside and see the cops were gone.

Jim's medial inversion, third line third foot, in those days would have us slapping our thighs in glee: "Get a load of *that*!"

His iambic style perfected itself in *Saint Judas*, for instance in the sonnet that supplies the title, which ends in a classic single line of resolution; only one ictus keeps it from the almost-rare fulfillment of the iambic paradigm: "I held the man for nothing in my arms." Three-quarters of us, if we had written the poem, would have wrecked the ending, diction and rhythm both, by a dead metaphor with an extra syllable: "I cradled the man for nothing in my arms." Jim's diction was as pure as his metric was resourceful and exact.

If *Saint Judas* was the best he could attain to, in the old mode, it was also the end of it. In 1958, in July, he wrote me a letter (I'm sure similar letters went to others) in which he announced that he was through writing poems. Another poet had mildly assaulted Jim in a review of the first *New Poets* anthology, and Jim's first reaction had been thirty scurrilous epigrams and an insulting letter . . . but now he turned his violence upon himself. In this letter he spoke of "denying the darker and wilder side of myself for the sake of subsisting on mere comfort—both academic and poetic." The first issue of Robert Bly's magazine, *The Fifties*, which he read at this crucial point, arrived like a reproach. (He did not yet know Bly.) He told me: "So I quit. I have been betraying whatever was true and courageous . . . in myself and in everyone else for so long, that I am still fairly convinced that I have killed it. So I quit." In the letter he called himself "a literary operator (and one of the slickest, cleverest, most 'charming' concoctors of the do-it-yourself *New Yorker* verse among all current failures). . . ." James Wright's readers will recognize that he is about to write "At the Executed Murderer's Grave."

A day later he wrote again, admitting that "I can't quit and go straight. I'm too deep in debt to the Olympian syndicate. They'd rub me out." (This is Roethke talk, who during mania often alluded to The Mob.) Later he said, "It was my old, shriveling, iambic self that struck. . . ." He continued to write iambic as he attacked his old iambic self; he was at the same time the fox and the hounds, turned upon himself in the corrosive iambics of "At the Executed Murderer's Grave," neatly berating himself for neatness—and of course beginning to find his way out. It was a way out, not really from iambic—arrangements of softer and louder syllables are guiltless—but from associations of diction and thought with iambic.

Jim visited Ann Arbor that August, an intense moment of talk and merriment. In these years we met several times—at an MLA convention, where we both looked for work; a poetry do at Wayne State in Detroit—and I discovered the pleasures of his companionship. He liked to laugh—a good storyteller, a fine mimic. With children he was especially inventive, playing little magic tricks; children could never get enough of him. For grown-ups he had another repertoire, mostly borrowed from comedians he admired. Like Roethke he did an exemplary W. C. Fields. He had yards of Jonathan Winters by heart. One brief bit I especially admired and asked him to perform a thousand times. He stood assuming a humble, even pathetic posture—head tilted, arms akimbo—and crooned in his handsome voice, "By day, a humble butcher . . ." Then manic energy leapt into his face, he smiled broadly, his fingers clicked at his sides, and he gave a three-second impression of Bojangles, while his lit-up voice announced: ". . . by night, a *fabulous tap dancer*!" Thinking of him now, ten years after his death, I remember what Ezra Pound said about his friend Gaudier-Brzeska, killed in France in 1915: "He was the best fun in the world."

On his quick August visit, we planned that he would return with his family in the autumn, after the birth of their second child. They would come for the weekend when the University of Minnesota played Michigan in football. I would get tickets. They would drive—or Liberty would; Jim never learned to drive—for a long weekend of football and poetry. But the October visit was a disaster. The drive to Ann Arbor seemed interminable, as Liberty parked at the side of the road when she needed to nurse the baby, a new son named Marshall. Then their car broke down; they bought another, and arrived later, exhausted, with Jim intensely nervous. He talked without stopping. He quoted page after page of prose and poetry, Dunbar's *Lament* at least twice. At one point, at a cocktail party we took them to, Jim recited German poetry for twenty minutes to an astonished assembly of mathematicians.

Jim and I sat at the football game for perhaps four hours, getting there early to watch the warm-ups, but I'm not sure I spoke at all. Jim talked about free verse, iambic, wit, images, Dickens, Dickinson, Pope, James Stephens, football, Robert Bly, James Dickey, Ted Roethke, boxing, Liberty, Franz, Marshall, basketball . . . His voice was like the sea, when you stand at the rail of a ship watching the waves all day.

Maybe that night, maybe the next, Jim's good-natured and affable—if unstoppable—tirade suddenly turned black. Late at night he decided that *they* wanted him to go back to the mills. He made a speech about how he would never go back to the mills, no matter how much *they* tried to push him there; he had fought *them* all his life. And he stormed upstairs to bed. In the morning, he walked outside in the frost of early morning without eating or speaking. He leaned against an old oak tree and smoked Pall Malls for two hours, while Liberty ate breakfast, fed Franz and Marshall, packed, and loaded the car. Continually I slipped outside to try to talk with him; he mumbled and shook his head. He did not seem angry; he would not talk now, but he would write a letter. It was cold, and the white of cigarette smoke mingled with the white of his breath. Feeling the cold, I would go back inside to warm up; then I would look out the window, see him there alone, and go back. When Liberty finished her chores they drove away.

A few days later, letters began arriving from Minneapolis. He remembered seeing me "forlorn and troubled in the wet leaves, both of you seeing us vanish. . . ." In this letter he told me about saving his soldier's pay while he was in Japan. "I knew musicians and possible poets and even ordinary lovable human beings, and I saw them with brutal regularity going into Wheeling Steel, turning into stupid and resigned slobs with beer bellies and glassy eyes." Every now and then, he said, this madness flashed over him.

Although Jim had been drinking over the weekend, the problem did not begin with alcohol. When he returned to Minneapolis, the considerable torment of his life turned worse. He entered a mental hospital, where he received electroshock for depression. In the new year, he and Liberty separated for the first time. They went back together, then parted again. Psychotherapy helped; it didn't cure. And—I suppose especially when separated from his family—the drinking turned worse. Once in a letter, 23 April 1959, he told me about attempting suicide by walking into the water near Seattle. His letters, like his poems, gave testimony to the day-to-day struggle of his life, which lasted—with restful respites, especially after his marriage to Annie—until he died, a struggle to live and make art, a struggle that the branch should not break.

This book is testimony that the branch did not break. However beaten he was—some poems record defeat—James Wright was resilient. Even in the letters of 1959, the struggle to make poetry continued; it was identical to the struggle to live at all. Working away from iambic, which for a while seemed glib or complacent, he asked me for instructions in making syllabics, which had been my own first alternative metric. Other poets excited him. He wrote enthusiastically about John Logan, Robert Bly, Vassar Miller, and Geoffrey Hill, whom he had come greatly to admire. Then there were terrible setbacks; on 3 September 1960, a woeful letter: "I really am sick this time."

In July of 1961, my family and I spent a week at the Blys' Minnesota farmhouse, visiting at the same time as the Simpsons with their two children. Jim was living alone, teaching summer school; he came out to join us for two weekends. From April on, his letters dwelt upon this possible getting-together, and in June he was writing agendas, numbered paragraphs of questions that we must take up with Robert when we were all together. He conspired with me against Robert because of Robert's perceived dogmatism about meter. (In his formal ambivalence, Jim was always sneaking off to write an iambic poem, showing it to me, and asking me not to tell Robert.) Out at the farm, Robert and Carol, Louis and Dorothy, and my wife and I lived an ebullient holiday, competing in badminton and swimming as well as in poetry and jokes. Jim came out from Minneapolis on the bus, a three- or four-hour ride. He was sad and lonesome, living a little to the side of the rest of us: because he was divorced, without his children, and drinking too much.

A couple of years earlier, Jim and I added another facet to our relationship. I became a poetry editor at Wesleyan University Press, which took Jim's second book for the beginning poetry series. When we accepted Jim's book, I became his editor, which meant that I gave him my opinions—as we had always done—and also gave him advice from the other editors. After *Saint Judas*, James submitted a collection of poems called *Amenities of Stone* that included old-style James Wright iambic poems as well as early surreal free verse. It was perhaps confused but it was powerful: Wesleyan's editors were unanimous in accepting it. Then, just after the Minnesota gathering, on 29 July 1961—with the book already scheduled for publication—Jim withdrew it. If the book had been published it would have shown Wright's transformation in process, almost in slow motion. Because he withdrew *Amenities*, James Wright's metamorphosis seemed shocking when *The Branch Will Not Break* came out in 1963. The change startled his old readers, and many reviewers disparaged it, but it gathered its own constituency, who preferred it to the earlier work. "The cool master of iambic," said the critical caricature, "sheds his costume and walks naked." It is difficult for people, even today, to love both sides of James Wright—Neruda and Robinson, Trakl and Hardy.

The critical caricature is distorted not only because it is a stick figure but also because of an invalid image: Nakedness is always a new costume. The many sides of James Wright are not nearly so discontinuous as they first appear to be. If we ignore either the discontinuities or the continuities, we ignore matters large in his poems. For my taste, there are three high moments in Wright's work. First came the height of traditional sound and structure, already handsome in *The Green Wall*, which rose to its zenith in a few poems of *Saint Judas*—including "At the Executed Murderer's Grave," which derides its own tradition and achievement. The second height was *The Branch Will Not Break*, a putative opposite, where simple images embody almost unbearable tension between deathward suffering and the desire to endure, to love, and to accept the world's pleasures. At best, the two come together, as in a famous enjambment: "I would break / into blossom." Sometimes the insistence on blossoming is contradicted (or even mocked) by clear evidence of breakage. Always the battle (conflict makes energy) takes place before us in these poems—as it takes place within us.

The third height, and best poetry of all, turns up in the last two books, but before he could reach this final eminence his work went through a lesser moment. Fine poems in *Shall We Gather at the River* mingle with slackness, which increases in the new poems of *Collected Poems* and in *Two Citizens*. An introduction to James Wright's complete poems is no place for dwelling on failures—all poets fail at times—but let me suggest that in his slack patches, Wright abandons oxymoronic images often to rely on a storyteller's voice—which rambles, and, proclaiming certainty, seems uncertain. Sometimes when he fails, he insists not on beauty (which is conflicted) but on prettiness (which isn't) against his own ugly experience.

At his best, from *The Green Wall* through the posthumous *This Journey*, Wright gathers true feeling—often feeling for the oppressed (internal and external)—into lines of great sensuous beauty; at his best, he had the best ear of his generation. *To a Blossoming Pear Tree* and *This Journey* include the highest of his poetic ranges. The stance of the storyteller or performer, awkward in *Two Citizens*, energizes the page in prose poems like "The Wheeling Gospel Tabernacle." Better still, in a poem like "The Best Days," or even more "The Last Days," everything comes together—vision and vowel, capacity for suffering and capacity for joy, even Ohio and Italy. Each of these poems begins with the epigraph from Virgil, *optima dies prima fugit*, and by the end of "The Last Days," when the poet rescues a bee drowning in the sweet juice of a pear, James Wright has found his Ohio in Virgil's Mantua:

> The best days are the first
> To flee, sang the lovely
> Musician born in this town
> So like my own.
> I let the bee go
> Among the gasworks at the edge of Mantua.

Of course Jim's Italy is not merely the peninsula, but also a literary tradition: Italy of Catullus, Virgil, Ovid; Italy of all the frosty Protestants looking for sun, crabbed northerners who come south and like the bee in the pear almost die in the ecstasy of southern flesh. The Germans made their sensuous pilgrimage, notably Jim's beloved Goethe with his *Italian Journey*; and of course there were the great poets of our language: Keats, Shelley, Landor, Browning, Pound; American novelists discovered an Italy also: Henry James, Edith Wharton, and William Dean Howells—the *other* literary figure born in Martins Ferry, Ohio.

In haste to arrive at Italy, I have bypassed some miseries. In 1963, the year he published *The Branch Will Not Break*, James Wright was fired by the University of Minnesota. Among the professors voting to deny him tenure was his friend the poet Allen Tate, which was hurtful. Jim missed classes because he got drunk; Jim got into barroom fistfights and spent time in the drunktank. It may be noted that Professor Berryman of the University of Minnesota, not renowned for sobriety, taught not in the Department of English but in the Department of Humanities.

Jim taught two years at Macalester College in St. Paul, then won a Guggenheim fellowship. In 1966, he took a good job at Hunter College in New York, where he remained until his death. Soon after he moved to New York, he met Edith Ann Runk—Annie—and they were married in Riverside Church in April of 1967. Although one cannot say that they lived happily ever after—Jim returned to the hospital with breakdowns—his fortunes in large part reversed themselves. Annie was tender, affectionate, and supportive of his poetry. Jim's work gained recognition, which can be tracked through prizes: In 1971 Brandeis gave him its prize in poetry; that year his *Collected Poems* appeared, for which he received the Pulitzer Prize; then the Academy of American Poets awarded him its ten-thousand-dollar fellowship. Increasingly, he and Annie spent summers in Italy or France; sometimes Jim took a term away from teaching and they would travel from hotel to hotel in Europe—quietly, soberly, enjoying pleasures of laziness, love, and work.

The year before he died was a good one, maybe more crowded with writing than any other time of his life. January through September of 1979, Jim and Annie traveled in Europe; he rose at four to work on his new poems. He wrote letters frequently, full of plans and vigor. Then, there was the sore throat.

Diagnosis was difficult. It was late in the autumn, back in New York, before his cancer was discovered, a little rough spot behind his tongue. At first it seemed curable: Oncology would shrink the tumor by X ray and surgery would cut it out. Jim was worried that the operation would curtail his speaking of poems. But the tumor would not shrink and there was no operation. Annie wrote old friends, who alerted each other by telephone. Jim's last outing was an appearance at President Carter's reception for poets at the White House in January of 1980. Then he entered Mount Sinai Hospital. Annie arranged visits from old friends of his generation. Galway Kinnell was teaching in Hawaii then, but found a reading in New York that allowed him to visit. Also came Philip Levine, Mark Strand, Robert Bly, Louis Simpson. . . . Jim reconciled two old friends who had quarreled. Because Jim looked bad—teeth out, hair patchy, thin—and because he was an old-fashioned male, he could not bear his women friends to see him. Jane Cooper, Jean Valentine, and Carolyn Kizer prevailed, but only for a moment.

When I visited him the first time, on Saturday the first of March, it was NCAA basketball tournament time, heading toward the confrontation of Michigan State with Indiana State, Magic Johnson with Larry Bird. Jim and I had always talked sports. Thus I arrived at Mount Sinai—to see my wretched racked friend—booming out praise for Larry Bird with a heartiness that tried to assuage my fear or panic. Jim was polite but he did not want to talk about sports. I quieted down; the subjects were poetry, friendship, and mortality.

It was a room for four—noisy, shabby, and dirty. Behind him on the wall were tacked dozens of photographs, mostly of his friends' children. Jim couldn't talk because of his tracheotomy, but he scrawled questions and answers on a yellow pad. The terrible thing was his coughing, as his throat tried to expel the machinery of its breathing-hole: Foam erupted, tinged with pink. Annie asked him if I could look at his new poems; he was still tinkering. So I first read *This Journey* as I sat beside Jim's bed in Mount Sinai, scarcely able to distinguish one word from another; I let my eyes scan across lines, down pages, and I murmured, "Wonderful, Jim, wonderful."

Three and a half weeks later, Annie called me, the afternoon of March 25, to say that Jim had died that morning. The funeral at Riverside Church—in the Little Chapel, where they had been married—was crowded with poets lamenting. The friends from California and Hawaii, who had visited Jim alive, did not fly in again for the memorial service, but Robert Bly was there, Louis Simpson, Gibbons Ruark, David Ignatow, Jane Cooper, Mark Strand, Tom Lux, John Haines, T. Weiss, Roger Hecht, Roland Flint, Belle Gardner, Paul Zweig, E. L. Doctorow, Stanley Moss, Bernie Kaplan, Sander Zulauf, Danielle Goseffi, Frank MacShane, William J. Smith, Joseph Langland . . . The organ played "Shall We Gather at the River" but we did not sing it. The eulogy did not avoid harsh things in Jim's life.

As it happened, I had seen him one more time—three days before he died, three weeks after my first visit. He had been moved to a hospice in the Bronx called Calvary. It was a relief to see him there after the squalor of Mount Sinai; his single room was quiet, clean, tidy. As I walked in the corridors while nurses attended to Jim, I saw a skeletal young girl with no hair, the skin tight on her skull; I saw a young man with a leg amputated, bandages over arms and head—*yet* tenderness and regard for life were palpable in Calvary's air. In the corridor a pretty young black woman sang softly to herself and with her arms clasped together danced a few steps. Jim's nurses and helpers touched him and called him tender names.

Annie was there with her niece Karin East; Jim was particularly fond of Karin. I stayed for a couple of hours, mostly without speaking. At one point Jim started to write me a note, and paused after the third word. On his yellow scratch pad I watched him write, "Don, I'm dying"—and then, after a tiny pause, as short as a line break— "to eat ice-cream from a tray." Jim stared continually at Annie as if he memorized her to take her with him. Once he stared fiercely at her back while she looked out the window at wet snow falling late in March in the dingy Bronx. He signaled to me that he wanted Annie. I relayed the message, and she stood above him while he gazed and his jaw shifted from side to side. He held her hands, then took them to his lips and kissed them.

When Annie left the room briefly, he was agitated. Although he was virtually speechless, he rasped one sentence: "Don, this is it." I nodded. When Annie returned, he took up the manuscript of *This Journey*, which he had asked Annie to photocopy for mailing to several friends, who would work with her to make the final book. Because I was there, he could hand it to me, and he improvised a small ritual. He wrote on the manila envelope, among other words, "I can do no more." Ceremonially, he asked Annie and Karin to sign as witnesses, and he added the date. Then he handed his last poems over.

Above the River

The Quest

In pasture where the leaf and wood
Were lorn of all delicious apple,
And underfoot a long and supple
Bough leaned down to dip in mud,
I came before the dark to stare
At a gray nest blown in a swirl,
As in the arm of a dead girl
Crippled and torn and laid out bare.

On a hill I came to a bare house,
And crept beside its bleary windows,
But no one lived in those gray hollows,
And rabbits ate the dying grass.
I stood upright, and beat the door,
Alone, indifferent, and aloof
To pebbles rolling down the roof
And dust that filmed the deadened air.

High and behind, where twilight chewed
Severer planes of hills away,
And the bonehouse of a rabbit lay
Dissolving by the darkening road,
I came, and rose to meet the sky,
And reached my fingers to a nest
Of stars laid upward in the west;
They hung too high; my hands fell empty.

So, as you sleep, I seek your bed
And lay my careful, quiet ear
Among the nestings of your hair,
Against your tenuous, fragile head,
And hear the birds beneath your eyes
Stirring for birth, and know the world
Immeasurably alive and good,
Though bare as rifted paradise.

Sitting in a Small Screenhouse
on a Summer Morning

Ten more miles, it is South Dakota.
Somehow, the roads there turn blue,
When no one walks down them.
One more night of walking, and I could have become
A horse, a blue horse, dancing
Down a road, alone.

I have got this far. It is almost noon. But never mind time:
That is all over.
It is still Minnesota.
Among a few dead cornstalks, the starving shadow
Of a crow leaps to his death.
At least, it is green here,
Although between my body and the elder trees
A savage hornet strains at the wire screen.
He can't get in yet.

It is so still now, I hear the horse
Clear his nostrils.
He has crept out of the green places behind me.
Patient and affectionate, he reads over my shoulder
These words I have written.
He has lived a long time, and he loves to pretend
No one can see him.
Last night I paused at the edge of darkness,
And slept with green dew, alone.
I have come a long way, to surrender my shadow
To the shadow of a horse.

From The Green Wall

For two Teds and two Jacks

A Fit against the Country

The stone turns over slowly,
Under the side one sees
The pale flint covered wholly
With whorls and prints of leaf.
After the moss rubs off
It gleams beneath the trees,
Till all the birds lie down.
Hand, you have held that stone.

The sparrow's throat goes hollow,
When the tense air forebodes
Rain to the sagging willow
And leaves the pasture moist.
The slow, cracked song is lost
Far up and down wet roads,
Rain drowns the sparrow's tongue.
Ear, you have heard that song.

Suddenly on the eye
Feathers of morning fall,
Tanagers float away
To sort the blackberry theft.
Though sparrows alone are left
To sound the dawn, and call
Awake the heart's gray dolor,
Eye, you have seen bright color.

Odor of fallen apple
Met you across the air,
The yellow globe lay purple
With bruises underfoot;
And, ravished out of thought,
Both of you had your share,
Sharp nose and watered mouth,
Of the dark tang of earth.

Yet, body, hold your humor
Away from the tempting tree,
The grass, the luring summer

That summon the flesh to fall.
Be glad of the green wall
You climbed across one day,
When winter stung with ice
That vacant paradise.

The Seasonless

When snows begin to fill the park,
It is not hard to keep the eyes
Secure against the flickering dark,
Aware of summer ghosts that rise.
The blistered trellis seems to move
The memory toward root and rose,
The empty fountain fills the air
With spray that spangled women's hair;
And men who walk this park in love
May bide the time of falling snows.

The trees recall their greatness now;
They were not always vague and bowed
With loads that build the slender bough
Till branches bear a tasteless fruit.
A month ago they rose and bore
Fleshes of berry, leaf, and shade:
How painlessly a man recalls
The stain of green on crooked walls,
The summer never known before,
The garden heaped to bloom and fade.

Beyond the holly bush and path
The city lies to meet the night,
And also there the quiet earth
Relies upon the lost delight
To rise again and fill the dark
With waterfalls and swallows' sound.
Beyond the city's lazy fume,
The sea repeats the fall of spume,

And gulls remember cries they made
When lovers fed them off the ground.

But lonely underneath a heap
Of overcoat and crusted ice,
A man goes by, and looks for sleep.
The spring of everlastingness.
Nothing about his face revives
A longing to evade the cold.
The night returns to keep him old,
And why should he, the lost and lulled,
Pray for the night of vanished lives,
The day of girls blown green and gold?

The Horse

> . . . the glory of his nostrils is terrible.
> Job 39:20

He kicked the world, and lunging long ago
Rose dripping with the dew of lawns,
Where new wind tapped him to a frieze
Against a wall of rising autumn leaves.
Some young foolhardy dweller of the barrows,
To grip his knees around the flanks,
Leaped from a tree and shivered in the air.
Joy clawed inside the bones
And flesh of the rider at the mane
Flopping and bounding over the dark banks.

Joy and terror floated on either side
Of the rider rearing. The supreme speed
Jerked to a height so spaced and wide
He seemed among the areas of the dead.
The flesh was free, the sky was rockless, clear,
The road beneath the feet was pure, the soul
Spun naked to the air
And lanced against a solitary pole
Of cumulus, to curve and roll

With the heave that disdains
Death in the body, stupor in the brains.

Now we have coddled the gods away.
The cool earth, the soft earth, we say:
Cover our eyes with petals, let the sky
Drift on while we are watching water pass
Among the drowsing mass
Of red and yellow algae in green lanes.
Yet earth contains
The horse as a remembrancer of wild
Arenas we avoid.

One day a stallion whirled my riding wife,
Whose saddle rocked her as a cradled child,
Gentle to the swell of water; yet her life
Poised perilously as on a shattered skiff.
The fear she rode, reminded of the void
That flung the ancient rider to the cold,
Dropped her down. I tossed my reins,

I ran to her with breath to make her rise,
And brought her back. Across my arms
She fumbled for the sunlight with her eyes.
I knew that she would never rest again,
For the colts of the dusk rear back their hooves
And paw us down, the mares of the dawn stampede
Across the cobbled hills till the lights are dead.
Here it is not enough to pray that loves
Draw grass over our childhood's lake of slime.
Run to the rocks where horses cannot climb,
Stable the daemon back to shaken earth,
Warm your hands at the comfortable fire,
Cough in a dish beside a wrinkled bed.

The Fishermen

We tossed our beer cans down among the rocks,
And walked away.

We turned along the beach to wonder
How many girls were out to swim and burn.
We found old men:

The driftwood faces
Sprawled in the air
And patterned hands half hidden in smoke like ferns;
The old men, fishing, letting the sea fall out,
Their twine gone slack.

You spoke of saurian beards
Grown into layers of lime,
Of beetles' shards and broad primeval moths
Lashing great ferns;
Of bent Cro-Magnon mothers beating
Their wheat to mash;
And salty stones
Stuck to the fin and scale
Of salmon skeleton,
And lonely fabulous whorls of wood
Drawn to the shore,
The carping nose, the claws, not to be known
From those dried fishermen:

Who watched the speedboat swaying in the scum
A mile offshore,
Or, nearer, leaping fish
Butting the baby ducks before their climb;
And last of all, before the eyes of age,
The calves of graceful women flashing fast
Into the fluffy towels and out of sight.

You pointed with a stick, and told me
How old men mourning the fall
Forget the splendid sea-top combed as clean as bone,
And the white sails.
You showed me how their faces withered
Even as we looked down
To find where they left off and sea began.

And though the sun swayed in the sea,
They were not moved:

Saurian faces still as layered lime,
The nostrils ferned in smoke behind their pipes,
The eyes resting in whorls like shells on driftwood,
The hands relaxing, letting out the ropes;
And they, whispering together,
The beaten age, the dead, the blood gone dumb.

A Girl in a Window

Now she will lean away to fold
The window blind and curtain back,
The yellow arms, the hips of gold,
The supple outline fading black,
Bosom availing nothing now,
And rounded shadow of long thighs.
How can she care for us, allow
The shade to blind imagined eyes?

Behind us, where we sit by trees,
Blundering autos lurch and swerve
On gravel, crawling on their knees
Around the unfamiliar curve;
Farther behind, a passing train
Ignores our lost identity;
So, reassured, we turn again
To see her vanish under sky.

Soon we must leave her scene to night,
To stars, or the indiscriminate
Pale accidents of lantern light,
A watchman walking by too late.
Let us return her now, my friends,
Her love, her body to the grave
Fancy of dreams where love depends.
She gave, and did not know she gave.

On the Skeleton of a Hound

Nightfall, that saw the morning-glories float
Tendril and string against the crumbling wall,
Nurses him now, his skeleton for grief,
His locks for comfort curled among the leaf.
Shuttles of moonlight weave his shadow tall,
Milkweed and dew flow upward to his throat.
Now catbird feathers plume the apple mound,
And starlings drowse to winter up the ground.
Thickened away from speech by fear, I move
Around the body. Over his forepaws, steep
Declivities darken down the moonlight now,
And the long throat that bayed a year ago
Declines from summer. Flies would love to leap
Between his eyes and hum away the space
Between the ears, the hollow where a hare
Could hide; another jealous dog would tumble
The bones apart, angry, the shining crumble
Of a great body gleaming in the air;
Quivering pigeons foul his broken face.
I can imagine men who search the earth
For handy resurrections, overturn
The body of a beetle in its grave;
Whispering men digging for gods might delve
A pocket for these bones, then slowly burn
Twigs in the leaves, pray for another birth.
But I will turn my face away from this
Ruin of summer, collapse of fur and bone.
For once a white hare huddled up the grass,
The sparrows flocked away to see the race.
I stood on darkness, clinging to a stone,
I saw the two leaping alive on ice,
On earth, on leaf, humus and withered vine:
The rabbit splendid in a shroud of shade,
The dog carved on the sunlight, on the air,
Fierce and magnificent his rippled hair,
The cockleburs shaking around his head.
Then, suddenly, the hare leaped beyond pain
Out of the open meadow, and the hound
Followed the voiceless dancer to the moon,

To dark, to death, to other meadows where
Singing young women dance around a fire,
Where love reveres the living.

                  I alone
Scatter this hulk about the dampened ground;
And while the moon rises beyond me, throw
The ribs and spine out of their perfect shape.
For a last charm to the dead, I lift the skull
And toss it over the maples like a ball.
Strewn to the woods, now may that spirit sleep
That flamed over the ground a year ago.
I know the mole will heave a shinbone over,
The earthworm snuggle for a nap on paws,
The honest bees build honey in the head;
The earth knows how to handle the great dead
Who lived the body out, and broke its laws,
Knocked down a fence, tore up a field of clover.

Three Steps to the Graveyard

When I went there first,
In the spring, it was evening,
It was long hollow thorn
Laid under the locust,
And near to my feet
The crowfoot, the mayapple
Trod their limbs down
Till the stalk blew over.
It grew summer, O riches
Of girls on the lawn,
And boys' locks lying
Tousled on knees,
The picnickers leaving,
The day gone down.

When I went there again,
I walked with my father
Who held in his hand

The crowfoot, the mayapple,
And under my hands,
To hold off the sunlight,
I saw him going,
Between two trees;
When the lawn lay empty
It was the year's end,
It was the darkness,
It was long hollow thorn
To wound the bare shade,
The sheaf and the blade.

O now as I go there
The crowfoot, the mayapple
Blear the gray pond;
Beside the still waters
The field mouse tiptoes,
To hear the air sounding
The long hollow thorn.
I lean to the hollow,
But nothing blows there,
The day goes down.
The field mice flutter
Like grass and are gone,
And a skinny old woman
Scrubs at a stone,
Between two trees.

Father

In paradise I poised my foot above the boat and said:
Who prayed for me?
                              But only the dip of an oar
In water sounded; slowly fog from some cold shore
Circled in wreaths around my head.

But who is waiting?
                              And the wind began,
Transfiguring my face from nothingness
To tiny weeping eyes. And when my voice

Grew real, there was a place
Far, far below on earth. There was a tiny man—

It was my father wandering round the waters at the wharf.
Irritably he circled and he called
Out to the marine currents up and down,
But heard only a cold unmeaning cough,
And saw the oarsman in the mist enshawled.

He drew me from the boat. I was asleep.
And we went home together.

Elegy in a Firelit Room

The window showed a willow in the west,
But windy dry. No folly weeping there.
A sparrow hung a wire about its breast
And spun across the air.

Instead of paying winter any mind,
I ran my fingerprints across the glass,
To feel the crystal forest sown by wind,
And one small face:

A child among the frozen bushes lost,
Breaking the white and rigid twigs between
Fingers more heavenly than hands of dust,
And fingernails more clean.

Beyond, the willow would not cry for cold,
The sparrow hovered long enough to stare;
The face between me and the wintered world
Began to disappear;

Because some friendly hands behind my back
Fumbled the coal and tended up the fire.
Warmth of the room waved to the window sash,
The face among the forest fell to air.

The glass began to weep instead of eyes,
A slow gray feather floated down the sky.
Delicate bone, finger and bush, and eyes
Yearned to the kissing fire and fell away.

Over the naked pasture and beyond,
A frozen bird lay down among the dead
Weeds, and the willow strode upon the wind
And would not bow its head.

Arrangements with Earth for Three Dead Friends

Sweet earth, he ran and changed his shoes to go
Outside with other children through the fields.
He panted up the hills and swung from trees
Wild as a beast but for the human laughter
That tumbled like a cider down his cheeks.
Sweet earth, the summer has been gone for weeks,
And weary fish already sleeping under water
Below the banks where early acorns freeze.
Receive his flesh and keep it cured of colds.
Button his coat and scarf his throat from snow.

And now, bright earth, this other is out of place
In what, awake, we speak about as tombs.
He sang in houses when the birds were still
And friends of his were huddled round till dawn
After the many nights to hear him sing.
Bright earth, his friends remember how he sang
Voices of night away when wind was one.
Lonely the neighborhood beneath your hill
Where he is waved away through silent rooms.
Listen for music, earth, and human ways.

Dark earth, there is another gone away,
But she was not inclined to beg of you
Relief from water falling or the storm.
She was aware of scavengers in holes

Of stone, she knew the loosened stones that fell
Indifferently as pebbles plunging down a well
And broke for the sake of nothing human souls.
Earth, hide your face from her where dark is warm.
She does not beg for anything, who knew
The change of tone, the human hope gone gray.

Lament for My Brother
on a Hayrake

Cool with the touch of autumn, waters break
Out of the pump at dawn to clear my eyes;
I leave the house, to face the sacrifice
Of hay, the drag and death. By day, by moon,
I have seen my younger brother wipe his face
And heave his arm on steel. He need not pass
Under the blade to waste his life and break;

The hunching of the body is enough
To violate his bones. That bright machine
Strips the revolving earth of more than grass;
Powered by the fire of summer, bundles fall
Folded to die beside a burlap shroud;
And so my broken brother may lie mown
Out of the wasted fallows, winds return,
Corn-yellow tassels of his hair blow down,
The summer bear him sideways in a bale
Of darkness to October's mow of cloud.

She Hid in the Trees
from the Nurses

She stands between the trees and holds
One hand in the other, still.
Now far away the evening folds
Around the silos and the hill.

She sees, slowly, the gardener
Return to check the gate before
The smoke begins to soften the air
And June bugs try the open door.

And through the windows, washing hands,
The patients have the mattress made,
Their trousers felt for colored stones,
The pleasures of the noon recalled:

For some were caught and held for hours
By spiders skating over a pond,
Some parted veils of hollyhocks
And looked for rabbit holes beyond.

But now the trousers lie in rows,
She sees the undressed shadows creep
Through half-illuminated minds
And chase the hare and flower to sleep.

She too must answer summons now,
And play the chimes inside her brain
When whistles of attendants blow;
Yet, for a while, she would remain,

And dabble her feet in the damp grass,
And lean against a yielding stalk,
And spread her name in dew across
The pebbles where the droplets walk.

Minutes away a nurse will come
Across the lawn and call for her;
The starlight calls the robin home,
The swans retire beneath their wings.

Surely her mind is clear enough
To hear her name among the trees.
She must remember home and love
And skirts that sway below her knees.

But why must she desert the shade
And sleep between the walls all night?

Why must a lonely girl run mad
To gain the simple, pure delight

Of staying, when the others leave,
To write a name or hold a stone?
Of hearing bobwhites flute their love
Though buildings loudly tumble down?

To a Defeated Savior

Do you forget the shifting hole
Where the slow swimmer fell aground
And floundered for your fishing pole
Above the snarl of string and sound?
You never seem to turn your face
Directly toward the river side,
Or up the bridge, or anyplace
Near where the skinny swimmer died.

You stand all day and look at girls,
Or climb a tree, or change a tire;
But I have seen the colored swirls
Of water flow to livid fire
Across your sleeping nose and jaws,
Transfiguring both the bone and skin
To muddy banks and sliding shoals
You and the drowned kid tumble in.

You see his face, upturning, float
And bob across your wavering bed;
His wailing fingers call your boat,
His voice throws up the ruddy silt,
The bleary vision prays for light
In sky behind your frozen hands;
But sinking in the dark all night,
You charm the shore with bloomless wands.

The circling tow, the shadowy pool
Shift underneath us everywhere.
You would have raised him, flesh and soul,

Had you been strong enough to dare;
You would have lifted him to breathe,
Believing your good hands would keep
His body clear of your own death:
This dream, this drowning in your sleep.

To a Troubled Friend

Weep, and weep long, but do not weep for me,
Nor, long lamenting, raise, for any word
Of mine that beats above you like a bird,
Your voice, or hand. But shaken clear, and free,
Be the bare maple, bough where nests are made
Snug in the season's wrinkled cloth of frost;
Be leaf, by hardwood knots, by tendrils crossed
On tendrils, stripped, uncaring; give no shade.

Give winter nothing; hold; and let the flake
Poise or dissolve along your upheld arms.
All flawless hexagons may melt and break;
While you must feel the summer's rage of fire,
Beyond this frigid season's empty storms,
Banished to bloom, and bear the birds' desire.

Poem for Kathleen Ferrier

1
I leaned to hear your song,
The breathing and the echo;
And when it dropped away,
I thought, for one deaf moment,
That I could never listen
To any other voice.

2
But the land is deep in sound.
The sleepy hares and crickets
Remember how to cry.

The birds have not forgotten
(The tanager, the sparrow)
The tumbled, rising tone.

3

The sounds go on, and on,
In spite of what the morning
Or evening dark has done.
We have no holy voices
Like yours to lift above us,
Yet we cannot be still.

4

All earth is loud enough.
Then why should I be sorry
(The owl scritches alive)
To stand before a shadow,
And see a cold piano
Half hidden by a drape?

5

No reason I can give.
Uttering tongues are busy,
Mount the diminished air
(The breathing and the echo)
Enough to keep the ear
Half satisfied forever.

A Song for the Middle of the Night

*By way of explaining to my son the following curse by
Eustace Deschamps: "Happy is he who has no children;
for babies bring nothing but crying and stench."*

Now first of all he means the night
        You beat the crib and cried
And brought me spinning out of bed
        To powder your backside.
I rolled your buttocks over
        And I could not complain:

Legs up, la la, legs down, la la,
    Back to sleep again.

Now second of all he means the day
    You dabbled out of doors
And dragged a dead cat Billy-be-damned
    Across the kitchen floors.
I rolled your buttocks over
    And made you sing for pain:
Legs up, la la, legs down, la la,
    Back to sleep again.

But third of all my father once
    Laid me across his knee
And solved the trouble when he beat
    The yowling out of me.
He rocked me on his shoulder
    When razor straps were vain:
Legs up, la la, legs down, la la,
    Back to sleep again.

So roll upon your belly, boy,
    And bother being cursed.
You turn the household upside down,
    But you are not the first.
Deschamps the poet blubbered too,
    For all his fool disdain:
Legs up, la la, legs down, la la,
    Back to sleep again.

A Presentation of Two Birds
to My Son

Chicken. How shall I tell you what it is,
And why it does not float with tanagers?
Its ecstasy is dead, it does not care.
Its children huddle underneath its wings,
And altogether lounge against the shack,
Warm in the slick tarpaulin, smug and soft.

You must not fumble in your mind
The genuine ecstasy of climbing birds
With that dull fowl.
When your grandfather held it by the feet
And laid the skinny neck across
The ragged chopping block,
The flop of wings, the jerk of the red comb
Were a dumb agony,
Stupid and meaningless. It was no joy
To leave the body beaten underfoot;
Life was a flick of corn, a steady roost.
Chicken. The sound is plain.

Look up and see the swift above the trees.
How shall I tell you why he always veers
And banks around the shaken sleeve of air,
Away from ground? He hardly flies on brains;
Pockets of air impale his hollow bones.
He leans against the rainfall or the sun.

You must not mix this pair of birds
Together in your mind before you know
That both are clods.
What makes the chimney swift approach the sky
Is ecstasy, a kind of fire
That beats the bones apart
And lets the fragile feathers close with air.
Flight too is agony,
Stupid and meaningless. Why should it be joy
To leave the body beaten underfoot,
To mold the limbs against the wind, and join
Those clean dark glides of Dionysian birds?
The flight is deeper than your father, boy.

To a Hostess Saying Good Night

Shake out the ruffle, turn and go,
Over the trellis blow the kiss.
Some of the guests will never know

Another night to shadow this.
Some of the birds awake in vines
Will never see another face
So frail, so lovely anyplace
Between the birdbath and the bines.

O dark come never down to you.
I look away and look away:
Over the moon the shadows go,
Over your shoulder, nebulae.
Some of the vast, the vacant stars
Will never see your face at all,
Your frail, your lovely eyelids fall
Between Andromeda and Mars.

A Poem about George Doty
in the Death House

Lured by the wall, and drawn
To stare below the roof,
Where pigeons nest aloof
From prowling cats and men,
I count the sash and bar
Secured to granite stone,
And note the daylight gone,
Supper and silence near.

Close to the wall inside,
Immured, empty of love,
A man I have wondered of
Lies patient, vacant-eyed.
A month and a day ago
He stopped his car and found
A girl on the darkening ground,
And killed her in the snow.

Beside his cell, I am told,
Hardy perennial bums
Complain till twilight comes

For hunger and for cold.
They hardly know of a day
That saw their hunger pass.
Bred to the dark, their flesh
Peacefully withers away.

The man who sits alone,
He is the one for wonder,
Who sways his fingers under
The cleanly shaven chin,
Who sees, in the shaving mirror
Pinned to the barren wall,
The uprooted ghost of all:
The simple, easy terror.

Caught between sky and earth,
Poor stupid animal,
Stripped naked to the wall,
He saw the blundered birth
Of daemons beyond sound.
Sick of the dark, he rose
For love, and now he goes
Back to the broken ground.

Now, as he grips the chain
And holds the wall, to bear
What no man ever bore,
He hears the bums complain;
But I mourn no soul but his,
Not even the bums who die,
Nor the homely girl whose cry
Crumbled his pleading kiss.

To a Fugitive

The night you got away, I dreamed you rose
Out of the earth to lean on a young tree.
Then they were there, hulking the moon away,
The great dogs rooting, snuffing up the grass.

You raise a hand, hungry to hold your lips
Out of the wailing air; but lights begin
Spidering the ground; oh they come closing in,
The beam searches your face like fingertips.

Hurry, Maguire, hammer the body down,
Crouch to the wall again, shackle the cold
Machine guns and the sheriff and the cars:
Divide the bright bars of the cornered bone,
Strip, run for it, break the last law, unfold,
Dart down the alley, race between the stars.

Eleutheria

Rubbing her mouth along my mouth she lost
Illusions of the sky, the dreams it offered:
The pale cloud walking home to winter, dust
Blown to a shell of sails so far above
That autumn landscape where we lay and suffered
The fruits of summer in the fields of love.

We lay and heard the apples fall for hours,
The stripping twilight plundered trees of boughs,
The land dissolved beneath the rabbit's heels,
And far away I heard a window close,
A haying wagon heave and catch its wheels,
Some water slide and stumble and be still.
The dark began to climb the empty hill.

If dark Eleutheria turned and lay
Forever beside me, who would care for years?
The throat, the supple belly, the warm thigh
Burgeoned against the earth; I lay afraid,
For who could bear such beauty under the sky?
I would have held her loveliness in air,
Away from things that lured me to decay:
The ground's deliberate riches, fallen pears,
Bewildered apples blown to mounds of shade.

Lovers' location is the first to fade.
They wander back in winter, but there is
No comfortable grass to couch a dress.
Musicians of the yellow weeds are dead.
And she, remembering something, turns to hear
Either a milkweed float or a thistle fall.
Bodiless shadow thrown along a wall,
She glides lightly; the pale year follows her.

The moments ride away, the locust flute
Is silvered thin and lost, over and over.
She will return some evening to discover
The tree uplifted to the very root,
The leaves shouldered away, with lichen grown
Among the interlacings of the stone,
October blowing dust, and summer gone
Into a dark barn, like a hiding lover.

Autumnal

Soft, where the shadow glides,
The yellow pears fell down.
The long bough slowly rides
The air of my delight.

Air, though but nothing, air
Falls heavy down your shoulder.
You hold in burdened hair
The color of my delight.

Neither the hollow pear,
Nor leaf among the grass,
Nor wind that wails the year
Against your leaning ear,
Will alter my delight:

That holds the pear upright
And sings along the bough,
Warms to the mellow sun.

The song of my delight
Gathers about you now,
Is whispered through, and gone.

The Shadow and the Real

There was no more than shadow where
She leaned outside the kitchen door,
Stood in the sun and let her hair
Loosely float in the air and fall.
She tossed her body's form before
Her feet, and laid it down the wall.
And how was I to feel, therefore,
Shadow no more than darker air?

I rose, and crossed the room, to find
Her hands, her body, her green dress;
But where she stood, the sun behind
Demolished her from touch and sight.
Her body burned to emptiness,
Her hair caught summer in the light;
I sought, bewildered, for her face,
No more than splendid air, gone blind.

Witches Waken the
Natural World in Spring

Warm in the underbough of dark
Willows is where the women go
To whisper how the barren park
Will shiver into blossom now.
It does not matter they are slim
Or plump as melons left too long
Upon the vine; beneath the dim
Spell of the willow they are strong.

And very seldom I remember
What revelations they have spoken.
I know I saw a willow tremble
In starlight once, a burdock broken,
Shaken by the voice of my girl
Who waved to heaven overhead;
And though she made a leaflet fall
I have forgotten what she said:

Except that spring was coming on
Or might have come already while
We lay beside a smooth-veined stone;
Except an owl sang half a mile
Away; except a starling's feather
Softened my face beside a root:
But how should I remember whether
She was the one who spoke, or not?

Morning Hymn to a Dark Girl

Summoned to desolation by the dawn,
I climb the bridge over the water, see
The Negro mount the driver's cabin and wave
Goodbye to the glum cop across the canal,
Goodbye to the flat face and empty eyes
Made human one more time. That uniform
Shivers and dulls against the pier, is stone.

Now in the upper world, the buses drift
Over the bridge, the gulls collect and fly,
Blown by the rush of rose; aseptic girls
Powder their lank deliberate faces, mount
The fog under the billboards. Over the lake
The windows of the rich waken and yawn.
Light blows across the city, dune on dune.

Caught by the scruff of the neck, and thrown out here
To the pale town, to the stone, to burial,
I celebrate you, Betty, flank and breast

Rich to the yellow silk of bed and floors;
Now half awake, your body blossoming trees;
One arm beneath your neck, your legs uprisen,
You blow dark thighs back, back into the dark.

Your shivering ankles skate the scented air;
Betty, burgeoning your golden skin, you poise
Tracing gazelles and tigers on your breasts,
Deep in the jungle of your bed you drowse;
Fine muscles of the rippling panthers move
And snuggle at your calves; under your arms
Mangoes and melons yearn; and glittering slowly,
Quick parakeets trill in your heavy trees,
O everywhere, Betty, between your boughs.

Pity the rising dead who fear the dark.
Soft Betty, locked from snickers in a dark
Brothel, dream on; scatter the yellow corn
Into the wilderness, and sleep all day.
For the leopards leap into the open grass,
Bananas, lemons fling air, fling odor, fall.
And, gracing darkly the dark light, you flow
Out of the grove to laugh at dreamy boys,
You greet the river with a song so low
No lover on a boat can hear, you slide
Silkily to the water, where you rinse
Your fluted body, fearless; though alive
Orangutans sway from the leaves and gaze,
Crocodiles doze along the oozy shore.

The Quail

Lost in the brush, bound by the other path
To find the house,
You let me know how many voices,
How many shifting bodies you possessed,
How you could flit away to follow birds,
And yet be near.

A quail implored the hollow for a home,
A covey of dark to lie in under stars;
And, when it sang, you left my hand
To voyage how softly down the even grass
And see the meadow where the quails lie down,
Flushed in the dark by hunters' broken guns.

You left my side before I knew the way
To find the house,
And soon you called across the hollow
To say you were alive and still on earth;
And, when you sang, the quail began to cry,
So I lost both.

The blue dusk bore feathers beyond our eyes,
Dissolved all wings as you, your hair dissolved,
Your frame of bone blown hollow as a house
Beside the path, were borne away from me
Farther than birds for whom I did not care,
Commingled with the dark complaining air.

I could have called the simple dark to fade,
To find the house,
And left you standing silent;
But stained away by maple leaves, and led
From tree to tree by wands of luring ghosts,
You knew my love,

You knew my feet would never turn away
From any forest where your body was,
Though vanished up the disembodied dark.
And when I found you laughing under trees,
The quail began to trill and flute away,
As far away as hands that reach for hands;
But, when it sang, you kissed me out of sound.

Sappho

*Ach, in den Armen hab ich sie alle verloren, du nur, du wirst
immer wieder geboren. . . .*
    —Rilke, *Die Aufzeichnungen des Malte Laurids Brigge*

The twilight falls; I soften the dusting feathers,
And clean again.
The house has lain and moldered for three days,
The windows smeared with rain, the curtains torn,
The mice come in,
The kitchen blown with cold.

I keep the house, and say no words.

It is true I am as twisted as the cactus
That gnarls and turns beside the milky light,
That cuts the fingers easily and means nothing,
For all the pain that shoots along the hand.
I dust the feathers down the yellow thorns,
I light the stove.

The gas curls round the iron fretwork, the flame
Floats above the lace,
And bounces like a dancer stayed on air.
Fire does not rest on iron, it drifts like a blue blossom
And catches on my breath;
Coiling, spinning, the blue foam of the gas fire
Writhes like a naked girl;
Turns up its face, like her.

She came to me in rain.
I did not know her, I did not know my name
After she left to bed her children down,
To phone her husband they were gone asleep,
And she, lying, a pure fire, in the feathers,
Dancing above the ironwork of her bed,
Roaring, and singeing nothing.
She had not wound her arms about me then,
She had not dared.
I only took her coat, and smiled to hear
How she had left her purse and her umbrella
In the theater, how she was sopping cold

With the fall rain; and mine was the one light
In the neighborhood. She came to my gas fire
And lay before it, sprawled, her pure bare shoulders
Folded in a doze, a clear, cold curve of stone.

I only leaned above the hair,
Turned back the quilt, arranged the feet, the arms,
And kissed the sleeping shoulder, lightly, like the rain;
And when she woke to wear her weathered clothes,
I sent her home.
She floated, a blue blossom, over the street.

And when she came again,
It was not long before she turned to me,
And let her shawl slide down her neck and shoulder,
Let her hair fall.
And when she came again,
It did not rain.

Her husband came to pluck her like an apple,
As the drunken farmer lurches against the tree,
Grips the green globe not long beyond its bloom,
And tears the skin, brutally, out of the bark,
Leaves the whole bough broken,
The orchard torn with many footprints,
The fence swung wide
On a raw hinge.

And now it is said of me
That my love is nothing because I have borne no children,
Or because I have fathered none;
That I twisted the twig in my hands
And cut the blossom free too soon from the seed;
That I lay across the fire,
And snuffed it dead sooner than draft or rain.

But I have turned away, and drawn myself
Upright to walk along the room alone.
Across the dark the spines of cactus plants
Remind me how I go—aloof, obscure,
Indifferent to the words the children chalk
Against my house and down the garden walls.
They cannot tear the garden out of me,

Nor smear my love with names. Love is a cliff,
A clear, cold curve of stone, mottled by stars,
Smirched by the morning, carved by the dark sea
Till stars and dawn and waves can slash no more,
Till the rock's heart is found and shaped again.

I keep the house and say no words, the evening
Falls like a petal down the shawl of trees.
I light the fire and see the blossom dance
On air alone; I will not douse that flame,
That searing flower; I will burn in it.
I will not banish love to empty rain.

For I know that I am asked to hate myself
For their sweet sake
Who sow the world with child.
I am given to burn on the dark fire they make
With their sly voices.

But I have burned already down to bone.
There is a fire that burns beyond the names
Of sludge and filth of which this world is made.
Agony sears the dark flesh of the body,
And lifts me higher than the smoke, to rise
Above the earth, above the sacrifice;
Until my soul flares outward like a blue
Blossom of gas fire dancing in mid-air:
Free of the body's work of twisted iron.

A Gesture by a Lady with an Assumed Name

Letters she left to clutter up the desk
Burned in the general gutter when the maid
Came in to do the room and take the risk
Of slipping off the necklace round her head.

Laundry she left to clutter up the floor
Hung to rachitic skeletons of girls

Who worked the bars or labored up the stair
To crown her blowsy ribbons on their curls.

Lovers she left to clutter up the town
Mourned in the chilly morgue and went away,
All but the husbands sneaking up and down
The stairs of that apartment house all day.

What were they looking for? The cold pretense
Of lamentation offered in a stew?
A note? A gift? A shred of evidence
To love when there was nothing else to do?

Or did they rise to weep for that unheard-
Of love, whose misery cries and does not care
Whether or not the madam hears a word
Or skinny children watch the trodden stair?

Whether or not, how could she love so many,
Then turn away to die as though for none?
I saw the last offer a child a penny
To creep outside and see the cops were gone.

Mutterings over the Crib of a Deaf Child

"How will he hear the bell at school
Arrange the broken afternoon,
And know to run across the cool
Grasses where the starlings cry,
Or understand the day is gone?"

Well, someone lifting curious brows
Will take the measure of the clock.
And he will see the birchen boughs
Outside sagging dark from the sky,
And the shade crawling upon the rock.

"And how will he know to rise at morning?
His mother has other sons to waken,
She has the stove she must build to burning
Before the coals of the nighttime die;
And he never stirs when he is shaken."

I take it the air affects the skin,
And you remember, when you were young,
Sometimes you could feel the dawn begin,
And the fire would call you, by and by,
Out of the bed and bring you along.

"Well, good enough. To serve his needs
All kinds of arrangements can be made.
But what will you do if his finger bleeds?
Or a bobwhite whistles invisibly
And flutes like an angel off in the shade?"

He will learn pain. And, as for the bird,
It is always darkening when that comes out.
I will putter as though I had not heard,
And lift him into my arms and sing
Whether he hears my song or not.

The Angel

Last night, before I came to bear
The clean edge of my wing upon the boulder,
I walked about the town.
The people seemed at peace that he was dead:
A beggar carried water out of a door,
And young men gathered round the corner
To spell the night.

I walked, like a folded bird, about the towers
And sang softly to the blue levels of evening,
I slid down treeless, featherless, bemused:
At curious faces whispering round a fire
And sniffing chestnuts sugared by a woman;

At a vague child heaving a beetle over
In dust, to see it swimming on its back.

Under an arch I found a woman lean
Weeping for loneliness: away from her
A young man whistle toward the crowds;
Out of an open window pigeons flew
And a slow dove fluted for nothing—the girl
Blew to the air a melody lost on me.

Laid in a pile of stone, how could he weep
For that calm town?
Looped in a yoke of darkened garden,
He murmured blood out of his heart for love,
Hallowed a soldier, took the savage kiss
And gave it back a warm caress;

Yet no one changed.

Tossing aside the worry of the place,
As someone threw an apple core across
A wall I walked beside, I sought delight
Pebble by pebble, song by song, and light
By light, singly, among the river boats.
Down to the river at the end I came.

But then a girl appeared, to wash her hair.
Struck stupid by her face,
I stood there, sick to love her, sick of sky.
The child, the beetle, chestnut fires, the song
Of girl and dove
Shuddered along my wings and arms.
She slipped her bodice off, and a last wave
Of shadow oiled her shoulder till it shone;
Lifting her arms to loosen the soft braids
She looked across the water. I looked down
And felt my wings waving aside the air,
Furious to fly. For I could never bear
Belly and breast and thigh against the ground.

Now, having heaved the hidden hollow open
As I was sent to do, seen Jesus waken
And guided the women there, I wait to rise.

To feel a weapon gouge between the ribs,
He hung with a shut mouth:
For curious faces round a chestnut fire,
For the slow fluting doves
Lost on a trellis, for the laughing girl
Who frightened me away.

But now I fumble at the single joy
Of dawn. On the pale ruffle of the lake
The ripples weave a color I can bear.
Under a hill I see the city sleep
And fade. The perfect pleasure of the eyes:
A tiny bird bathed in a bowl of air,
Carving a yellow ripple down the bines,
Posing no storm to blow my wings aside
As I drift upward dropping a white feather.

The Assignation

After the winter thawed away, I rose,
Remembering what you said. Below the field
Where I was dead, the crinkled leaf and blade
Summoned my body, told me I must go.
Across the road I saw some other dead
Revive their little fires, and bow the head
To someone still alive and long ago.
Low in the haze a pall of smoke arose.

Inside the moon's hollow is a hale gray man
Who washed his hands, and waved me where to go:
Up the long hill, the mound of lunar snow,
Around three lapping pebbles, over the crossed
Arms of an owl nailed to the southern sky.
I spun three times about, I scattered high,
Over my shoulder, clouds of salt and dust.
The earth began to clear. I saw a man.

He said the sun was falling toward the trees,
The picnic nearly over. Small on the lake
The sails were luring lightning out of dark,

While quieter people guided slim canoes.
I hid in bushes, shy. Already cars
Shuttled away, the earliest evening stars
Blurred in a cloud. A lone child left his shoes
Half in the sand, and slept beneath the trees.

With fires demolished, everybody gone
To root in bushes, congregate by trees
Or haul the yellow windows down to haze,
I lost my way. Water in water fell,
The badgers nibbled rootlets up the shore,
For dancing more than food, where long before
Women had gossiped. Chanting a soft farewell,
Canaries swung. Then everything was gone.

No hurry for me there, I let my dress
Fall to the lawn, the pleasure of the silk
Wind with the subtle grass, berries and milk
Of skin sweeten me. Snuggling, I lay prone,
Barren yet motherly for what might come
Out of the emptied branches, man or flame.
I shivered slightly. Everything was gone,
Everyone gone. I kicked aside my dress.

O then it was you I waited for, to hold
The soft leaves of my bones between your hands
And warm them back to life, to fashion wands
Out of my shining arms. O it was you
I loved before my dying and long after,
You, you I could not find. The air fell softer,
My snatch of breath gave out, but no one blew
My name in hallowed weeds. Lonely to hold

Some hand upon me, lest it float away
And be as dead as I, thrown in a sack
Of air to drown in air, I rose, lay back
In trees, and died again. The spiders care
For trellises they hold against the sky,
Except for walls of air the houses die
And fall; and only for my flesh of air
Your flesh of earth would lean and drift away;

But you cared nothing, living, false to me.
What could I do but take a daemon then
And slouch about in dust, eager for pain
Or anything, to keep your memory clear?
A thing came down from the dark air on wings
And rummaged at my limbs, to hold my wings
Down in the dirt; I could not see for fear.
The thing withdrew, full of the dark and me.

And I was riven. Even my poor ghost
Can never stand beside your window now;
I stir the wind, I chatter at a bough,
But make no sound. Your cowardice may keep
You from your assignation with my ghost,
The love you promised me when I was dust,
Not air. And yet I cannot even sleep,
I cannot die, but I will feel my ghost

Driven to find this orchard every year,
This picnic ground, and wait till everyone
Tires of the sundown, turns the headlights on,
To float them off like moths into the dark.
I will stand up to strip my hunger off,
And stare, and mumble, knowing all your love
Is cut beside my name on the white rock,
While you forget the promise and the year.

You sat beside the bed, you took my hands;
And when I lay beyond all speech, you said,
You swore to love me after I was dead,
To meet me in a grove and love me still,
Love the white air, the shadow where it lay.
Dear love, I called your name in air today,
I saw the picnic vanish down the hill,
And waved the moon awake, with empty hands.

Come Forth

Lazarus lay to see the body turn.
The femur first removed itself from arms,
The elbows folded under each other soon.

The clavicle and vertebrae and shin
Divided like the stars and let the air
Caress the flesh awake before it fell.

Only the torpid brain would not remove.
From far away beyond the granite walls
A vowel of longing tore the wind in two.

Come forth, it said. *But who is this who cried?*
For I have left the human long ago,
My flesh a synagogue the flame has eaten.

Before the voice the worms began to pray,
And fled away howling into the granite.
The shin returned to spring a leaping leg,

The skull rounded itself upon the brain,
The heart arose and cried with joy for pain,
The arteries assumed a thud again.

And the hair furied on the shocking head,
And muscles blossomed like the thunderhead
That trumpets the pale tropics to green storm.

The stones rolling away and the air thrust
Into the lung of the cave, Lazarus knew
The unholy and indifferent sting of wind

Across the flesh of man. Outside, the sun
Flayed the same bone as before. Nevertheless
His treading skeleton clattered like a choir

And waved him forward on a crest of praise.
A wall or two away the calling voice
Shook like a pacing father, and was still.

O blessed fire, O harsh and loving air.

Erinna to Sappho

I saw your shoulder swell and pitch
Alive, your fingers, curving, turn
To summon me above that ditch
    Where I lay down.

Yet as I came, you turned about
And waved to someone out of sight,
Someone you could not do without
    That very night.

Who was she? for I only saw
Mellifluous berries fall from vines,
Long apple blooms depress a bough,
    Clustering wines

Dripping their liquor as they hung
In spray and tendril, curling hair.
You flickered your inviting tongue
    At no one there;

No one but air, garden, the hewn
Poet above his pedestal,
Lyre in the marble, song in stone,
    The trees, the wall;

Unless there was, before I rose,
One of the hollow things who walk
The world in anguish, wearing clothes
    Just before dark;

And you were calling out to her
Or him, whatever bodiless
Presences hollow spirits bear
    Beneath their dress.

Whether I knew or did not know,
Under the misery of my skin,

What pale plunderer looted you
    Outside and in,

I leaped, above the ditch of earth,
Bodily, clung my arms around
Your poising knees, and brought us both
    Back to the ground,

Where we belong, if anywhere,
To hide in our own hollowed dust.
Whatever I gave, I gave no bare
    Pain of a ghost.

I offered, worshiping, that sweet
Cluster of liquors caught in globes,
I burst the riches till they wet
    Your tousled robes;

And though I stole from you no more
Than fireflies gain of the soft moon,
You turned to me, long, long before
    The ghost was gone,

If ghost it was, or melon rind,
Or stag's skeleton hung to dry,
Lover, or song, or only wind
    Sighing your sigh.

A Little Girl on Her Way
to School

When the dark dawn humped off to die
The air sang, clearly the country bells
Rang in the light from trees to wells
And silkened every catbird cry.

Webbed in a gown of yellow-white,
Gauzed as a robin where the tree

Blows down over the eyelids, she
Limped on beyond me in the light.

One bell before I woke, the stones
Under the balls of her soft feet
Cried out to her, the leaves in the wet
All tumbled toward her name at once.

And while my waking hung in poise
Between the air and the damp earth,
I saw her startle to the breath
Of birds beginning in her voice.

Be careful of holes, the catbird said,
His nest hanging below her hair,
Nudging the robins windward there,
Whorling the air of glint and shade.

Fall in the hole, the pigeon swore,
His feathers beckoning her to ground,
Burling the sparrows out of sound,
Whorling the glints of shade and air.

Cling to the edge, cling to the edge,
Here, step lightly, touch my beak.
She listened, but she would not speak,
Following the white swan through the hedge.

My Grandmother's Ghost

She skimmed the yellow water like a moth,
Trailing her feet across the shallow stream;
She saw the berries, paused and sampled them
Where a slight spider cleaned his narrow tooth.
Light in the air, she fluttered up the path,
So delicate to shun the leaves and damp,
Like some young wife, holding a slender lamp
To find her stray child, or the moon, or both.

Even before she reached the empty house,
She beat her wings ever so lightly, rose,
Followed a bee where apples blew like snow;
And then, forgetting what she wanted there,
Too full of blossom and green light to care,
She hurried to the ground, and slipped below.

Saint Judas

They answered
and said unto him,
Thou wast altogether born in sin,
and dost thou teach us?
And they
cast him out.

To Philip Timberlake, my teacher,
and to Sonjia Urseth, my student

I stop my habitual thinking, as if the plow had suddenly run deeper in its furrow through the crust of the world. How can I go on, who have just stepped over such a bottomless skylight in the bog of my life? Suddenly old Time winked at me, — Ah you know me, you rogue, — and news had come that IT was well. . . . Heal yourselves, doctors; by God I live.

—Thoreau, *A Week on the Concord and Merrimack Rivers*

I. Lunar Changes

Complaint

She's gone. She was my love, my moon or more.
She chased the chickens out and swept the floor,
Emptied the bones and nut-shells after feasts,
And smacked the kids for leaping up like beasts.
Now morbid boys have grown past awkwardness;
The girls let stitches out, dress after dress,
To free some swinging body's riding space
And form the new child's unimagined face.
Yet, while vague nephews, spitting on their curls,
Amble to pester winds and blowsy girls,
What arm will sweep the room, what hand will hold
New snow against the milk to keep it cold?
And who will dump the garbage, feed the hogs,
And pitch the chickens' heads to hungry dogs?
Not my lost hag who dumbly bore such pain:
Childbirth and midnight sassafras and rain.
New snow against her face and hands she bore,
And now lies down, who was my moon or more.

Paul

I used to see her in the door,
Lifting up her hand to wave
To citizens, or pass the hour
With neighboring wives who did not have
Anything more than time to say.

I used to see her in the door,
Simple and quiet woman, slim;
And so, I think, Paul cared the more

The night they carried her from him,
The night they carried her away.

The doctor did not even ask
For any neighborly advice;
He knew he had a simple task,
And it was obvious from his eyes
There was not anything to say.

The doctor had a word for Paul;
He said that she was resting now,
And would not wake, and that was all.
And then he walked into the snow,
Into the snow he walked away.

And did Paul shriek and curse the air,
And did he pummel with his fist
Against the wall, or tear his hair
And rush outside to bite the mist
That did not have a thing to say?

He sat upon her ruffled bed
And did not even look at me.
She was lovely, she was dead.
Some sparrows chirruped on a tree
Outside, and then they flew away.

An Offering for Mr. Bluehart

That was a place, when I was young,
Where two or three good friends and I
Tested the fruit against the tongue
Or threw the withered windfalls by.
The sparrows, angry in the sky,
Denounced us from a broken bough.
They limp along the wind and die.
The apples all are eaten now.

Behind the orchard, past one hill
The lean satanic owner lay

And threatened us with murder till
We stole his riches all away.
He caught us in the act one day
And damned us to the laughing bone,
And fired his gun across the gray
Autumn where now his life is done.

Sorry for him, or any man
Who lost his labored wealth to thieves,
Today I mourn him, as I can,
By leaving in their golden leaves
Some luscious apples overhead.
Now may my abstinence restore
Peace to the orchard and the dead.
We shall not nag them any more.

Old Man Drunk

He sits before me now, reptilian, cold,
Worn skeletal with sorrow for his child.
He would have lied to her, were he not old:
An old man's fumbling lips are not defiled
By the sweet lies of love. Yet one must be
Skillful to bring it off; that treachery
Whips back to lash the bungler of its art.
He curses his ineptitude of heart.

He knows the quivering eye of youth is blind.
The pale ears, roaring deep as shell, are deaf
To the half-drowning cry of love behind
The skull. His daughter struck him in her grief
Across the face, hearing her lover dead.
He stood behind her chair, he bowed his head,
Knowing that even death cannot prolong
The quick hysteric angers of the young.

I can say nothing. I will see him sit
Under the vacant clock, till I grow old.
The barkeep's wife returns to throw her fit
And pitch us out into the early cold.

I touch his shoulder, but he does not move,
Lost in the blind bewilderment of love,
The meaningless despair that could not keep
His daughter long from falling off to sleep.

Meanwhile, the many faces of old age
Flutter before me in the tavern haze.
He cannot let me see him weep and rage
Into his wrinkled pillow. Face by face,
He grins to entertain, he fills my glass,
Cold to the gestures of my vague *alas*,
Gay as a futile god who cannot die
Till daylight, when the barkeep says goodbye.

Sparrows in a Hillside Drift

Pitiful dupes of old illusion, lost
And fallen in the white, they glitter still
Sprightly as when they bathed in summer dust,
Then fade among the crystals on the hill.

Lonely for warm days when the season broke,
Alert to wing and fire, they must have flown
To rest among those toughened boughs of oak
That brood above us, now the fire is gone.

Walking around to breathe, I kick aside
The soft brown feather and the brittle beak.
All flesh is fallen snow. The days deride
The wings of these deluded, once they break.

Somewhere the race of wittier birds survive,
Southering slowly with the cooling days.
They pause to quiver in the wind alive
Like some secure felicity of phrase.

But these few blunderers below my hands
Assault the ear with silence on the wind.

I lose their words, though winter understands.
Man is the listener gone deaf and blind.

The oak above us shivers in the bleak
And lucid winter day; and, far below
Our gathering of the cheated and the weak,
A chimney whispers to a cloud of snow.

A Note Left in Jimmy Leonard's Shack

Near the dry river's water-mark we found
    Your brother Minnegan,
Flopped like a fish against the muddy ground.
Beany, the kid whose yellow hair turns green,
Told me to find you, even in the rain,
    And tell you he was drowned.

I hid behind the chassis on the bank,
    The wreck of someone's Ford:
I was afraid to come and wake you drunk:
You told me once the waking up was hard,
The daylight beating at you like a board.
    Blood in my stomach sank.

Beside, you told him never to go out
    Along the river-side
Drinking and singing, clattering about.
You might have thrown a rock at me and cried
I was to blame, I let him fall in the road
    And pitch down on his side.

Well, I'll get hell enough when I get home
    For coming up this far,
Leaving the note, and running as I came.
I'll go and tell my father where you are.
You'd better go find Minnegan before
    Policemen hear and come.

Beany went home, and I got sick and ran,
　　You old son of a bitch.
You better hurry down to Minnegan;
He's drunk or dying now, I don't know which,
Rolled in the roots and garbage like a fish,
　　The poor old man.

At Thomas Hardy's Birthplace, 1953

1

The nurse carried him up the stair
Into his mother's sleeping room.
The beeches lashed the roof and dragged the air
　　Because of storm.

Wind could have overturned the dead.
Moth and beetle and housefly crept
Under the door to find the lamp, and cowered:
　　But still he slept.

The ache and sorrow of darkened earth
Left pathways soft and meadows sodden;
The small Frome overflowed the firth,
　　And he lay hidden

In the arms of the tall woman gone
To soothe his mother during the dark;
Nestled against the awkward flesh and bone
　　When the rain broke.

2

Last night at Stinsford where his heart
Is buried now, the rain came down.
Cold to the hidden joy, the secret hurt,
　　His heart is stone.

But over the dead leaves in the wet
The mouse goes snooping, and the bird.

Something the voiceless earth does not forget
     They come to guard,

Maybe, the heart who would not tell
Whatever secret he learned from the ground,
Who turned aside and heard the human wail,
     That other sound.

More likely, though, the laboring feet
Of fieldmouse, hedgehog, moth and hawk
Seek in the storm what comfort they can get
     Under the rock

Where surely the heart will not wake again
To endure the unending beat of the air,
Having been nursed beyond the sopping rain,
     Back down the stair.

Evening

I called him to come in,
The wide lawn darkened so.
Laughing, he held his chin
And hid beside a bush.
The light gave him a push,
Shadowy grass moved slow.
He crept on agile toes
Under a sheltering rose.

His mother, still beyond
The bare porch and the door,
Called faintly out of sound,
And vanished with her voice.
I caught his curious eyes
Measuring me, and more—
The light dancing behind
My shoulder in the wind.

Then, struck beyond belief
By the child's voice I heard,
I saw his hair turn leaf,
His dancing toes divide
To hooves on either side,
One hand become a bird.
Startled, I held my tongue
To hear what note he sang.

Where was the boy gone now?
I stood on the grass, alone.
Swung from the apple bough
The bees ignored my cry.
A dog roved past, and I
Turned up a sinking stone,
But found beneath no more
Than grasses dead last year.

Suddenly lost and cold,
I knew the yard lay bare.
I longed to touch and hold
My child, my talking child,
Laughing or tame or wild—
Solid in light and air,
The supple hands, the face
To fill that barren place.

Slowly, the leaves descended,
The birds resolved to hands;
Laugh, and the charm was ended,
The hungry boy stepped forth.
He stood on the hard earth,
Like one who understands
Fairy and ghost—but less
Our human loneliness.

Then, on the withering lawn,
He walked beside my arm.
Trees and the sun were gone,
Everything gone but us.
His mother sang in the house,
And kept our supper warm,

And loved us, God knows how,
The wide earth darkened so.

Dog in a Cornfield

Fallow between the horny trees
    The empty field
Lay underneath the motions of the cloud.
My master called for bobwhites on his knees,
    And suddenly the wind revealed
The body pitching forward in the mud.

My master leaped alive at first,
    And cried, and ran
Faster than air could echo feet and hands.
The lazy maples wailed beyond the crust
    Of earth and artificial man.
Here lay one death the autumn understands.

How could I know he ran to lie,
    And joke with me,
Beside the toppled scarecrow there, as though
His body, like the straw, lay beaten dry?
    Growling, I circled near a tree,
Indifferent to a solitary crow.

Down on the stubble field the pair
    Lay side by side,
Scarecrow and master. I could hardly tell
Body from body, and the color of hair
    Blended, to let my master hide.
His laughter thickened like a droning bell.

I called him out of earth, to come
    And walk with me,
To leave that furrow where the man's shape broke,
To let the earth collapse, and come on home.
    The limber scarecrow knew the way
To meet the wind, that monumental joke;

But once the real man tumbled down,
    Funny or not,
The broomstick and the straw might leap and cry.
Scared of the chance to wrestle wood and stone,
    I howled into the air, forgot
How scarecrows stumble in a field to die.

Snarling, I leaped the rusty fence,
    I ran across
The shock of leaves, blundering as I tore
Into the scarecrow in the man's defense.
    My master rolled away on grass
And saw me scatter legs and arms in air.

And saw me summon all my force
    To shake apart
The brittle shoes, the tough blades of the brains
Back to the ground; the brutal formlessness,
    The twisted knot of its arid heart
Back to the sweet roots of the autumn rains.

Where do the sticks and stones get off,
    Mocking the shape
Of eyes younger than summer, of thoughtful hands?
The real man falls to nothing fast enough.
    I barked into the air, to keep
The man quick to a joy he understands.

On Minding One's
Own Business

Ignorant two, we glide
On ripples near the shore.
The rainbows leap no more,
And men in boats alight
To see the day subside.

All evening fins have drowned
Back in the summer dark.

Above us, up the bank,
Obscure on lonely ground,
A shack receives the night.

I hold the left-hand oar
Out of the wash, and guide
The skiff away so wide
We wander out of sight
As soundless as before.

We will not land to bear
Our will upon that house,
Nor force on any place
Our dull offensive weight.

Somebody may be there,
Peering at us outside
Across the even lake,
Wondering why we take
Our time and stay so late.

Long may the lovers hide
In viny shacks from those
Who thrash among the trees,
Who curse, who have no peace,
Who pitch and moan all night
For fear of someone's joys,
Deploring the human face.

From prudes and muddying fools,
Kind Aphrodite, spare
All hunted criminals,
Hoboes, and whip-poor-wills,
And girls with rumpled hair,
All, all of whom might hide
Within that darkening shack.
Lovers may live, and abide.

Wherefore, I turn my back,
And trawl our boat away,
Lest someone fear to call
A girl's name till we go

Over the lake so slow
We hear the darkness fall.

The Morality of Poetry

to Gerald Enscoe

Would you the undulation of one wave,
its trick to me transfer. . . .
                              —Whitman

I stood above the sown and generous sea
Late in the day, to muse about your words:
Your human images come to pray for hands
To wipe their vision clear, your human voice
Flinging the poem forward into sound.
Below me, roaring elegies to birds,
Intricate, cold, the waters crawled the sands,
Heaving and groaning, casting up a tree,
A shell, a can to clamber over the ground:
Slow celebration, cluttering ripple on wave.

I wondered when the complicated sea
Would tear and tangle in itself and die,
Sheer outrage hammering itself to death:
Hundreds of gulls descending to the froth,
Their bodies clumped and fallen, lost to me.
Counting those images, I meant to say
A hundred gulls decline to nothingness;
But, high in cloud, a single naked gull
Shadows a depth in heaven for the eye.
And, for the ear, under the wail and snarl
Of groping foghorns and the winds grown old,
A single human word for love of air
Gathers the tangled discords up to song.
Summon the rare word for the rare desire.
It thrives on hunger, and it rises strong
To live above the blindness and the noise
Only as long as bones are clean and spare,
The spine exactly set, the muscles lean.
Before you let a single word escape,

Starve it in darkness; lash it to the shape
Of tense wing skimming on the sea alone. . . .

So through my cold lucidity of heart
I thought to send you careful rules of song.
But gulls ensnare me here; the sun fades; thought
By thought the tide heaves, bobbing my words' damp wings;
Mind is the moon-wave roiling on ripples now.
Sun on the bone-hulled galleons of those gulls
Charms my immense irrelevance away,
And lures wings moonward. Openly she soars,
A miracle out of all gray sounds, the moon,
Deepening and rifting swell and formal sky.
Woman or bird, she plumes the ashening sound,
Flaunting to nothingness the rules I made.
Scattering cinders, widening, over the sand
Her cold epistle falls. To plumb the fall
Of silver on ripple, evening ripple on wave,
Quick celebration where she lives for light,
I let all measures die. My voice is gone,
My words to you unfinished, where they lie
Common and bare as stone in diamond veins.
Where the sea moves the word moves, where the sea
Subsides, the slow word fades with lunar tides.
Now still alive, my skeletal words gone bare,
Lapsing like dead gulls' brittle wings and drowned,
In a mindless dance, beneath the darkening air,
I send you shoreward echoes of my voice:
The dithyrambic gestures of the moon,
Sun-lost, the mind plumed, Dionysian,
A blue sea-poem, joy, moon-ripple on wave.

At the Slackening of the Tide

Today I saw a woman wrapped in rags
Leaping along the beach to curse the sea.
Her child lay floating in the oil, away
From oarlock, gunwale, and the blades of oars.

The skinny lifeguard, raging at the sky,
Vomited sea, and fainted on the sand.

The cold simplicity of evening falls
Dead on my mind,
And underneath the piles the water
Leaps up, leaps up, and sags down slowly, farther
Than seagulls disembodied in the drag
Of oil and foam.

Plucking among the oyster shells a man
Stares at the sea, that stretches on its side.
Now far along the beach, a hungry dog
Announces everything I knew before:
Obliterate naiads weeping underground,
Where Homer's tongue thickens with human howls.

I would do anything to drag myself
Out of this place:
Root up a seaweed from the water,
To stuff it in my mouth, or deafen me,
Free me from all the force of human speech;
Go drown, almost.

Warm in the pleasure of the dawn I came
To sing my song
And look for mollusks in the shallows,
The whorl and coil that pretty up the earth,
While far below us, flaring in the dark,
The stars go out.

What did I do to kill my time today,
After the woman ranted in the cold,
The mellow sea, the sound blown dark as wine?
After the lifeguard rose up from the waves
Like a sea-lizard with the scales washed off?
Sit there, admiring sunlight on a shell?

Abstract with terror of the shell, I stared
Over the waters where
God brooded for the living all one day.
Lonely for weeping, starved for a sound of mourning,

I bowed my head, and heard the sea far off
Washing its hands.

All the Beautiful Are Blameless

Out of a dark into the dark she leaped
Lightly this day.
Heavy with prey, the evening skiffs are gone,
And drowsy divers lift their helmets off,
Dry on the shore.

Two stupid harly-charlies got her drunk
And took her swimming naked on the lake.
The waters rippled lute-like round the boat,
And far beyond them, dipping up and down,
Unmythological sylphs, their names unknown,
Beckoned to sandbars where the evenings fall.

Only another drunk would say she heard
A natural voice
Luring the flesh across the water.
I think of those unmythological
Sylphs of the trees.

Slight but orplidean shoulders weave in dusk
Before my eyes when I walk lonely forward
To kick beer-cans from tracked declivities.
If I, being lightly sane, may carve a mouth
Out of the air to kiss, the drowned girl surely
Listened to lute-song where the sylphs are gone.
The living and the dead glide hand in hand
Under cool waters where the days are gone.
Out of the dark into a dark I stand.

The ugly curse the world and pin my arms
Down by their grinning teeth, sneering a blame.
Closing my eyes, I look for hungry swans
To plunder the lake and bear the girl away,

Back to the larger waters where the sea
Sifts, judges, gathers the body, and subsides.

But here the starved, touristic crowd divides
And offers the dead
Hell for the living body's evil:
The girl flopped in the water like a pig
And drowned dead drunk.

So do the pure defend themselves. But she,
Risen to kiss the sky, her limbs still whole,
Rides on the dark tarpaulin toward the shore;
And the hired saviors turn their painted shell
Along the wharf, to list her human name.
But the dead have no names, they lie so still,
And all the beautiful are blameless now.

In a Viennese Cemetery

There Hugo Wolf is buried: fully formed
Out of the stone a naked woman leans
Kissing the uncut stone, the solid void
Of granite cold to sound and song unmade.
She holds her body to the rock, unwarmed
By any sculptor's trick. The climbing vines
Fail to relieve what barren death destroyed:
The life half over, and the song gone dead.

Somewhere unborn inside the stone a mouth
Hungered severely for her starving kiss.
Reaching his lover's hands across the dark,
Maybe the dead musician underneath
Whispers to touch the woman's nakedness,
To strike a fire inside the yearning rock.

Brush aside that fantasy, I feel
The wind of early autumn cross the ground,
I turn among the stones to let it blow
Clearly across my face as over stone.

Bodiless yearnings make no music fall;
Breath of the body bears the living sound.
This dour musician died so long ago
Even his granite beard is softened down.

An age or so will wear away his grave,
The lover who attains the girl be rain,
The granite underneath be carved no more.
Only the living body calls up love,
That shadow risen casually from stone
To clothe the nakedness of bare desire.

A Prayer in My Sickness

la muerte entra y sale

You hear the long roll of the plunging ground,
The whistle of stones, the quail's cry in the grass.
I stammer like a bird, I rasp like stone,
I mutter, with gray hands upon my face.
The earth blurs, beyond me, into dark.
Spinning in such bewildered sleep, I need
To know you, whirring above me, when I wake.
Come down. Come down. I lie afraid.
I have lain alien in my self so long,
How can I understand love's angry tongue?

The Cold Divinities

I should have been delighted there to hear
The woman and the boy,
Singing along the shore together.
Lightly the shawl and shoulder of the sea
Upbore the plume and body of one gull
Dropping his lines.

Loping behind a stone too large for waves
To welter down like pumice without sound,

Laughing his languages awake, that boy
Flung to his mother, on a wrack of weeds,
Delicate words, a whisper like a spume
Fluting along the edges of the shore.

I should have been delighted that the cries
Of fishermen and gulls
Faded among the swells, to let me
Gather into the fine seines of my ears
The frail fins of their voices as they sang:
My wife and child.

Lovely the mother shook her hair, so long
And glittering in its darkness, as the moon
In the deep lily-heart of the hollowing swells
Flamed toward the cold caves of the evening sea:
And the fine living frieze of her Greek face;
The sea behind her, fading, and the sails.

I should have been delighted for the gaze,
The billowing of the girl,
The bodying skirt, the ribbons falling;
I should have run to gather in my arms
The mother and the child who seemed to live
Stronger than stone and wave.

But slowly twilight gathered up the skiffs
Into its long gray arms; and though the sea
Grew kind as possible to wrack-splayed birds;
And though the sea like woman vaguely wept;
She could not hide her clear enduring face,
Her cold divinities of death and change.

The Revelation

Stress of his anger set me back
To musing over time and space.
The apple branches dripping black
Divided light across his face.

Towering beneath the broken tree,
He seemed a stony shade to me.
He spoke no language I could hear
For long with my distracted ear.

Between his lips and my delight
In blowing wind, a bird-song rose.
And soon in fierce, blockading light
The planet's shadow hid his face.
And all that strongly molded bone
Of chest and shoulder soon were gone,
Devoured among the solid shade.
Assured his angry voice was dead,

And satisfied his judging eyes
Had given over plaguing me,
I stood to let the darkness rise—
My darkness, gathering in the tree,
The field, the swollen shock of hay,
Bank of the creek half washed away.
Lost in my self, and unaware
Of love, I took the evening air.

I blighted, for a moment's length,
My father out of sight and sound;
Prayed to annihilate his strength,
The proud legs planted on the ground.
Why should I hear his angry cry
Or bear the damning of his eye?
Anger for anger I could give,
And murder for my right to live.

The moon rose. Lucidly the moon
Ran skimming shadows off the trees.
To strip all shadow but its own
Down to the perfect mindlessness.
Yet suddenly the moonlight caught
My father's fingers reaching out,
The strong arm begging me for love,
Loneliness I knew nothing of.

And weeping in the nakedness
Of moonlight and of agony,
His blue eyes lost their barrenness
And bore a blossom out to me.
And as I ran to give it back,
The apple branches, dripping black,
Trembled across the lunar air
And dropped white petals on his hair.

A Winter Day in Ohio

P. W. T. died in late Spring, 1957

Clever, defensive, seasoned animals
Plato and Christ deny your grave. But man,
Who slept for years alone, will turn his face
Alone to the common wall before his time.
Between the woodchuck and the cross, alone
All afternoon, I take my time to mourn.
I am too cold to cry against the snow
Of roots and stars, drifting above your face.

II. A Sequence of Love Poems

Thou know'st, the first time that we smell the air
We wawl and cry.
                                        —*King Lear*

A Breath of Air

I walked, when love was gone,
Out of the human town,
For an easy breath of air.
Beyond a break in the trees,
Beyond the hangdog lives
Of old men, beyond girls:
The tall stars held their peace.
Looking in vain for lies
I turned, like earth, to go.
An owl's wings hovered, bare
On the moon's hills of snow.

And things were as they were.

In Shame and Humiliation

*He will launch a curse upon the world, and as only man
can curse (it is his privilege, the primary distinction between
him and other animals), maybe by his curse alone he will at-
tain his object—that is, convince himself that he is a man
and not a piano-key!*
                    —Dostoyevsky, *Notes from Underground*

What can a man do that a beast cannot,
A bird, a reptile, any fiercer thing?
    He can amaze the ground
With anger never hissed in a snake's throat
    Or past a bitch's fang,
Though, suffocate, he cannot make a sound.

He can out-rage the forked tongue with a word,
The iron forged of his pain, over and over,
    Till the cold blade can fall
And beak an enemy's heart quick as a bird,
    And then retire to cover,
To vines of hair, declivities of skull.

Outright the snake, faster than man, can kill.
A mongrel's teeth can snarl as man's cannot.
    And a bird, unbodied soul
Soaring and dazzling, in the cloud at will
    Outbeautifies the flight
Of halt man's clavicles that flop and wheel.

Their cries last longer. Sinew of wing and coil,
Or sprung thighs of hounds impinge their iron
    Easy and quick, to leap
Over the brooks, the miles and days, like oil
    Flung on a surge of green.
A man limps into nothing more than sleep.

But under the dream he always dreams too late,
That stark abounding dream of wretchedness
    Where stones and very trees
Ignore his name, and crows humiliate,
    And fiends below the face,
Serpents, women, and dogs dance to deny his face—

He will not deny, he will not deny his own.
Thrashing in lakes or pools of broken glass,
    He hunches over to look
And feel his mouth, his nostrils, feel of the bone,
    A man's ultimate face:
The individual bone, that burns like ice.

That fire, that searing cold is what I claim:
What makes me man, that dogs can never share,
    Woman or brilliant bird,
The beaks that mock but cannot speak the names
    Of the blind rocks, of the stars.
Sprawling in dark, I burn my sudden pride.

Let my veins wither now, my words revolt
Serpent or bird or pure untroubled mind.
        I will avow my face
Unto my face and, through the spirit's vault,
        Deliberate underground,
Devour the locusts of my bitterness.

That angel, wheeled upon my heart, survives,
Nourished by food the righteous cannot eat
        And loathe to move among.
They die, fastidious, while the spirit thrives
        Out of its own defeat.
The pure, the pure! will never live so long.

The Accusation

I kissed you in the dead of dark,
And no one knew, or wished to know,
You bore, across your face, a mark
From birth, those shattered years ago.
Now I can never keep in mind
The memory of your ugliness
At a clear moment. Now my blind
Fingers alone can read your face.

Often enough I had seen that slash
Of fire you quickly hid in shame;
You flung your scarf across the flesh,
And turned away, and said my name.
Thus I remember daylight and
The scar that made me pity you.
God damn them both, you understand.
Pity can scar love's face, I know.

I loved your face because your face
Was broken. When my hands were heavy,
You kissed me only in a darkness
To make me daydream you were lovely.
All the lovely emptiness

On earth is easy enough to find.
You had no right to turn your face
From me. Only the truth is kind.

I cannot dream of you by night.
I half-remember what you were.
And I remember the cold daylight,
And pity your disgusting scar
As any light-eyed fool could pity,
Who sees you walking down the street.
I lose your stark essential beauty,
I dream some face I read about.

If I were given a blind god's power
To turn your daylight on again,
I would not raise you smooth and pure:
I would bare to heaven your uncommon pain,
Your scar I had a right to hold,
To look on, for the pain was yours.
Now you are dead, and I grow old,
And the doves cackle out of doors,

And lovers, flicking on the lights,
Turn to behold each lovely other.
Let them remember fair delights.
How can I ever love another?
You had no right to banish me
From that scarred truth of wretchedness,
Your face, that I shall never see
Again, though I search every place.

The Ghost

I cannot live nor die.
Now shadows rise nor fall,
Whisper aloud nor weep.
Struck beyond time and change
To a claw, a withering thigh,
A breath, a slackening call

To cold throats out of range,
I fade to a broken hope.

What good may mourning do,
The sigh, the soft lament,
The poised turning away
To name one faded name?
I will not name it now.
The day, the heart lie spent.
I find, now that I came,
Love that I cannot say.

The wind builds hock and tongue
Up from the sinewy ground.
But how may the blind air tell
A gnat from a lark? Alone,
Weighed by the laboring sound
Of wind on muscle and hair,
White as a thistle and bare,
I close the gate of hell.

Neat, shallow, hell is here,
Here, where I speak to lips
At one with stone and me,
Living and dead at one:
Love's cry, the shock of fear,
The shadow of rain that drips,
A mirror of gleaming stone,
The hands that cannot see,

Ears stricken blind, and eyes
That cannot speak nor sing,
And arms that barely breathe
Above ground or below.
Lumbering from hell, I gaze
Down at the earth so long,
I need no further go.
Here is the gate of wreath.

Love need no further go
Than back to the earth, to die.
The living need not seek

For love but underfoot.
The first star rises slow
And brambles lash my eye
And lichens trip my foot,
And yet, I cannot speak.

I will stand here, till dawn.
I will not fall down, to pray.
Dark bells may summon you
Out of your dream to cry.
Then I will tread your lawn
Through a soft break of day,
To see your day go by,
Who stare, and stare me through.

The Alarm

When I came back from my last dream, when I
Whirled in the morning snowfall up the lawn,
I looked behind me where my wings were gone.
Rusting above the snow, for lack of care,
A pile of rakes and shovels rotted away.
Tools of the world were crumbling into air,
And I, neither the living nor the dead,
Paused in the dusk of dawn to wonder why
Any man clambers upward out of shade
To rake and shovel all his dust away.

I found my body sprawled against the bed.
One hand flopped back as though to ward away
Shovels of light. The body wakes to burial:
But my face rebelled; the lids and lips were gray,
And spiders climbed their webs above my head.
I stood above my wreck of flesh and skull:
A foot reclined over the wrenching thigh,
And suddenly, before I joined my face,
The eyelids opened, and it stared across
The window pane, into the empty sky.

Neither the living nor the dead I stood,
Longing to leave my poor flesh huddled there
Heaped up for burning under the last laments.
I moved, to leap on spider webs and climb.
But where do spiders fling those filaments,
Those pure formalities of blood and air,
Both perfect and alive? I did no good.
The hands of daylight hammered down my ghost,
And I was home now, bowing into my dust,
To quicken into stupor one more time,
One of the living buried like the dead.

A Girl Walking into a Shadow

The mere trees cast no coolness where you go.
Your small feet press no darkness into the grass.
I know your weight of days, and mourn I know.
All hues beneath the ground are bare grayness.

When I was young, I might have touched your hair,
Gestured my warning, how that fire will gray,
Slight arms and delicate hands fall heavier,
And pale feet hasten to a dark delay.

Now old, I love you slowly, through my sound.
Lightly alive, you cannot mourn for trees.
You cannot care how grass, above the ground,
Gathers to mold your shadow's quick caress.

Heavy for you, I hear the futile speech
Of air in trees, of shadows in your hair.
Quick to go by me now, beyond my reach,
You pause. With darkness deepening everywhere,

Something of light falls, pitiful and kind.
Something of love forgot the dark embrace
Of evening, where the lover's eyes go blind
With dreaming on the hollows of your face.

But Only Mine

I dreamed that I was dead, as all men do,
And feared the dream, though hardly for the sake
Of any thrust of pain my flesh might take
Below the softening shales. Bereft of you,
I lay for days and days alone, I knew
Somewhere above me boughs were burning gold,
And women's frocks were loose, and men grew old.

Grew old. And shrivelled. Asked the time of day.
And then forgot. Turned. Looked among the grass.
Tripped on a twig. Frightened some leaves away.
Children. And girls. I knew, above my face,
Rabbit and jay flocked, wondering how to cross
An empty field stripped naked to the sun.
They halted into a shadow, huddled down.

Rabbit and jay, old man, and girl, and child,
All moved above me, dreaming of broad light.
I heard you walking through the empty field.
Startled awake, I found my living sight:
The grave drifted away, and it was night,
I felt your soft despondent shoulders near.
Out of my dream, the dead rose everywhere.

I did not dream your death, but only mine.

III. The Part Nearest Home

From the uttermost part of the earth have we heard songs, even glory to the righteous. But I said, My leanness, my leanness, woe unto me.

—Isaiah 24:16

What the Earth Asked Me

"Why did you kiss the girl who cried
For lovers through her lonely mind,
Homely as sin and sick of pride?"

    In pity for my kind.

"What good will pity do the lost
Who flutter in the driven wind,
Wild for the body, ghost on ghost?"

    No good, no good to me.

"Why did you hammer with your fist
That beetle on the window-blind,
Withered in summer's holocaust?"

    In pity for my kind.

"What good will pity do the found
Who flutter in the driven wind,
Wild to be ghosts below the ground?"

    No good, no good to me.

"The living and the dead together
Flutter before, flutter behind.
Why do you try to change the weather?"

    In pity for my kind.

"What good will pity do the kiss
That shrivels on the mouth of grief?
Have you been calling me for this?"

No good to me, no good to me.

The Refusal

When we get back, the wagon will be gone,
The porchlight empty in the wind, no doubt;
    And everybody here,
Who damned us for the conscience of a stone,
    Will tell us to get out
And do our sniffling in the dark somewhere.

It may not be delight to hear that word,
The pride of mourners mocking in our faces.
    I offer no delight,
Neither a soft life, nor a grave deferred.
    I have known other places
Ugly as this, and shut them from my sight.

Inside the house, somebody we could love,
Who labored for us till the taut string gave,
    Stares from a half-closed eye.
Why should we gaze back in that pit of love?
    All the beloved lie
In the perpetual savagery of graves.

Come here to me; I will not let you go
To suffer on some relative's hard shoulder—
    Weeping woman or man.
God, I have died so many days ago,
    The funeral began
When I was born, and will go on forever:—

Unless I shut the door myself, and take
Your elbow, drag you bodily, out of breath
    And let the house grow dark.

Inside, that lamentation for the sake
    Of numbers on a rock
Starves me and freezes you, and kills us both.

Must we reel with the wine of mourning like a drunk?
Look there, the doors are latched, the windows close,
    And we are told to go.
When we come back, the granite will be sunk
    An inch or more below
The careful fingers of the healing snows.

Preacher and undertaker follow the cars;
They claimed the comfort of the earth, and lied.
    Better to trust the moon
Blown in the soft bewilderment of stars;
    The living lean on pain,
The hard stones of the earth are on our side.

American Twilights, 1957

to Caryl Chessman

1

The buckles glitter, billies lean
Supple and cold as men on walls.
The trusties' faces, yawning green,
Summon up heart, as someone calls
For light, for light! and evening falls.

Checking the cells, the warden piles
Shadow on shadow where he goes
Beyond the catwalk, down the files,
Sneering at one who thumbs his nose.
One weeps, and stumbles on his toes.

Tear and tormented snicker and heart
Click in the darkness; close, and fade.
Clean locks together mesh and part,
And lonely lifers, foot and head,
Huddle against the bed they made.

2

Lie dark, beloved country, now.
Trouble no dream, so still you lie.
Citizens drawl their dreams away;
Stupored, they hid their agony
Deep in the rock; but men must die.

Tall on the earth I would have sung
Heroes of hell, could I have learned
Their names to marvel on my tongue;
The land is dark where they have turned,
And now their very names are burned.

But buried under trestled rock
The broken thief and killer quake:
Tower by tower and clock by clock
Citizens wind the towns asleep.
God, God have pity when they wake.

Haunted by gallows, peering in dark,
I conjure prisons out of wet
And strangling pillows where I mark
The misery man must not forget,
Though I have found no prison yet.

Lo now, the desolation man
Has tossed away like a gnawed bone
Will hunt him where the sea began,
Summon him out of tree and stone,
Damn him, before his dream be gone:—

Seek him behind his bars, to crack
Out the dried kernel of his heart.
God, God have pity if he wake,
Have mercy on man who dreamed apart.
God, God have pity on man apart.

Devotions

I longed to kill you once, when I was young,
Because you laughed at me before my friends.
    And now the baffled prose
Of a belated vengeance numbs my tongue.
    Come back, before the last wind bends
Your body to the void beyond repose.

Standing alone before your grave, I read
The name, the season, every decent praise
    A chisel might devise—
Deliberate scrawls to guard us from the dead.
    And yet I lift my strength, to raise
Out of the mossy wallow your pig's eyes.

The summons fell, but I could not come home
To gloat above the hackling and the rasp
    Caught in your corded throat;
And, many towns away, I heard your doom
    Tolling the hate beyond my grasp,
Thieving the poisons of my angry thought.

After so many years to lose the vision
Of your last anguish! Furious at the cheat,
    After your burial
I traveled here, to lay my weak derision
    Fresh as a garland at your feet.
All day I have gathered curses, but they fail.

I cannot even call to mind so clearly,
As once I could, your confident thin voice
    Banishing me to nothing.
Your hand crumbles, your sniffing nostrils barely
    Evoke the muscles of my loathing:
And I too die, who came here to rejoice.

Lost mocker of my childhood, how the moss
Softens your hair, how deeply nibbling fangs
    Sink in the careless ground.
Seasons of healing grasses weave across
    Your caving lips, and dull my strange
Terror of failures. Shaken, I have found

Nothing to mark you off in earth but stone.
Walking here lonely and strange now, I must find
    A grave to prod my wrath
Back to its just devotions. Miserable bone,
    Devouring jaw-hinge, glare gone blind,
Come back, be damned of me, your aftermath.

At the Executed Murderer's Grave

for J. L. D.

*Why should we do this? What good is it to us? Above all, how
can we do such a thing? How can it possibly be done?*
                              —Freud

1

My name is James A. Wright, and I was born
Twenty-five miles from this infected grave,
In Martins Ferry, Ohio, where one slave
To Hazel-Atlas Glass became my father.
He tried to teach me kindness. I return
Only in memory now, aloof, unhurried,
To dead Ohio, where I might lie buried,
Had I not run away before my time.
Ohio caught George Doty. Clean as lime,
His skull rots empty here. Dying's the best
Of all the arts men learn in a dead place.
I walked here once. I made my loud display,
Leaning for language on a dead man's voice.
Now sick of lies, I turn to face the past.
I add my easy grievance to the rest:

2

Doty, if I confess I do not love you,
Will you let me alone? I burn for my own lies.
The nights electrocute my fugitive,
My mind. I run like the bewildered mad
At St. Clair Sanitarium, who lurk,
Arch and cunning, under the maple trees,
Pleased to be playing guilty after dark.
Staring to bed, they croon self-lullabies.

Doty, you make me sick. I am not dead.
I croon my tears at fifty cents per line.

3
Idiot, he demanded love from girls,
And murdered one. Also, he was a thief.
He left two women, and a ghost with child.
The hair, foul as a dog's upon his head,
Made such revolting Ohio animals
Fitter for vomit than a kind man's grief.
I waste no pity on the dead that stink,
And no love's lost between me and the crying
Drunks of Belaire, Ohio, where police
Kick at their kidneys till they die of drink.
Christ may restore them whole, for all of me.
Alive and dead, those giggling muckers who
Saddled my nightmares thirty years ago
Can do without my widely printed sighing
Over their pains with paid sincerity.
I do not pity the dead, I pity the dying.

4
I pity myself, because a man is dead.
If Belmont County killed him, what of me?
His victims never loved him. Why should we?
And yet, nobody had to kill him either.
It does no good to woo the grass, to veil
The quicklime hole of a man's defeat and shame.
Nature-lovers are gone. To hell with them.
I kick the clods away, and speak my name.

5
This grave's gash festers. Maybe it will heal,
When all are caught with what they had to do
In fear of love, when every man stands still
By the last sea,
And the princes of the sea come down
To lay away their robes, to judge the earth
And its dead, and we dead stand undefended everywhere,
And my bodies—father and child and unskilled criminal—
Ridiculously kneel to bare my scars,
My sneaking crimes, to God's unpitying stars.

6

Staring politely, they will not mark my face
From any murderer's, buried in this place.
Why should they? We are nothing but a man.

7

Doty, the rapist and the murderer,
Sleeps in a ditch of fire, and cannot hear;
And where, in earth or hell's unholy peace,
Men's suicides will stop, God knows, not I.
Angels and pebbles mock me under trees.
Earth is a door I cannot even face.
Order be damned, I do not want to die,
Even to keep Belaire, Ohio, safe.
The hackles on my neck are fear, not grief.
(Open, dungeon! Open, roof of the ground!)
I hear the last sea in the Ohio grass,
Heaving a tide of gray disastrousness.
Wrinkles of winter ditch the rotted face
Of Doty, killer, imbecile, and thief:
Dirt of my flesh, defeated, underground.

Saint Judas

When I went out to kill myself, I caught
A pack of hoodlums beating up a man.
Running to spare his suffering, I forgot
My name, my number, how my day began,
How soldiers milled around the garden stone
And sang amusing songs; how all that day
Their javelins measured crowds; how I alone
Bargained the proper coins, and slipped away.

Banished from heaven, I found this victim beaten,
Stripped, kneed, and left to cry. Dropping my rope
Aside, I ran, ignored the uniforms:
Then I remembered bread my flesh had eaten,
The kiss that ate my flesh. Flayed without hope,
I held the man for nothing in my arms.

Some Translations
(from *Collected Poems*
and new translations)

In memory of Betty Kray

Ten Short Poems

From the Spanish of Juan Ramón Jiménez

1

Rose of the Sea

The white moon takes the sea away from the sea
and gives it back to the sea. Beautiful,
conquering by means of the pure and tranquil,
the moon compels the truth to delude itself
that it is truth become whole, eternal, solitary,
though it is not so.
                    Yes.
                          Divine plainness,
you pierce the familiar certainty, you place
a new soul into whatever is real.
Unpredictable rose! you took the rose away
from the rose, and you could give back
the rose to the rose.

From Diario de Poeta y Mar

2

To the bridge of love,
old stone between tall cliffs
    —eternal meeting place, red evening—,
I come with my heart.
    —My beloved is only water,
that always passes away, and does not deceive,
that always passes away, and does not change,
that always passes away, and does not end.

From Eternidades

3

The dawn brings with it
that sadness of arriving, by train,
at a station that is not one's own.
    How disagreeable, those rumblings
of a new day that one knows cannot last long—
    —Oh my life!—
Overhead, as the day breaks, a child is crying.

From Eternidades

4

Rosebushes

It is the sea, in the earth.
Colors of the south, in the winter sun,
contain the noisy shiftings
of the sea and the coasts . . .
Tomorrow in the sea!—I say, rather, in the earth
that moves, now, into the sea!

From *Diario de Poeta y Mar*

5

Dreaming

—No, no!
        and the dirtyneck boy starts crying and running
without getting away, in a moment, on the streets.
        His hands,
he's got something in his hands!
He doesn't know what it is, but he runs to the dawn
With his hidden prize.
Endlessly beforehand, we know what his trophy is:
something ignored, that the soul keeps awake in us.
We almost start to glitter inside his gold
with extravagant nakedness . . .
    —No, no!
        and the dirtyneck boy starts crying and running
without getting away, in a moment, on the street.
The arm is strong, it could easily grab him . . .
The heart, also a beggar, lets him go.

From *Diario de Poeta y Mar*

6

How close to becoming spirit something is,
when it is still so immensely far away
from hands!
        like starlight,
like a nameless voice
in a dream, like faraway horses,
that we hear, as we breathe heavily,
one ear placed to the ground;
like the sea on the telephone . . .

And life begins to grow
within us, the delightful daylight
that cannot be switched off,
that is thinning, now, somewhere else.
    Ah, how lovely, how lovely,
truth, even if it is not real, how lovely!

From Diario de Poeta y Mar

7

On the City Ramparts of Cádiz

The sea is enormous,
just as everything is,
yet it seems to me I am still with you . . .
Soon only water will separate us,
water, restlessly shifting,
water, only water!

From Diario de Poeta y Mar

8

Stormclouds
give their morose faces to the sea.

    The water, worked up out of iron,
is a hard, flat landscape,
of exhausted mines,
in a state of collapse,
ruins.

    Nothingness! That word, for me,
here, today, comes home,
the cadaver of a word,
laid out, naturally,
in its own grave.
            Nothingness!

From Diario de Poeta y Mar

9

Moguer

Moguer. Mother and brothers.
The house, clean and warm.

What sunlight there is, what rest
in the whitening cemetery!
In a moment, love grows remote.
The sea does not exist; the field
of vineyards, reddish and level,
is the world, like a bright light shining on nothing,
and flimsy, like a bright light shining on nothing.

Here I have been cheated enough!
Here, the only healthy thing to do is die.
This is the way out, that I wanted so badly,
that escapes into the sunset.

Moguer. If only I could rise up, sanctified!
Moguer. Brothers and sisters.

From *Diario de Poeta y Mar*

10

Life

What I used to regard as a glory shut in my face,
was a door, opening
toward this clarity:
Country without a name:

Nothing can destroy it, this road
of doors, opening, one after another,
always toward reality:
Life without calculation!

From *Eternidades*

I Want to Sleep

From the Spanish of Jorge Guillén

I shall be still stronger,
Still clearer, purer, so let
The sweet invasion of oblivion come on.
I want to sleep.

If I could forget myself, if I were only
A tranquil tree,
Branches to spread out the silence,
Trunk of mercy.

The great darkness, grown motherly,
Deepens little by little,
Brooding over this body that the soul—
After a pause—surrenders.

It may even embark from the endless world,
From its accidents,
And, scattering into stars at the last,
The soul will be daybreak.

Abandoning myself to my accomplice,
My boat,
I shall reach on my ripples and mists
Into the dawn.

I do not want to dream of useless phantoms,
I do not want a cave.
Let the huge moonless spaces
Hold me apart, and defend me.

Let me enjoy so much harmony
Thanks to the ignorance
Of this being, that is so secure
It pretends to be nothing.

Night with its darkness, solitude with its peace,
Everything favors
My delight in the emptiness
That soon will come.

Emptiness, O paradise
Rumored about so long:
Sleeping, sleeping, growing alone
Very slowly.

Darken me, erase me,
Blessed sleep,

As I lie under a heaven that mounts
Its guard over me.

Earth, with your darker burdens,
Drag me back down,
Sink my being into my being:
Sleep, sleep.

Nature Alive

From the Spanish of Jorge Guillén

The panel board of the table,
That smooth plane precisely
True to a hair, holds up
Its level form, sustained

By an idea: pure, exact,
The mind's image before
The mind's eyes! And yet,
Full assurance needs the touch

That explores and discovers
How the formal idea sags back
Down to the rich heaviness
Of kindling, trunk and timber

Of walnut. The walnut wood,
Secure in its own whorls
And grains, assured of its long
Season of so much strength

Now fused into the heart
Of this quiet vigor, the stuff
Of a table board, remains
Always, always wild!

Love Song to a Morning

From the Spanish of Jorge Guillén

Morning, clear morning,
If only I were your lover!

With every step I take on your margin,
I should long for you all the more.

My word hurries to gather
All of your fresh beauty.

Here we are, on our path.
Let me understand you.

Loveliness, held lightly
To the blade of nothingness!

The blue rosemary
Smells of the real earth.

How much of the world does the mallow
Grasp from her stone?

The cricket trills endlessly.
I bow to his patience.

How much joy the honeybee
Leaves to the flower!

And he plunges, laboring
In the heat of the mine.

Now the cricket is hurrying
His song. Is there yet more spring?

Whoever loses all this, loses himself.
So much green, and the field mine!

Heaven that the eye cannot fathom:
It is love that wins you.

Don't I deserve such a morning?
My heart earns it.

Clarity, uttermost strength;
My soul is fulfilled in you.

Anguish of Death

From the Spanish of Pablo Neruda

In Cajamarca, the anguish of death began.

The youthful Atahualpa, sky-blue stamen,
illustrious tree, listened to the wind
carry the faint murmur of steel.
There was a confused
light, an earth-tremor from the coast,
an unbelievable galloping—
rearing and power—
from iron and iron, among the weeds.
The governors were arriving.
The Inca came out to the music
surrounded by his nobles.

The visitors
from another planet, sweaty and bearded,
go to do reverence.
The chaplain,
Valverde, treacherous heart, rotten jackal,
brings forward a strange object, a piece
of a basket, a fruit,
perhaps from the same planet from which the horses come.
Atahualpa takes it. He does not know
what it is made of; it doesn't shine, it makes no noise,
and he lets it fall, smiling.

"Death;
vengeance, kill, I will absolve you,"
the jackal of the murderous cross cries out.
Thunder draws near the robbers.

Our blood is shed in its cradle.
The young princes gather like a chorus
around the Inca, in the hour of the anguish of death.

Ten thousand Peruvians fell
under crosses and swords, the blood
moistened the robes of Atahualpa.
Pizarro, the cruel hog from western Spain,
had the slender arms of the Inca
tied up. Night has now come down
over Peru like a live coal that is black.

Some Beasts

From the Spanish of Pablo Neruda

It was the twilight of the iguana.
From the rainbow-arch of the battlements,
his long tongue like a lance
sank down in the green leaves,
and a swarm of ants, monks with feet chanting,
crawled off into the jungle;
the guanaco, thin as oxygen
in the wide peaks of cloud,
went along, wearing his shoes of gold,
while the llama opened his honest eyes
on the breakable neatness
of a world full of dew.
The monkeys braided a sexual
thread that went on and on
along the shores of the dawn,
demolishing walls of pollen
and startling the butterflies of Muzo
into flying violets.
It was the night of the alligators,
the pure night, crawling
with snouts emerging from ooze,
and out of the sleepy marshes
the confused noise of scaly plates
returned to the ground where they began.

The jaguar brushes the leaves
with a luminous absence,
the puma runs through the branches
like a forest fire,
while the jungle's drunken eyes
burn from inside him.
The badgers scratch the river's
feet, scenting the nest
whose throbbing delicacy
they attack with red teeth.

And deep in the huge waters
the enormous anaconda lies
like the circle around the earth,
covered with ceremonies of mud,
devouring, religious.

The Heights of Machu Picchu, III

From the Spanish of Pablo Neruda

The human soul was threshed out like maize in the endless
granary of defeated actions, of mean things that happened,
to the very edge of endurance, and beyond,
and not only death, but many deaths, came to each one:
each day a tiny death, dust, worm, a light
flicked off in the mud at the city's edge, a tiny death
        with coarse wings
pierced into each man like a short lance
and the man was besieged by the bread or by the knife,
the cattle-dealer: the child of sea-harbors, or the dark
        captain of the plough,
or the rag-picker of snarled streets:

everybody lost heart, anxiously waiting for death, the
        short death of every day:
and the grinding bad luck of every day was
like a black cup that they drank, with their hands shaking.

Trumpets

From the German of Georg Trakl

Under the trimmed willows, where brown children
    are playing
And leaves tumbling, the trumpets blow. A quaking
    of cemeteries.
Banners of scarlet rattle through a sadness of maple trees,
Riders along rye-fields, empty mills.

Or shepherds sing during the night, and stags step delicately
Into the circle of their fire, the grove's sorrow immensely old,
Dancing, they loom up from one black wall;
Banners of scarlet, laughter, insanity, trumpets.

De Profundis

From the German of Georg Trakl

It is a stubble field, where a black rain is falling.
It is a brown tree, that stands alone.
It is a hissing wind, that encircles empty houses.
How melancholy the evening is.

Beyond the village,
The soft orphan garners the sparse ears of corn.
Her eyes graze, round and golden, in the twilight
And her womb awaits the heavenly bridegroom.

On the way home
The shepherd found the sweet body
Decayed in a bush of thorns.

I am a shadow far from darkening villages.
I drank the silence of God
Out of the stream in the trees.

Cold metal walks on my forehead.
Spiders search for my heart.
It is a light that goes out in my mouth.

At night, I found myself in a pasture,
Covered with rubbish and the dust of stars.
In a hazel thicket
Angels of crystal rang out once more.

The Rats

From the German of Georg Trakl

In the farmyard the white moon of autumn shines.
Fantastic shadows fall from the eaves of the roof.
A silence is living in the empty windows;
Now from it the rats emerge softly

And skitter here and there, squeaking.
And a gray malodorous mist from the latrine
Follows behind them, sniffing:
Through the mist the ghostly moonlight quivers.

And the rats squeak eagerly as if insane
And go out to fill houses and barns
Which are filled full of fruit and grain.
Icy winds quarrel in the darkness.

A Winter Night

From the German of Georg Trakl

It has been snowing. Past midnight, drunk on purple wine,
you leave the gloomy shelters of men, and the red fire of their
fireplaces. Oh the darkness of night.

Black frost. The ground is hard, the air has a bitter taste.
Your stars make unlucky figures.

With a stiff walk, you tramp along the railroad embankment
with huge eyes, like a soldier charging a dark machinegun nest.
Onward!

Bitter snow and moon.

A red wolf, that an angel is strangling. Your trouser legs rustle, as you walk, like blue ice, and a smile full of suffering and pride petrifies your face, and your forehead is white before the ripe desire of the frost;

or else it bends down silently over the doze of the night-watchman, slumped down in his wooden shack.

Frost and smoke. A white shirt of stars burns on your clothed shoulders, and the hawk of God strips flesh out of your hard heart.

Oh the stony hill. The cool body, forgotten and silent, is melting away in the silver snow.

Sleep is black. For a long time the ear follows the motion of the stars deep down in the ice.

When you woke, the churchbells were ringing in the town. Out of the door in the east the rose-colored day walked with silver light.

Sleep

From the German of Georg Trakl

Not your dark poisons again,
White sleep!
This fantastically strange garden
Of trees in deepening twilight
Fills up with serpents, nightmoths,
Spiders, bats.
Approaching the stranger! Your abandoned shadow
In the red of evening
Is a dark pirate ship
On the salty oceans of confusion.
White birds from the outskirts of the night

Flutter out over the shuddering cities
Of steel.

I Am Freed

From the Spanish of César Vallejo

I am freed from the burdens of the sea
when the waters come toward me.

Let us always sail out. Let us taste
the marvellous song, the song spoken
by the lower lips of desire.
Oh beautiful virginity.
The saltless breeze passes.

From the distance, I breathe marrows,
hearing the profound score, as the surf
hunts for its keys.

And if we banged
into the absurd,
we shall cover ourselves with the gold of owning nothing,
and hatch the still unborn wing
of the night, sister
of the orphaned wing of the day,
that is not really a wing since it is only one.

White Rose

From the Spanish of César Vallejo

I feel all right. Now
a stoical frost shines
in me.
It makes me laugh, this ruby-colored
rope
that creaks in my body.

Endless rope,
like a spiral
descending
from
evil . . .
rope, bloody and clumsy,
shaped by
a thousand waiting daggers.

Because it goes in this way, braiding
its rolls of funeral crepe,
and because it ties the quivering cat
of Fear to the frozen nest,
to the final fire.

Now surrounded by light
I am calm.
And out on my Pacific
a shipwrecked coffin mews.

A Divine Falling of Leaves

From the Spanish of César Vallejo

Moon: royal crown of an enormous head,
dropping leaves into yellow shadows as you go.
Red crown of a Jesus who broods
tragically, softly over emeralds!

Moon: reckless heart in heaven,
why do you row toward the west
in that cup filled with blue wine,
whose hull is defeated and sad?

Moon: it is no use flying anyway,
so you go up in a flame of scattered opals:
maybe you are my heart, who is like a gypsy,
who loafs in the sky, shedding poems like tears! . . .

Down to the Dregs

From the Spanish of César Vallejo

This afternoon it rains as never before; and I
don't feel like staying alive, heart.

The afternoon is pleasant. Why shouldn't it be?
It is wearing grace and pain; it is dressed like a woman.

This afternoon in Lima it is raining. And I remember
the cruel caverns of my ingratitude;
my block of ice laid on her poppy,
stronger than her crying "Don't be this way!"

My violent black flowers; and the barbarous
and staggering blow with a stone; and the glacial pause.
And the silence of her dignity will pour
scalding oils on the end of the sentence.

Therefore, this afternoon, as never before, I walk
with this owl, with this heart.

And other women go past; and seeing me sullen,
they sip a little of you
in the abrupt furrow of my deep grief.

This afternoon it rains, rains endlessly. And I
don't feel like staying alive, heart.

Our Daily Bread

From the Spanish of César Vallejo
    for Alejandro Gamboa

Breakfast is drunk down . . . Damp earth
of the cemetery gives off the fragrance of the precious blood.
City of winter . . . the mordant crusade
of a cart that seems to pull behind it
an emotion of fasting that cannot get free!

I wish I could beat on all the doors,
and ask for somebody; and then
look at the poor, and, while they wept softly,
give bits of fresh bread to them.
And plunder the rich of their vineyards
with those two blessed hands
which blasted the nails with one blow of light,
and flew away from the Cross!

Eyelash of morning, you cannot lift yourselves!
Give us our daily bread,
Lord . . . !

Every bone in me belongs to others;
and maybe I robbed them.
I came to take something for myself that maybe
was meant for some other man;
and I start thinking that, if I had not been born,
another poor man could have drunk this coffee.
I feel like a dirty thief . . . Where will I end?

And in this frigid hour, when the earth
has the odor of human dust and is so sad,
I wish I could beat on all the doors
and beg pardon from someone,
and make bits of fresh bread for him
here, in the oven of my heart . . . !

The Eternal Dice

From the Spanish of César Vallejo

> For Manuel González Prada, this wild and unique
> feeling—one of those emotions which the great mas-
> ter has admired most in my work

My God, I am weeping for the life that I live;
I am sorry to have stolen your bread;
but this wretched, thinking piece of clay
is not a crust formed in your side:
you have no Marys that abandon you!

My God, if you had been man,
today you would know how to be God;
but you always lived so well,
that now you feel nothing of your own creation.
And the man who suffers you: he is God!

Today, when there are candles in my witchlike eyes,
as in the eyes of a condemned man,
God of mine, you will light all your lamps,
and we will play with the old dice . . .
Gambler, when the whole universe, perhaps,
is thrown down,
the circled eyes of Death will turn up,
like two final aces of clay.

My God, in this muffled, dark night,
you can't play any more, because the Earth
is already a die nicked and rounded
from rolling by chance;
and it can stop only in a hollow place,
in the hollow of the enormous grave.

The Big People

From the Spanish of César Vallejo

What time are the big people
going to come back?
Blind Santiago is striking six
and already it's very dark.

Mother said that she wouldn't be delayed.

Aguedita, Nativa, Miguel,
be careful of going over there, where
doubled-up griefs whimpering their memories
have just gone
toward the quiet poultry yard, where
the hens are still getting settled,
who have been startled so much.

We'd better just stay here.
Mother said that she wouldn't be delayed.

And we shouldn't be sad. Let's go see
the boats—mine is prettier than anybody's!—
we were playing with them the whole blessed day,
without fighting among ourselves, as it should be:
they stayed behind in the puddle, all ready,
loaded with pleasant things for tomorrow.

Let's wait like this, obedient
and helpless, for the homecoming, the apologies
of the big people, who are always the first
to abandon the rest of us in the house—
as if we couldn't get away too!

Aguedita, Nativa, Miguel?
I am calling, I am feeling around for you in the darkness.
Don't leave me behind by myself,
to be locked in all alone.

Across the Fields . . .

From the German of Hermann Hesse

Across the sky, the clouds move,
Across the fields, the wind,
Across the fields the lost child
Of my mother wanders.

Across the street, leaves blow,
Across the trees, birds cry—
Across the mountains, far away,
My home must be.

Ravenna (1)

From the German of Hermann Hesse

I, too, have been in Ravenna.
It is a little dead city
That has churches and a good many ruins.
You can read about it in books.

You walk back through it and look around you:
The streets are so muddy and damp, and so
Dumbstruck for a thousand years,
And moss and grass, everywhere.

That is what old songs are like—
You listen to them, and nobody laughs
And everybody draws back into
His own time till night falls into him.

Ravenna (2)

From the German of Hermann Hesse

The women of Ravenna,
With their deep gazes and affectionate gestures,
Carry a knowledge of the days
Of the old city, their festivals.

The women of Ravenna
Weep like children who won't tell you: deep, light.
And when they laugh, a glittering song
Rises in the sludge of the text.

The women of Ravenna pray
Like children: gentle, fully contented.
They can speak love's words without even knowing
Themselves they are lying.

The women of Ravenna kiss
Rarely and deep, they kiss back.

And all they know about life is that
We all have to die.

The Poet

From the German of Hermann Hesse

Only on me, the lonely one,
The unending stars of the night shine,
The stone fountain whispers its magic song,
To me alone, to me the lonely one
The colorful shadows of the wandering clouds
Move like dreams over the open countryside.
Neither house nor farmland,
Neither forest nor hunting privilege is given to me,
What is mine belongs to no one,
The plunging brook behind the veil of the woods,
The frightening sea,
The bird whir of children at play,
The weeping and singing, lonely in the evening, of a man
    secretly in love.
The temples of the gods are mine also, and mine
The aristocratic groves of the past.
And no less, the luminous
Vault of heaven in the future is my home:
Often in full flight of longing my soul storms upwards,
To gaze on the future of blessed men,
Love, overcoming the law, love from people to people.
I find them all again, nobly transformed:
Farmer, king, tradesman, busy sailors,
Shepherd and gardener, all of them
Gratefully celebrate the festival of the future world.
Only the poet is missing,
The lonely one who looks on,
The bearer of human longings, the pale image
Of whom the future, the fulfillment of the world
Has no further need. Many garlands
Wilt on his grave,
But no one remembers him.

The First Flowers

From the German of Hermann Hesse

Beside the brook
Towards the willows,
During these days
So many yellow flowers have opened
Their eyes into gold.
I have long since lost my innocence, yet memory
Touches my depth, the golden hours of morning, and gazes
Brilliantly upon me out of the eyes of flowers.
I was going to pick flowers;
Now I leave them all standing
And walk home, an old man.

Opening Poem

From the Spanish of Miguel Hernández

The field has drawn back
when it saw man, muscles
tightened, rush into it.

What an abyss appears
between the olive tree and man!

The animal who sings:
the animal who is able
to weep and to sink roots,
remembered his claws.

Claws that he adorned
with silkiness and flowers
but at last allows to be bare
in all their cruelty.

My claws are snapping on my hands.
Keep away from them, my son.
I am liable to plunge them,

I am liable to thrust them
into your fragile body.

I have turned back into the tiger.
Keep away, or I will destroy you.

Today love is death,
and man is a hunter of man.

The Wounded Man

From the Spanish of Miguel Hernández
  for the wall of a hospital in the front lines

 1

The wounded stretch out across the battlefields.
And from that stretched field of bodies that fight
a wheat-field of warm fountains springs up and spreads out
into streams with husky voices.

Blood always rains upwards towards the sky.
And the wounds lie there making sounds like seashells,
if inside the wounds there is the swiftness of flight,
essence of waves.

Blood smells like the sea, and tastes like the sea, and the wine-
      cellar.
The wine-cellar of the sea, of rough wine, breaks open
where the wounded man drowns, shuddering,
and he flowers and finds himself where he is.

I am wounded: look at me: I need more lives.
The one I have is too small for the consignment
of blood that I want to lose through wounds.
Tell me who has not been wounded.

My life is a wound with a happy childhood.
Pity the man who is not wounded, who doesn't feel
wounded by life, and never sleeps in life,
joyfully wounded.

If a man goes towards the hospitals joyfully,
they change into gardens of half-opened wounds,
of flowering oleanders in front of the surgery room
with its bloodstained doors.

2

Thinking of freedom I bleed, struggle, manage to live on.
Thinking of freedom, like a tree of blood
that is generous and imprisoned, I give my eyes and hands
to the surgeons.

Thinking of freedom I feel more hearts than grains of sand
in my chest: my veins give up foam,
and I enter the hospitals and I enter the rolls of gauze
as if they were lilies.

Thinking of freedom I break loose in battle
from those who have rolled her statue through the mud.
And I break loose from my feet, from my arms,
from my house, from everything.

Because where some empty eye-pits dawn,
she will place two stones that see into the future,
and cause new arms and new legs to grow
in the lopped flesh.

Bits of my body I lose in every wound
will sprout once more, sap-filled, autumnless wings.
Because I am like the lopped tree, and I sprout again:
because I still have my life.

July 18, 1936–July 18, 1938

From the Spanish of Miguel Hernández

It is blood. It is not hail, battering my temples.
It is two years of blood; two enormous bloods.
Blood that acts like the sun, you come devouring,
till all the balconies are left drowned and empty.

Blood that is the best of all riches.
Blood that stored up its gifts for love.
See it stirring up seas, surprising trains,
breaking bulls' spirits as it heartens lions.

Time is blood. Time circulates through my veins.
In the presence of the clock and daybreak, I am more than
     wounded,
and I hear blood colliding, of every shape and size.

Blood where even death could hardly bathe:
moving brilliance of blood that has not grown pale,
because my eyes, a thousand years old, have given it shelter.

"The Cemetery"
From the Spanish of Miguel Hernández

The cemetery lies near
where you and I are sleeping,
among blue prickly-pear,
blue century-plants and children
who cry out with such life
if a dead body throws its shadow on the road.

From here to the cemetery, everything
is blue, golden, clear.
Four steps and the dead.
Four steps and the living.

Clear, blue, and golden
my son, there, seems far away.

Boxer
From the Yiddish of Aleph Katz

Storm wind,
Waiting blind in his arms,

Charges the ferocious lightning through his fists
That chase the sparks
Of his eyes.

Jungle nights, bleeding fountains of fire,
Burgeon up from the ring,
And light up an auto-da-fé to heaven
In a forest of eyes.

The woods are burning,
A cry bears itself forth—
An eternity,
And silences the last sob
Of the defeated, and sings forever the song
Of accidental strength,
The winner of nothing.

Bowery Motifs—I

From the Yiddish of Aleph Katz

Dust and dirt,
Bread begged for,
A dead life.

A cursed blessing,
Broken world,
Stink of money.

Man a mistake,
A ghost of lice,
Fear of mice.

An outraged city
Deafens a secret,
And laughs at God.

Bowery Motifs—II

From the Yiddish of Aleph Katz

The mountain is high,
And the avid merchant stingy:
The market is full of buyers,
And the diver brings back few pearls.

The shadow strangles,
The glance gulps down
and dies.
The way is forbidden,
Blocked.

Wishes are trampled;
The heart, a dead body.
Alone, one surrenders and waits, trembling.
For a miracle.

Bowery Motifs—III

From the Yiddish of Aleph Katz

Heart thrown into the garbage,
Its terrible burden too heavy,
The fields of the spirit lie desolate,
The mast of fortune broken.

Better to live this way,
A lone thorn in the field,
Than the golden way of the world
That charges a quick death
For its straw, its bread.

Not in Marble Palaces

From the Spanish of Pedro Salinas

Not in marble palaces,
not in months, no, not in ciphers,
never touching ground:
in weightless, fragile worlds
we have lived together.
Time was beaten out,
but hardly by minutes:
one minute was a hundred years,
one life, one love.
Roofs sheltered us,
less than roofs, clouds;
less than clouds, heavens;
even less, air, nothing.
Crossing oceans
formed out of twenty tears,
ten yours and ten mine,
we arrived at the golden
beads of a necklace,
clear islands, deserted,
without flowers, without bodies;
a harbor, so tiny,
made of glass, for a love
that in itself was enough
for the largest longing,
and we asked neither ships
nor time for help.
Opening
enormous tunnels
in grains of sand,
we discovered the mines
of flames and of chance.
And everything
hanging from that thread
that held up . . . what?
That's why our life
doesn't appear to be lived:
slippery, evasive,
it left behind neither wakes

nor footprints. If you want
to remember it, don't look
where you always look for traces
and recollections.
Don't look at your soul,
your shadow or your lips.
Look carefully into the palm
of your hand, it's empty.

Anacreon's Grave

From the German of Goethe

Here, where the rose opens,
Where delicate vines and bay leaves embrace each other,
Where the young dove is calling,
Where the little cricket is glad,
Whose grave is this,
That all the gods have planted and trimmed with
    living things?
This is Anacreon's bed.
The happy poet enjoyed spring, summer, and autumn;
Now this small hill shelters him from the winter.

The Branch Will Not Break

Ach, könnt' ich dorthin kommen,
Und dort mein Herz erfreu'n,
Und aller Qual entnommen,
Und frei und selig sein.

Ach, jenes Land der Wonne!
Das seh' ich oft im Traum.
Doch kommt die Morgensonne,
Zerfliesst's wie eitel Schaum.

Eleutheria

Μνασεσθαι τινα φαιμ υστερου αμμεοιν
—*Sappho*

As I Step over a Puddle at the End of Winter, I Think of an Ancient Chinese Governor

And how can I, born in evil days
And fresh from failure, ask a kindness of Fate?
—Written A.D. 819

Po Chu-i, balding old politician,
What's the use?
I think of you,
Uneasily entering the gorges of the Yang-Tze,
When you were being towed up the rapids
Toward some political job or other
In the city of Chungshou.
You made it, I guess,
By dark.

But it is 1960, it is almost spring again,
And the tall rocks of Minneapolis
Build me my own black twilight
Of bamboo ropes and waters.
Where is Yuan Chen, the friend you loved?
Where is the sea, that once solved the whole loneliness
Of the Midwest? Where is Minneapolis? I can see nothing
But the great terrible oak tree darkening with winter.
Did you find the city of isolated men beyond mountains?
Or have you been holding the end of a frayed rope
For a thousand years?

Goodbye to the Poetry of Calcium

Dark cypresses—
The world is uneasily happy:
It will all be forgotten.
—Theodor Storm

Mother of roots, you have not seeded
The tall ashes of loneliness
For me. Therefore,
Now I go.
If I knew the name,

Your name, all trellises of vineyards and old fire
Would quicken to shake terribly my
Earth, mother of spiralling searches, terrible
Fable of calcium, girl. I crept this afternoon
In weeds once more,
Casual, daydreaming you might not strike
Me down. Mother of window sills and journeys,
Hallower of scratching hands,
The sight of my blind man makes me want to weep.
Tiller of waves or whatever, woman or man,
Mother of roots or father of diamonds,
Look: I am nothing.
I do not even have ashes to rub into my eyes.

In Fear of Harvests

It has happened
Before: nearby,
The nostrils of slow horses
Breathe evenly,
And the brown bees drag their high garlands,
Heavily,
Toward hives of snow.

Three Stanzas from Goethe

That man standing there, who is he?
His path lost in the thicket,
Behind him the bushes
Lash back together,
The grass rises again,
The waste devours him.

Oh, who will heal the sufferings
Of the man whose balm turned poison?
Who drank nothing
But hatred of men from love's abundance?

Once despised, now a despiser,
He kills his own life,
The precious secret.
The self-seeker finds nothing.

Oh, Father of Love,
If your psaltery holds one tone
That his ear still might echo,
Then quicken his heart!
Open his eyes, shut off by clouds
From the thousand fountains
So near him, dying of thirst
In his own desert.

(Note: These three stanzas are from Goethe's poem "Harzreise im
Winter." They are the stanzas which Brahms detached from the
poem and employed as the text for his "Alto Rhapsody" of 1869.)

Autumn Begins in Martins Ferry, Ohio

In the Shreve High football stadium,
I think of Polacks nursing long beers in Tiltonsville,
And gray faces of Negroes in the blast furnace at Benwood,
And the ruptured night watchman of Wheeling Steel,
Dreaming of heroes.

All the proud fathers are ashamed to go home.
Their women cluck like starved pullets,
Dying for love.

Therefore,
Their sons grow suicidally beautiful
At the beginning of October,
And gallop terribly against each other's bodies.

Lying in a Hammock
at William Duffy's Farm
in Pine Island, Minnesota

Over my head, I see the bronze butterfly,
Asleep on the black trunk,
Blowing like a leaf in green shadow.
Down the ravine behind the empty house,
The cowbells follow one another
Into the distances of the afternoon.
To my right,
In a field of sunlight between two pines,
The droppings of last year's horses
Blaze up into golden stones.
I lean back, as the evening darkens and comes on.
A chicken hawk floats over, looking for home.
I have wasted my life.

The Jewel

There is this cave
In the air behind my body
That nobody is going to touch:
A cloister, a silence
Closing around a blossom of fire.
When I stand upright in the wind,
My bones turn to dark emeralds.

In the Face of Hatred

I am frightened by the sorrow
Of escaping animals.
The snake moves slowly
Beyond his horizon of yellow stone.
A great harvest of convicts has shaken loose
And hurries across the wall of your eyes.
Most of them, all moving alike,
Are gone already along the river.

Only two boys,
Trailed by shadows of rooted police,
Turn aimlessly in the lashing elderberries.
One cries for his father's death,
And the other, the silent one,
Listens into the hallway
Of a dark leaf.

Fear Is What Quickens Me

1

Many animals that our fathers killed in America
Had quick eyes.
They stared about wildly,
When the moon went dark.
The new moon falls into the freight yards
Of cities in the south,
But the loss of the moon to the dark hands of Chicago
Does not matter to the deer
In this northern field.

2

What is that tall woman doing
There, in the trees?
I can hear rabbits and mourning doves whispering together
In the dark grass, there
Under the trees.

3

I look about wildly.

A Message Hidden in an Empty Wine Bottle That I Threw into a Gully of Maple Trees One Night at an Indecent Hour

Women are dancing around a fire
By a pond of creosote and waste water from the river
In the dank fog of Ohio.

They are dead.
I am alone here,
And I reach for the moon that dangles
Cold on a dark vine.
The unwashed shadows
Of blast furnaces from Moundsville, West Virginia,
Are sneaking across the pits of strip mines
To steal grapes
In heaven.
Nobody else knows I am here.
All right.
Come out, come out, I am dying.
I am growing old.
An owl rises
From the cutter bar
Of a hayrake.

Stages on a Journey Westward

1

I began in Ohio.
I still dream of home.
Near Mansfield, enormous dobbins enter dark barns in autumn,
Where they can be lazy, where they can munch little apples,
Or sleep long.
But by night now, in the bread lines my father
Prowls, I cannot find him: So far off,
1500 miles or so away, and yet
I can hardly sleep.
In a blue rag the old man limps to my bed,
Leading a blind horse
Of gentleness.
In 1932, grimy with machinery, he sang me
A lullaby of a goosegirl.
Outside the house, the slag heaps waited.

2

In western Minnesota, just now,
I slept again.
In my dream, I crouched over a fire.
The only human beings between me and the Pacific Ocean

Were old Indians, who wanted to kill me.
They squat and stare for hours into small fires
Far off in the mountains.
The blades of their hatchets are dirty with the grease
Of huge, silent buffaloes.

3

It is dawn.
I am shivering,
Even beneath a huge eiderdown.
I came in last night, drunk,
And left the oil stove cold.
I listen a long time, now, to the flurries.
Snow howls all around me, out of the abandoned prairies.
It sounds like the voices of bums and gamblers,
Rattling through the bare nineteenth-century whorehouses
In Nevada.

4

Defeated for re-election,
The half-educated sheriff of Mukilteo, Washington,
Has been drinking again.
He leads me up the cliff, tottering.
Both drunk, we stand among the graves.
Miners paused here on the way up to Alaska.
Angry, they spaded their broken women's bodies
Into ditches of crab grass.
I lie down between tombstones.
At the bottom of the cliff
America is over and done with.
America,
Plunged into the dark furrows
Of the sea again.

How My Fever Left

I can still hear her.
She hobbles downstairs to the kitchen.
She is swearing at the dishes.
She slaps her grease rags
Into a basket,

And slings it over her skinny forearm, crooked
With hatred, and stomps outside.
I can hear my father downstairs,
Standing without a coat in the open back door,
Calling to the old bat across the snow.
She's forgotten her black shawl,
But I see her through my window, sneering,
Flapping upward
Toward some dark church on the hill.
She has to meet somebody else, and
It's no use, she won't listen,
She's gone.

Miners

1

The police are probing tonight for the bodies
Of children in the black waters
Of the suburbs.

2

Below the chemical riffles of the Ohio River,
Grappling hooks
Drag delicately about, between skiff hulks and sand shoals,
Until they clasp
Fingers.

3

Somewhere in a vein of Bridgeport, Ohio;
Deep in a coal hill behind Hanna's name;
Below the tipples, and dark as a drowsy woodchuck;
A man, alone,
Stumbles upon the outside locks of a grave, whispering
Oh let me in.

4

Many American women mount long stairs
In the shafts of houses,
Fall asleep, and emerge suddenly into tottering palaces.

In Ohio

White mares lashed to the sulky carriages
Trot softly
Around the dismantled fairgrounds
Near Buckeye Lake.

The sandstone blocks of a wellspring
Cool dark green moss.

The sun floats down, a small golden lemon dissolves
In the water.
I dream, as I lean over the edge, of a crawdad's mouth.

The cellars of haunted houses are like ancient cities,
Fallen behind a big heap of apples.

A widow on a front porch puckers her lips
And whispers.

Two Poems about President Harding

One: His Death
In Marion, the honey locust trees are falling.
Everybody in town remembers the white hair,
The campaign of a lost summer, the front porch
Open to the public, and the vaguely stunned smile
Of a lucky man.

"Neighbor, I want to be helpful," he said once.
Later, "You think I'm honest, don't you?"
Weeping drunk.

I am drunk this evening in 1961,
In a jag for my countryman,
Who died of crab meat on the way back from Alaska.
Everyone knows that joke.

How many honey locusts have fallen,
Pitched rootlong into the open graves of strip mines,
Since the First World War ended
And Wilson the gaunt deacon jogged sullenly
Into silence?
Tonight,
The cancerous ghosts of old con men
Shed their leaves.
For a proud man,
Lost between the turnpike near Cleveland
And the chiropractors' signs looming among dead mulberry trees,
There is no place left to go
But home.

"Warren lacks mentality," one of his friends said.

Yet he was beautiful, he was the snowfall
Turned to white stallions standing still
Under dark elm trees.

He died in public. He claimed the secret right
To be ashamed.

Two: His Tomb in Ohio
>   *". . . he died of a busted gut."*
>   —Mencken, on Bryan

A hundred slag piles north of us,
At the mercy of the moon and rain,
He lies in his ridiculous
Tomb, our fellow citizen.
No, I have never seen that place,
Where many shadows of faceless thieves
Chuckle and stumble and embrace
On beer cans, stogie butts, and graves.

One holiday, one rainy week
After the country fell apart,
Hoover and Coolidge came to speak
And snivel about his broken heart.
His grave, a huge absurdity,
Embarrassed cops and visitors.

Hoover and Coolidge crept away
By night, and women closed their doors.

Now junkmen call their children in
Before they catch their death of cold;
Young lovers let the moon begin
Its quick spring; and the day grows old;
The mean one-legger who rakes up leaves
Has chased the loafers out of the park;
Minnegan Leonard half-believes
In God, and the poolroom goes dark;

America goes on, goes on
Laughing, and Harding was a fool.
Even his big pretentious stone
Lays him bare to ridicule.
I know it. But don't look at me.
By God, I didn't start this mess.
Whatever moon and rain may be,
The hearts of men are merciless.

Eisenhower's Visit to Franco, 1959

". . . we die of cold, and not of darkness."
—Unamuno

The American hero must triumph over
The forces of darkness.
He has flown through the very light of heaven
And come down in the slow dusk
Of Spain.

Franco stands in a shining circle of police.
His arms open in welcome.
He promises all dark things
Will be hunted down.

State police yawn in the prisons.
Antonio Machado follows the moon
Down a road of white dust,

To a cave of silent children
Under the Pyrenees.
Wine darkens in stone jars in villages.
Wine sleeps in the mouths of old men, it is a dark red color.

Smiles glitter in Madrid.
Eisenhower has touched hands with Franco, embracing
In a glare of photographers.
Clean new bombers from America muffle their engines
And glide down now.
Their wings shine in the searchlights
Of bare fields,
In Spain.

In Memory of a Spanish Poet

Take leave of the sun, and of the wheat, for me.
—Miguel Hernández,
written in prison, 1942

I see you strangling
Under the black ripples of whitewashed walls.
Your hands turn yellow in the ruins of the sun.
I dream of your slow voice, flying,
Planting the dark waters of the spirit
With lutes and seeds.

Here, in the American Midwest,
Those seeds fly out of the field and across the strange heaven of
    my skull.
They scatter out of their wings a quiet farewell,
A greeting to my country.

Now twilight gathers,
A long sundown.
Silos creep away toward the west.

The Undermining of the
Defense Economy

Stairway, face, window,
Mottled animals
Running over the public buildings.
Maple and elm.
In the autumn
Of early evening,
A pumpkin
Lies on its side,
Turning yellow as the face
Of a discharged general.
It's no use complaining, the economy
Is going to hell with all these radical
Changes,
Girls the color of butterflies
That can't be sold.
Only after nightfall,
Little boys lie still, awake,
Wondering, wondering,
Delicate little boxes of dust.

Twilights

The big stones of the cistern behind the barn
Are soaked in whitewash.
My grandmother's face is a small maple leaf
Pressed in a secret box.
Locusts are climbing down into the dark green crevices
Of my childhood. Latches click softly in the trees. Your hair is
    gray.

The arbors of the cities are withered.
Far off, the shopping centers empty and darken.

A red shadow of steel mills.

Two Hangovers

Number One

I slouch in bed.
Beyond the streaked trees of my window,
All groves are bare.
Locusts and poplars change to unmarried women
Sorting slate from anthracite
Between railroad ties:
The yellow-bearded winter of the depression
Is still alive somewhere, an old man
Counting his collection of bottle caps
In a tarpaper shack under the cold trees
Of my grave.

I still feel half drunk,
And all those old women beyond my window
Are hunching toward the graveyard.

Drunk, mumbling Hungarian,
The sun staggers in,
And his big stupid face pitches
Into the stove.
For two hours I have been dreaming
Of green butterflies searching for diamonds
In coal seams;
And children chasing each other for a game
Through the hills of fresh graves.
But the sun has come home drunk from the sea,
And a sparrow outside
Sings of the Hanna Coal Co. and the dead moon.
The filaments of cold light bulbs tremble
In music like delicate birds.
Ah, turn it off.

Number Two:
I Try to Waken and Greet the World Once Again

In a pine tree,
A few yards away from my window sill,
A brilliant blue jay is springing up and down, up and down,
On a branch.

I laugh, as I see him abandon himself
To entire delight, for he knows as well as I do
That the branch will not break.

Depressed by a Book of Bad Poetry, I Walk toward an Unused Pasture and Invite the Insects to Join Me

Relieved, I let the book fall behind a stone.
I climb a slight rise of grass.
I do not want to disturb the ants
Who are walking single file up the fence post,
Carrying small white petals,
Casting shadows so frail that I can see through them.
I close my eyes for a moment, and listen.
The old grasshoppers
Are tired, they leap heavily now,
Their thighs are burdened.
I want to hear them, they have clear sounds to make.
Then lovely, far off, a dark cricket begins
In the maple trees.

Two Horses Playing in the Orchard

Too soon, too soon, a man will come
To lock the gate, and drive them home.
Then, neighing softly through the night,
The mare will nurse her shoulder bite.
Now, lightly fair, through lock and mane
She gazes over the dusk again,
And sees her darkening stallion leap
In grass for apples, half asleep.

Lightly, lightly, on slender knees
He turns, lost in a dream of trees.
Apples are slow to find this day,

Someone has stolen the best away.
Still, some remain before the snow,
A few, trembling on boughs so low
A horse can reach them, small and sweet:
And some are tumbling to her feet.

Too soon, a man will scatter them,
Although I do not know his name,
His age, or how he came to own
A horse, an apple tree, a stone.
I let those horses in to steal
On principle, because I feel
Like half a horse myself, although
Too soon, too soon, already. Now.

By a Lake in Minnesota

Upshore from the cloud—
The slow whale of country twilight—
The spume of light falls into valleys
Full of roses.

And below,
Out of the placid waters,
Two beavers, mother and child,
Wave out long ripples
To the dust of dead leaves
On the shore.

And the moon walks,
Hunting for hidden dolphins
Behind the darkening combers
Of the ground.

And downshore from the cloud,
I stand, waiting
For dark.

Beginning

The moon drops one or two feathers into the field.
The dark wheat listens.
Be still.
Now.
There they are, the moon's young, trying
Their wings.
Between trees, a slender woman lifts up the lovely shadow
Of her face, and now she steps into the air, now she is gone
Wholly, into the air.
I stand alone by an elder tree, I do not dare breathe
Or move.
I listen.
The wheat leans back toward its own darkness,
And I lean toward mine.

From a Bus Window in Central Ohio, Just Before a Thunder Shower

Cribs loaded with roughage huddle together
Before the north clouds.
The wind tiptoes between poplars.
The silver maple leaves squint
Toward the ground.
An old farmer, his scarlet face
Apologetic with whiskey, swings back a barn door
And calls a hundred black-and-white Holsteins
From the clover field.

March

A bear under the snow
Turns over to yawn.
It's been a long, hard rest.

Once, as she lay asleep, her cubs fell
Out of her hair,
And she did not know them.

It is hard to breathe
In a tight grave:

So she roars,
And the roof breaks.
Dark rivers and leaves
Pour down.

When the wind opens its doors
In its own good time,
The cubs follow that relaxed and beautiful woman
Outside to the unfamiliar cities
Of moss.

Trying to Pray

This time, I have left my body behind me, crying
In its dark thorns.
Still,
There are good things in this world.
It is dusk.
It is the good darkness
Of women's hands that touch loaves.
The spirit of a tree begins to move.
I touch leaves.
I close my eyes, and think of water.

Two Spring Charms

Fragments from the Norwegian

1

Now it is late winter.

Years ago,

I walked through a spring wind
Bending green wheat
In a field near Trondhjem.

2

Black snow,
Like a strange sea creature,
Draws back into itself,
Restoring grass to earth.

Spring Images

Two athletes
Are dancing in the cathedral
Of the wind.

A butterfly lights on the branch
Of your green voice.

Small antelopes
Fall asleep in the ashes
Of the moon.

Arriving in the Country Again

The white house is silent.
My friends can't hear me yet.
The flicker who lives in the bare tree at the field's edge
Pecks once and is still for a long time.
I stand still in the late afternoon.
My face is turned away from the sun.
A horse grazes in my long shadow.

In the Cold House

I slept a few minutes ago,
Even though the stove has been out for hours.
I am growing old.
A bird cries in bare elder trees.

Snowstorm in the Midwest

Though haunches of whales
Slope into whitecap doves,
It is hard to drown here.

Between two walls,
A fold of echoes,
A girl's voice walks naked.

I step into the water
Of two flakes.
The crowns of white birds rise
To my ankles,
To my knees,
To my face.

Escaping in silence
From locomotive and smoke,
I hunt the huge feathers of gulls
And the fountains of hills,
I hunt the sea, to walk on the waters.

A splayed starling
Follows me down a long stairway
Of white sand.

Having Lost My Sons, I Confront the Wreckage of the Moon: Christmas, 1960

After dark
Near the South Dakota border,
The moon is out hunting, everywhere,
Delivering fire,
And walking down hallways
Of a diamond.

Behind a tree,
It lights on the ruins
Of a white city:
Frost, frost.

Where are they gone,
Who lived there?

Bundled away under wings
And dark faces.

I am sick
Of it, and I go on,
Living, alone, alone,
Past the charred silos, past the hidden graves
Of Chippewas and Norwegians.

This cold winter
Moon spills the inhuman fire
Of jewels
Into my hands.

Dead riches, dead hands, the moon
Darkens,
And I am lost in the beautiful white ruins
Of America.

American Wedding

She dreamed long of waters.
Inland today, she wakens
On scraped knees, lost
Among locust thorns.

She gropes for
The path backward, to
The pillows of the sea.

Bruised trillium
Of wilderness, she
May rest on briar leaves,
As long as the wind cares to pause.

Now she is going to learn
How it is that animals
Can save time:
They sleep a whole season
Of lamentation and snow,
Without bothering to weep.

A Prayer to Escape from
the Market Place

I renounce the blindness of the magazines.
I want to lie down under a tree.
This is the only duty that is not death.
This is the everlasting happiness
Of small winds.
Suddenly,
A pheasant flutters, and I turn
Only to see him vanishing at the damp edge
Of the road.

Rain

It is the sinking of things.

Flashlights drift over dark trees,
Girls kneel,
An owl's eyelids fall.

The sad bones of my hands descend into a valley
Of strange rocks.

Today I Was Happy,
So I Made This Poem

As the plump squirrel scampers
Across the roof of the corncrib,
The moon suddenly stands up in the darkness,
And I see that it is impossible to die.
Each moment of time is a mountain.
An eagle rejoices in the oak trees of heaven,
Crying
This is what I wanted.

Mary Bly

I sit here, doing nothing, alone, worn out by long winter.
I feel the light breath of the newborn child.
Her face is smooth as the side of an apricot,
Eyes quick as her blond mother's hands.
She has full, soft, red hair, and as she lies quiet
In her tall mother's arms, her delicate hands
Weave back and forth.
I feel the seasons changing beneath me,
Under the floor.
She is braiding the waters of air into the plaited manes
Of happy colts.

They canter, without making a sound, along the shores
Of melting snow.

To the Evening Star: Central Minnesota

Under the water tower at the edge of town
A hugh Airedale ponders a long ripple
In the grass fields beyond.
Miles off, a whole grove silently
Flies up into the darkness.
One light comes on in the sky,
One lamp on the prairie.

Beautiful daylight of the body, your hands carry seashells.
West of this wide plain,
Animals wilder than ours
Come down from the green mountains in the darkness.
Now they can see you, they know
The open meadows are safe.

I Was Afraid of Dying

Once,
I was afraid of dying
In a field of dry weeds.
But now,
All day long I have been walking among damp fields,
Trying to keep still, listening
To insects that move patiently.
Perhaps they are sampling the fresh dew that gathers slowly
In empty snail shells
And in the secret shelters of sparrow feathers fallen on the
        earth.

A Blessing

Just off the highway to Rochester, Minnesota,
Twilight bounds softly forth on the grass.
And the eyes of those two Indian ponies
Darken with kindness.
They have come gladly out of the willows
To welcome my friend and me.
We step over the barbed wire into the pasture
Where they have been grazing all day, alone.
They ripple tensely, they can hardly contain their happiness
That we have come.
They bow shyly as wet swans. They love each other.
There is no loneliness like theirs.
At home once more,
They begin munching the young tufts of spring in the darkness.
I would like to hold the slenderer one in my arms,
For she has walked over to me
And nuzzled my left hand.
She is black and white,
Her mane falls wild on her forehead,
And the light breeze moves me to caress her long ear
That is delicate as the skin over a girl's wrist.
Suddenly I realize
That if I stepped out of my body I would break
Into blossom.

Milkweed

While I stood here, in the open, lost in myself,
I must have looked a long time
Down the corn rows, beyond grass,
The small house,
White walls, animals lumbering toward the barn.
I look down now. It is all changed.
Whatever it was I lost, whatever I wept for
Was a wild, gentle thing, the small dark eyes
Loving me in secret.
It is here. At a touch of my hand,

The air fills with delicate creatures
From the other world.

A Dream of Burial

Nothing was left of me
But my right foot
And my left shoulder.
They lay white as the skein of a spider floating
In a field of snow toward a dark building
Tilted and stained by wind.
Inside the dream, I dreamed on.

A parade of old women
Sang softly above me,
Faint mosquitoes near still water.

So I waited, in my corridor.
I listened for the sea
To call me.
I knew that, somewhere outside, the horse
Stood saddled, browsing in grass,
Waiting for me.

Shall We Gather at the River

Und wenn der Mensch in seiner Qual verstummt,
Gab mir ein Gott zu sagen, was ich leide.
                                        —Goethe

Jenny

A Christmas Greeting

Good evening, Charlie. Yes, I know. You rise,
Two lean gray spiders drifting through your eyes.
Poor Charlie, hobbling down the hill to find
The last bootlegger who might strike them blind,
Be dead. A child, I saw you hunch your spine,
Wrench your left elbow round, to hold in line
The left-hand hollow of your back, as though
The kidney prayed for mercy. Years ago.
The kidneys do not pray, the kidneys drip.
Urine stains at the liver; lip by lip,
Affectionate, the snub-nosed demons kiss
And sting us back to such a world as this.
Charlie, the moon drips slowly in the dark,
The mill smoke stains the snow, the gray whores walk,
The left-hand hollow fills up, like the tide
Drowning the moon, skillful with suicide.
Charlie, don't ask me. Charlie go away,
I feel my own spine hunching. If I pray,
I lose all meaning. I don't know my kind:
Sack me, or bury me among the blind.
What should I pray for? what can they forgive?
You died because you could not bear to live,
Pitched off the bridge in Brookside, God knows why.
Well, don't remind me. I'm afraid to die,
It hurts to die, although the lucky do.
Charlie, I don't know what to say to you
Except Good Evening, Greetings, and Good Night,
God Bless Us Every One. Your grave is white.
What are you doing here?

The Minneapolis Poem

to John Logan

1

I wonder how many old men last winter
Hungry and frightened by namelessness prowled
The Mississippi shore

Lashed blind by the wind, dreaming
Of suicide in the river.
The police remove their cadavers by daybreak
And turn them in somewhere.
Where?
How does the city keep lists of its fathers
Who have no names?
By Nicollet Island I gaze down at the dark water
So beautifully slow.
And I wish my brothers good luck
And a warm grave.

2

The Chippewa young men
Stab one another shrieking
Jesus Christ.
Split-lipped homosexuals limp in terror of assault.
High school backfields search under benches
Near the Post Office. Their faces are the rich
Raw bacon without eyes.
The Walker Art Center crowd stare
At the Guthrie Theater.

3

Tall Negro girls from Chicago
Listen to light songs.
They know when the supposed patron
Is a plainclothesman.
A cop's palm
Is a roach dangling down the scorched fangs
Of a light bulb.
The soul of a cop's eyes
Is an eternity of Sunday daybreak in the suburbs
Of Juárez, Mexico.

4

The legless beggars are gone, carried away
By white birds.
The Artificial Limbs Exchange is gutted
And sown with lime.
The whalebone crutches and hand-me-down trusses
Huddle together dreaming in a desolation
Of dry groins.

I think of poor men astonished to waken
Exposed in broad daylight by the blade
Of a strange plough.

5

All over the walls of comb cells
Automobiles perfumed and blindered
Consent with a mutter of high good humor
To take their two naps a day.
Without sound windows glide back
Into dusk.
The sockets of a thousand blind bee graves tier upon tier
Tower not quite toppling.
There are men in this city who labor dawn after dawn
To sell me my death.

6

But I could not bear
To allow my poor brother my body to die
In Minneapolis.
The old man Walt Whitman our countryman
Is now in America our country
Dead.
But he was not buried in Minneapolis
At least.
And no more may I be
Please God.

7

I want to be lifted up
By some great white bird unknown to the police,
And soar for a thousand miles and be carefully hidden
Modest and golden as one last corn grain,
Stored with the secrets of the wheat and the mysterious lives
Of the unnamed poor.

Inscription for the Tank

My life was never so precious
To me as now.

I gape unbelieving at those two lines
Of my words, caught and frisked naked.

If they loomed secret and dim
On the wall of the drunk-tank,
Scraped there by a raw fingernail
In the trickling crusts of gray mold,

Surely the plainest thug who read them
Would cluck with the ancient pity.
Men have a right to thank God for their loneliness.
The walls are hysterical with their dank messages.

But the last hophead is gone
With the quick of his name
Bleeding away down a new wall
Blank as his nails.

I wish I had walked outside
To wade in the sea, drowsing and soothed;
I wish I had copied some words from Isaiah,
Kabir, Ansari, oh Whitman, oh anyone, anyone.

But I wrote down mine, and now
I must read them forever, even
When the wings in my shoulders cringe up
At the cold's fangs, as now.

Of all my lives, the one most secret to me,
Folded deep in a book never written,
Locked up in a dream of a still place,
I have blurted out.

I have heard weeping in secret
And quick nails broken.
Let the dead pray for their own dead.
What is their pity to me?

In Terror of Hospital Bills

I still have some money
To eat with, alone
And frightened, knowing how soon
I will waken a poor man.

It snows freely and freely hardens
On the lawns of my hope, my secret
Hounded and flayed. I wonder
What words to beg money with.

Pardon me, sir, could you?
Which way is St. Paul?
I thirst.
I am a full-blooded Sioux Indian.

Soon I am sure to become so hungry
I will have to leap barefoot through gas-fire veils of shame,
I will have to stalk timid strangers
On the whorehouse corners.

Oh moon, sow leaves on my hands,
On my seared face, oh I love you.
My throat is open, insane,
Tempting pneumonia.

But my life was never so precious
To me as now.
I will have to beg coins
After dark.

I will learn to scent the police,
And sit or go blind, stay mute, be taken for dead
For your sake, oh my secret,
My life.

I Am a Sioux Brave,
He Said in Minneapolis

1

He is just plain drunk.
He knows no more than I do
What true waters to mourn for
Or what kind of words to sing
When he dies.

2

The black caterpillar
Crawls out, what with one thing
And another, across
The wet road.
How lonely the dead must be.

Gambling in Stateline, Nevada

The great cracked shadow of the Sierra Nevada
Hoods over the last road.

I came down here from the side of
A cold cairn where a girl named Rachel
Just made it inside California
And died of bad luck.

Here, across from the keno board,
An old woman
Has been beating a strange machine
In its face all day.

Dusk limps past in the street.
I step outside.
It's gone.
I finger a worthless agate
In my pocket.

The Poor Washed Up
by Chicago Winter

Well, I still have a train ticket valid.
I can get out.
The faces of unimaginably beautiful blind men
Glide among mountains.
What pinnacles should they gaze upon
Except the moon?
Eight miles down in the secret canyons and ranges
Of six o'clock, the poor
Are mountainously blind and invisible.
Do they die?
Where are they buried?
They fill the sea now.
When you glide in, men cast shadows
You can trace from an airplane.
Their shoulders are huge with the barnacles
That God has cast down into the deep places.
The Sixth Day remained evening, deepening further down,
Further and further down, into night, a wounded black angel
Forgotten by Genesis.
If only the undulating of the shadows would pause.
The sea can stand anything.
I can't.

I can remember the evening.
I can remember the morning.
I am too young
To live in the sea alone without
Any company.
I can either move into the McCormick Theological Seminary
And get a night's sleep,
Or else get hauled back to Minneapolis.

An Elegy for the Poet
Morgan Blum

Morgan the lonely,
Morgan the dead,

Has followed his only
Child into a vast
Desolation.
When I heard he was going
I tried to blossom
Into the boat beside him,
But I had no money.

When I went in to see him,
The nurse said no.
So I snuck in behind her.
And there they were.
They were there, for a moment.
Red Jacket, Robert Hayman,
H. Phelps Putnam,
And sweet Ted Roethke,
A canary and a bear.

They looked me over,
More or less alive.
They looked at me, more
Or less out of place.
They said, get out,
Morgan is dying.
They said, get out,
Leave him alone.

We have no kings
In this country,
They kept saying.
But we have one
Where the dead rise
On the other shore.
And they hear only
The cold owls throwing
Salt over
Their secret shoulders.

So I left Morgan,
And all of them alone.
And now I am so lonely
For the air I want to breathe.

Come breathe me, dark prince.
And Morgan lay there
Clean shaved like a baby
By the nurse who said no.
And so a couple
Of years ago,
The old poets died
Young.

And now the young,
Scarlet on their wings, fly away
Over the marshes.

Old Age Compensation

There are no roads but the frost,
And the pumpkins look haggard.
The ants have gone down to the grave, crying
God spare them one green blade.
Failing the grass, they have abandoned the grass.
All creatures who have died today of old age
Have gone more than ten miles already.
All day I have slogged behind
And dreamed of them praying for one candle,
Only one.
Fair enough. Only, from where I stand,
I can see one last night nurse shining in one last window
In the Home for Senior Citizens.
The white uniform flickers, the town is gone.
What do I do now? I have one candle,
But what's the use?
If only they can catch up with twilight,
They'll be safe enough.
Their boats are moored there, among the cattails
And the night-herons' nests.
All they have to do now
Is to get one of those lazy birds awake long enough
To guide them across the river.
Herons fly low, too.

All it will take is one old man trawling one oar.
Anybody can follow a blue wing,
They don't need my candle.
But I do.

Before a Cashier's Window in
a Department Store

1

The beautiful cashier's white face has risen once more
Behind a young manager's shoulder.
They whisper together, and stare
Straight into my face.
I feel like grabbing a stray child
Or a skinny old woman
And diving into a cellar, crouching
Under a stone bridge, praying myself sick,
Till the troops pass.

2

Why should he care? He goes.
I slump deeper.
In my frayed coat, I am pinned down
By debt. He nods,
Commending my flesh to the pity of the daws of God.

3

Am I dead? And, if not, why not?
For she sails there, alone, looming in the heaven of the beautiful.
She knows
The bulldozers will scrape me up
After dark, behind
The officers' club.
Beneath her terrible blaze, my skeleton
Glitters out. I am the dark. I am the dark
Bone I was born to be.

4

Tu Fu woke shuddering on a battlefield
Once, in the dead of night, and made out

The mangled women, sorting
The haggard slant-eyes.
The moon was up.

5

I am hungry. In two more days
It will be spring. So this
Is what it feels like.

Speak

To speak in a flat voice
Is all that I can do.
I have gone every place
Asking for you.
Wondering where to turn
And how the search would end
And the last streetlight spin
Above me blind.

Then I returned rebuffed
And saw under the sun
The race not to the swift
Nor the battle won.
Liston dives in the tank,
Lord, in Lewiston, Maine,
And Ernie Doty's drunk
In hell again.

And Jenny, oh my Jenny
Whom I love, rhyme be damned,
Has broken her spare beauty
In a whorehouse old.
She left her new baby
In a bus-station can,
And sprightly danced away
Through Jacksontown.

Which is a place I know,
One where I got picked up

A few shrunk years ago
By a good cop.
Believe it, Lord, or not.
Don't ask me who he was.
I speak of flat defeat
In a flat voice.

I have gone forward with
Some, a few lonely some.
They have fallen to death.
I die with them.
Lord, I have loved Thy cursed,
The beauty of Thy house:
Come down. Come down. Why dost
Thou hide thy face?

Outside Fargo, North Dakota

Along the sprawled body of the derailed
    Great Northern freight car,
I strike a match slowly and lift it slowly.
No wind.

Beyond town, three heavy white horses
Wade all the way to their shoulders
In a silo shadow.

Suddenly the freight car lurches.
The door slams back, a man with a flashlight
Calls me good evening.
I nod as I write good evening, lonely
And sick for home.

Living by the Red River

Blood flows in me, but what does it have to do
With the rain that is falling?

In me, scarlet-jacketed armies march into the rain
Across dark fields. My blood lies still,
Indifferent to cannons on the ships of imperialists
Drifting offshore.
Sometimes I have to sleep
In dangerous places, on cliffs underground,
Walls that still hold the whole prints
Of ancient ferns.

To Flood Stage Again

In Fargo, North Dakota, a man
Warned me the river might rise
To flood stage again.
On the bridge, a girl hurries past me, alone,
Unhappy face.
Will she pause in wet grass somewhere?
Behind my eyes she stands tiptoe, yearning for confused sparrows
To fetch a bit of string and dried wheatbeard
To line her outstretched hand.
I open my eyes and gaze down
At the dark water.

A Poem Written under an Archway in a Discontinued Railroad Station, Fargo, North Dakota

Outside the great clanging cathedrals of rust and smoke,
The locomotives browse on sidings.
They pause, exhausted by the silence of prairies.
Sometimes they leap and cry out, skitterish.
They fear dark little boys in Ohio,
Who know how to giggle without breathing,
Who sneak out of graveyards in summer twilights
And lay crossties across rails.
The rattle of coupling pins still echoes
In the smoke stains,

The Cincinnati of the dead.
Around the bend now, beyond the grain elevators,
The late afternoon limited wails
Savage with the horror and loneliness of a child, lost
And dragged by a glad cop through a Chicago terminal.
The noose tightens, the wail stops, and I am leaving.
Across the street, an arthritic man
Takes coins at the parking lot.
He smiles with the sinister grief
Of old age.

Late November in a Field

Today I am walking alone in a bare place,
And winter is here.
Two squirrels near a fence post
Are helping each other drag a branch
Toward a hiding place; it must be somewhere
Behind those ash trees.
They are still alive, they ought to save acorns
Against the cold.
Frail paws rifle the troughs between cornstalks when the moon
Is looking away.
The earth is hard now,
The soles of my shoes need repairs.
I have nothing to ask a blessing for,
Except these words.
I wish they were
Grass.

The Frontier

The man on the radio mourns
That another endless American winter
Daybreak is beginning to fall
On Idaho, on the mountains.

How many scrawny children
Lie dead and half-hidden among frozen ruts
In my body, along my dark roads.
Lean coyotes pass among clouds
On mountain trails, and smile,
And pass on in snow.

A girl stands in a doorway.
Her arms are bare to the elbows,
Her face gray, she stares coldly
At the daybreak.
When the howl goes up, her eyes
Flare white, like a mare's.

Listening to the Mourners

Crouched down by a roadside windbreak
At the edge of the prairie,
I flinch under the baleful jangling of wind
Through the telephone wires, a wilderness of voices
Blown for a thousand miles, for a hundred years.
They all have the same name, and the name is lost.
So: it is not me, it is not my love
Alone lost.
The grief that I hear is my life somewhere.
Now I am speaking with the voice
Of a scarecrow that stands up
And suddenly turns into a bird.
This field is the beginning of my native land,
This place of skull where I hear myself weeping.

Youth

Strange bird,
His song remains secret.
He worked too hard to read books.
He never heard how Sherwood Anderson

Got out of it, and fled to Chicago, furious to free himself
From his hatred of factories.
My father toiled fifty years
At Hazel-Atlas Glass,
Caught among girders that smash the kneecaps
Of dumb honyaks.
Did he shudder with hatred in the cold shadow of grease?
Maybe. But my brother and I do know
He came home as quiet as the evening.

He will be getting dark, soon,
And loom through new snow.
I know his ghost will drift home
To the Ohio River, and sit down, alone,
Whittling a root.
He will say nothing.
The waters flow past, older, younger
Than he is, or I am.

Rip

It can't be the passing of time that casts
That white shadow across the waters
Just offshore.
I shiver a little, with the evening.
I turn down the steep path to find
What's left of the river gold.
I whistle a dog lazily, and lazily
A bird whistles me.
Close by a big river, I am alive in my own country,
I am home again.
Yes: I lived here, and here, and my name,
That I carved young, with a girl's, is healed over, now,
And lies sleeping beneath the inward sky
Of a tree's skin, close to the quick.
It's best to keep still.
But:
There goes that bird that whistled me down here
To the river a moment ago.

Who is he? A little white barn owl from Hudson's Bay,
Flown out of his range here, and lost?
Oh, let him be home here, and, if he wants to,
He can be the body that casts
That white shadow across the waters
Just offshore.

The Life

Murdered, I went, risen,
Where the murderers are,
That black ditch
Of river.

And if I come back to my only country
With a white rose on my shoulder,
What is that to you?
It is the grave
In blossom.

It is the trillium of darkness,
It is hell, it is the beginning of winter,
It is a ghost town of Etruscans who have no names
Any more.

It is the old loneliness.
It is.
And it is
The last time.

Three Sentences for a Dead Swan

1
There they are now,
The wings,
And I heard them beginning to starve
Between two cold white shadows,

But I dreamed they would rise
Together,
My black Ohioan swan.

2

Now one after another I let the black scales fall
From the beautiful black spine
Of this lonesome dragon that is born on the earth at last,
My black fire,
Ovoid of my darkness,
Machine-gunned and shattered hillsides of yellow trees
In the autumn of my blood where the apples
Purse their wild lips and smirk knowingly
That my love is dead.

3

Here, carry his splintered bones
Slowly, slowly
Back into the
Tar and chemical strangled tomb,
The strange water, the
Ohio river, that is no tomb to
Rise from the dead
From.

Brush Fire

In this field,
Where the small animals ran from a brush fire,
It is a voice
In burned weeds, saying
I love you.
Still, when I go there,
I find only two gray stones,
And, lying between them,
A dead bird the color of slate.
It lies askew in its wings,
Its throat bent back as if at the height of some joy too great
To bear to give.

And the lights are going out
In a farmhouse, evening
Stands, in a gray frock, silent, at the far side
Of a raccoon's grave.

The Lights in the Hallway

The lights in the hallway
Have been out a long time.
I clasp her,
Terrified by the roundness of the earth
And its apples and the voluptuous rings
Of poplar trees, the secret Africas,
The children they give us.
She is slim enough.
Her knee feels like the face
Of a surprised lioness
Nursing the lost children
Of a gazelle by pure accident.
In that body I long for,
The Gabon poets gaze for hours
Between boughs toward heaven, their noble faces
Too secret to weep.
How do I know what color her hair is? I float among
Lonely animals, longing
For the red spider who is God.

The Small Blue Heron

1

He is not the last one.
I wish he were. Do I?
My friends brought him into the kitchen
In a waste basket and
Took him out and
Set him down.
I stroked his long throat

On the floor. I was glad to hear him
Croaking with terror.

2

The Nazis assigned
A dour man
To drive a truck every morning.
They called him "King of the Jews."
One evening, a dour man,
An Old Jew, sought out the King.
"You! Schmo! When you pick me up tomorrow,
Put me on top of the stack,
I've got asthma."

3

He is not the last one. There is a darkening place
Among the cattails on the other side of the river.
The blue heron has gone there this evening,
Darkening into a reed that the fastidious fox
Never dreamed of.

Willy Lyons

My uncle, a craftsman of hammers and wood,
Is dead in Ohio.
And my mother cries she is angry.
Willy was buried with nothing except a jacket
Stitched on his shoulder bones.
It is nothing to mourn for.
It is the other world.
She does not know how the roan horses, there,
Dead for a century,
Plod slowly.
Maybe they believe Willy's brown coffin, tangled heavily in moss,
Is a horse trough drifted to shore
Along that river under the willows and grass.
Let my mother weep on, she needs to, she knows of cold winds.
The long box is empty.
The horses turn back toward the river.

Willy planes limber trees by the waters,
Fitting his boat together.
We may as well let him go.
Nothing is left of Willy on this side
But one cracked ball-peen hammer and one suit,
Including pants, his son inherited,
For a small fee, from Hesslop's funeral home;
And my mother,
Weeping with anger, afraid of winter
For her brothers' sake:
Willy, and John, whose life and art, if any,
I never knew.

A Prayer to the Lord Ramakrishna

1

The anguish of a naked body is more terrible
To bear than God.
And the rain goes on falling.

2

When I stand up to cry out,
She laughs.
On the window sill, I lean
My bare elbows.
One blue wing, torn whole out of heaven,
Soaks in the black rain.

3

Blind, mouth sealed, a face blazes
On my pillow of cold ashes.

4

No!
I kneel down, naked, and ask forgiveness.
A cold drizzle blows into the room,
And my shoulders flinch to the bone.
You have nothing to do with us.
Sleep on.

In Memory of Leopardi

I have gone past all those times when the poets
Were beautiful as only
The rich can be. The cold bangles
Of the moon grazed one of my shoulders,
And so to this day,
And beyond, I carry
The sliver of a white city, the barb of a jewel
In my left clavicle that hunches.
Tonight I sling
A scrambling sack of oblivions and lame prayers
On my right good arm. The Ohio River
Has flown by me twice, the dark jubilating
Isaiah of mill and smoke marrow. Blind son
Of a meadow of huge horses, lover of drowned islands
Above Steubenville, blind father
Of my halt gray wing:
Now I limp on, knowing
The moon strides behind me, swinging
The scimitar of the divinity that struck down
The hunchback in agony
When he saw her, naked, carrying away his last sheep
Through the Asian rocks.

Two Postures beside a Fire

1

Tonight I watch my father's hair,
As he sits dreaming near his stove.
Knowing my feather of despair,
He sent me an owl's plume for love,
Lest I not know, so I've come home.
Tonight Ohio, where I once
Hounded and cursed my loneliness,
Shows me my father, who broke stones,
Wrestled and mastered great machines,
And rests, shadowing his lovely face.

2

Nobly his hands fold together in his repose.
He is proud of me, believing
I have done strong things among men and become a man
Of place among men of place in the large cities.
I will not awaken him.
I have come home alone, without wife or child
To delight him. Awake, solitary and welcome,
I too sit near his stove, the lines
Of an ugly age scarring my face, and my hands
Twitch nervously about.

For the Marsh's Birthday

As a father to his son, as a friend to
his friend, Be pleased to show mercy, O God.

I was alone once, waiting
For you, what you might be.
I heard your grass birds, fluting
Down a long road, to me.
Wholly for you, for you,
I was lonely, lonely.

For how was I to know
Your voice, or understand
The Irish cockatoo?
Never on sea or land
Had I heard a voice that was
Greener than grass.

Oh the voice lovelier was
Than a crow's dreaming face,
His secret face, that smiles
Alive in a dead place.
Oh I was lonely, lonely:
What were the not to me?

The not were nothing then.
Now, let the not become

Nothing, and so remain,
Till the bright grass birds come
Home to the singing tree.
Then, let them be.

Let them be living, then,
They have been dead so long.
Love, I am sick of pain
And sick with my longing,
My Irish cockatoo,
To listen to you.

Now you are all alive
And not a dream at all;
Now there are more than five
Voices I listen to
Call, call, call, call, call, call:
My Irish cockatoo.

Lifting Illegal Nets by Flashlight

The carp are secrets
Of the creation: I do not
Know if they are lonely.
The poachers drift with an almost frightening
Care under the bridge.
Water is a luminous
Mirror of swallows' nests. The stars
Have gone down.
What does my anguish
Matter? Something
The color
Of a puma has plunged through this net, and is gone.
This is the firmest
Net I ever saw, and yet something
Is gone lonely
Into the headwaters of the Minnesota.

Confession to J. Edgar Hoover

Hiding in the church of an abandoned stone,
A Negro soldier
Is flipping the pages of the Articles of War,
That he can't read.

Our father,
Last evening I devoured the wing
Of a cloud.
And, in the city, I sneaked down
To pray with a sick tree.

I labor to die, father,
I ride the great stones,
I hide under stars and maples,
And yet I cannot find my own face.
In the mountains of blast furnaces,
The trees turn their backs on me.

Father, the dark moths
Crouch at the sills of the earth, waiting.
And I am afraid of my own prayers.
Father, forgive me.
I did not know what I was doing.

To the Poets in New York

You strolled in the open, leisurely and alone,
Daydreaming of a beautiful human body
That had undressed quietly and slipped into the river
And become the river:
The proud body of an animal that would transform
The snaggled gears and the pulleys
Into a plant that grows under water.
You went searching gently for the father of your own agony,
The camellia of your death,
The voice that would call out to you clearly and name the fires
Of your hidden equator.

Solitary,
Patient for the last voices of the dusk to die down, and the dusk
To die down, listener waiting for courteous rivers
To rise and be known,
You kept a dark counsel.
It is not seemly a man should rend open by day
The huge roots of his blood trees.
A man ought to hide sometimes on the banks
Of the sky,
And some human beings
Have need of lingering back in the fastidious half-light
Even at dawn.

The River Down Home

Under the enormous pier-shadow,
Hobie Johnson drowned in a suckhole.
I cannot even remember
His obliterated face.
Outside my window, now, Minneapolis
Drowns, dark.
It is dark.
I have no life.

What is left of all of it?
Blind hoboes sell American flags
And bad poems of patriotism
On Saturday evenings forever in the rain,
Between the cathouses and the slag heaps
And the river, down home.
Oh Jesus Christ, the Czechoslovakians
Are drunk again, clambering
Down the sand-pitted walls
Of the grave.

In Response to a Rumor That the Oldest Whorehouse in Wheeling, West Virginia, Has Been Condemned

I will grieve alone,
As I strolled alone, years ago, down along
The Ohio shore.
I hid in the hobo jungle weeds
Upstream from the sewer main,
Pondering, gazing.

I saw, down river,
At Twenty-third and Water Streets
By the vinegar works,
The doors open in early evening.
Swinging their purses, the women
Poured down the long street to the river
And into the river.

I do not know how it was
They could drown every evening.
What time near dawn did they climb up the other shore,
Drying their wings?

For the river at Wheeling, West Virginia,
Has only two shores:
The one in hell, the other
In Bridgeport, Ohio.

And nobody would commit suicide, only
To find beyond death
Bridgeport, Ohio.

Poems to a Brown Cricket

1
I woke,
Just about daybreak, and fell back
In a drowse.

A clean leaf from one of the new cedars
Has blown in through the open window.
How long ago a huge shadow of wings pondering and hovering
        leaned down
To comfort my face.
I don't care who loved me.
Somebody did, so I let myself alone.
I will stand watch for you, now.
I lay here awake a long time before I looked up
And found you sunning yourself asleep
In the Secret Life of Jakob Boehme
Left open on the desk.

2

Our friends gave us their love
And this room to sleep in.
Outside now, not a sound.
Instead of rousing us out for breakfast,
Our friends love us and grant us our loneliness.
We shall waken again
When the courteous face of the old horse David
Appears at our window,
To snuffle and cough gently.
He, too, believes we may long for
One more dream of slow canters across the prairie
Before we come home to our strange bodies
And rise from the dead.

3

As for me, I have been listening,
For an hour or so, now, to the scampering ghosts
Of Sioux ponies, down the long road
Toward South Dakota.
They just brought me home, leaning forward, by both hands
        clinging
To the joists of the magnificent dappled feathers
Under their wings.

4

As for you, I won't press you to tell me
Where you have gone.
I know. I know how you love to edge down

The long trails of canyons.
At the bottom, along willow shores, you stand, waiting for
    twilight,
In the silence of deep grass.
You are safe there, guarded, for you know how the dark faces
Of the cliffs forbid easy plundering
Of their beautiful pueblos:
White cities concealed delicately in their chasms
As the new eggs of the mourning dove
In her ground nest,
That only the spirit hunters
Of the snow can find.

    5
Brown cricket, you are my friend's name.
I will send back my shadow for your sake, to stand guard
On the solitude of the mourning dove's young.
Here, I will stand by you, shadowless,
At the small golden door of your body till you wake
In a book that is shining.

To the Muse

It is all right. All they do
Is go in by dividing
One rib from another. I wouldn't
Lie to you. It hurts
Like nothing I know. All they do
Is burn their way in with a wire.
It forks in and out a little like the tongue
Of that frightened garter snake we caught
At Cloverfield, you and me, Jenny
So long ago.

I would lie to you
If I could.
But the only way I can get you to come up
Out of the suckhole, the south face

Of the Powhatan pit, is to tell you
What you know:

You come up after dark, you poise alone
With me on the shore.
I lead you back to this world.

Three lady doctors in Wheeling open
Their offices at night.
I don't have to call them, they are always there.
But they only have to put the knife once
Under your breast.
Then they hang their contraption.
And you bear it.

It's awkward a while. Still, it lets you
Walk about on tiptoe if you don't
Jiggle the needle.
It might stab your heart, you see.
The blade hangs in your lung and the tube
Keeps it draining.
That way they only have to stab you
Once. Oh Jenny.

I wish to God I had made this world, this scurvy
And disastrous place. I
Didn't, I can't bear it
Either, I don't blame you, sleeping down there
Face down in the unbelievable silk of spring,
Muse of black sand,
Alone.

I don't blame you, I know
The place where you lie.
I admit everything. But look at me.
How can I live without you?
Come up to me, love,
Out of the river, or I will
Come down to you.

New Poems
(from *Collected Poems*)

The Idea of the Good

I am bone lonely
Down on the black rock.
Now once again I take
My way, my own way,
Alone till the black
Rock opens into ground
And closes and I die.
Two hundred feet below me two deer fled past just now.
I want an owl to poise on my grave
Without sound, but
In this mean time
I want bone feet borne down
Cold on stone.
I dream of my poor Judas walking along and alone
And alone and alone and alone till his wound
Woke and his bowels
Broke.
Jenny, I gave you that unhappy
Book that nobody knows but you
And me, so give me
A little life back.
Or at least send me the owl's feather
Again, and I promise I will give it
To no one. How could I?
Nobody else will follow
This poem but you,
But I don't care.
My precious secret, how
Could they know
You or me?
Patience.

Blue Teal's Mother

How do I know it was a fox?
It might have been nothing
But the late snow.

All I know is
My friend brought home
The five blue babies, caressing their feathers.
One followed after another across
The moulting road, and they
Had no mother, they had
No father, they had only
The humpbacked old Chevrolet
They came home in.

In three days, they were gone.
A weasel got them.

The weasel turns white in the snow,
And becomes an ermine,
That some women wear dead.

Set free the weasel,
Set free the fox,
And the cold groundhog
Outwitting the sun.

Give even the living
A chance.

I, too, live,
Even in my pain.
Why, look here, one night
When I was drunk,
A bulk tree got in my way.
Never mind what I thought when dawn broke.
In the dark, the night before,
I knew perfectly well I could have knocked
The bulk tree down.
Well, cut it up, anyway.

I didn't hurt it.
I gathered it into my arms.
You may not believe this, but
It turned into a slender woman.
Stop nagging me. I know
What I just said.
It turned into a slender woman.

Moon

I am so delighted
With you, because I know you
And I know you
Came down to me, answering.
I walked up hill
After you went all the way down.
I hadn't seen you,
But I believed in you,
And I believed you were dividing three cones
Of sky down beyond
The left shoulder of the white oak
In Warnock,
Ohio, and I remember and I pray
Come down to me love and bring me
One panther of silver and one happy
Evening of snow,
And I will give you
My life, my own, and now
My beloved has come to me and we have gone walking
Below you beside the East
River in the snow, all
Three of us, leaving
Six prints of panther, kind
Woman, and happy
Man,
And I love you,
Sky full of laurels and arrows,
White shadow of cities where the scars
Of forgotten swans
Waken into feathers
And new leaves.

A Poem about Breasts

Already she seems bone thin
When her clothes are on.
The lightest wind blows
Her dress toward the doorways.

Everybody thinks he can see
Her body longing to follow
Helpless and miserable,
Dreaming itself
Into an apparition of loneliness,
A spirit of vine wondering
At a grape here and there,
As the September spider,
The master, ascends
Her long spine.

Already she weighs more, yet
She still bows down slightly,
As I stand in her doorway.
It's not hunching, it's only
That children have been reaching
Upward for years to gather
Sweetness of her face.
They are innocent and passionate
Thieves of the secret hillsides.
Now she rises, tall, round, round.
And round again, and, again, round.

Sun Tan at Dusk

When was the last time
You remembered you
Had gone out? A bee
Blew past me. Jays
Raised hell down stream,
You rose up
Slow out of the mountain pool.
Color of doe out of green
Against dark.
The fawn's honey weeping down stream.
I just got up. This is
When I wake.

A Mad Fight Song for William S. Carpenter, 1966

Varus, varus, gib mir meine Legionen wieder

Quick on my feet in those Novembers of my loneliness,
I tossed a short pass,
Almost the instant I got the ball, right over the head
Of Barrel Terry before he knocked me cold.

When I woke, I found myself crying out
Latin conjugations, and the new snow falling
At the edge of a green field.

Lemoyne Crone had caught the pass, while I lay
Unconscious and raging
Alone with the fire ghost of Catullus, the contemptuous
        graces tossing
Garlands and hendecasyllabics over the head
Of Cornelius Nepos the mastodon,
The huge volume.

At the edges of Southeast Asia this afternoon
The quarterbacks and the lines are beginning to fall,
A spring snow,

And terrified young men
Quick on their feet
Lob one another's skulls across
Wings of strange birds that are burning
Themselves alive.

(Note: Carpenter, a West Pointer, called for his own troops to be na-
palmed rather than have them surrender. General Westmoreland
called him "hero" and made him his aide, and President Johnson
awarded him a Silver Star for courage.)

The Pretty Redhead

From the French of Apollinaire

I stand here in the sight of everyone a man full of sense
Knowing life and knowing of death what a living man can know

Having gone through the griefs and happinesses of love
Having known sometimes how to impose his ideas
Knowing several languages
Having travelled more than a little
Having seen war in the artillery and the infantry
Wounded in the head trepanned under chloroform
Having lost his best friends in the horror of battle

I know as much as one man alone can know
Of the ancient and the new
And without troubling myself about this war today
Between us and for us my friends
I judge this long quarrel between tradition and imagination
Between order and adventure

You whose mouth is made in the image of God's mouth
Mouth which is order itself
Judge kindly when you compare us
With those who were the very perfection of order
We who are seeking everywhere for adventure

We are not your enemies
Who want to give ourselves vast strange domains
Where mystery flowers into any hands that long for it
Where there are new fires colors never seen
A thousand fantasies difficult to make sense out of
They must be made real
All we want is to explore kindness the enormous country where
        everything is silent
And there is time which somebody can banish or welcome home
Pity for us who fight always on the frontiers
Of the illimitable and the future
Pity our mistakes pity our sins

Here summer is coming the violent season
And so my youth is as dead as spring
Oh Sun it is the time of reason grown passionate
And I am still waiting
To follow the forms she takes noble and gentle
So I may love her alone

She comes and draws me as a magnet draws filaments of iron
She has the lovely appearance
Of an adorable redhead
Her hair turns golden you would say
A beautiful lightning flash that goes on and on
Or the flames that spread out their feathers
In wilting tea roses

But laugh laugh at me
Men everywhere especially people from here
For there are so many things that I don't dare to tell you
So many things that you would not let me say
Have pity on me

Echo for the Promise of
Georg Trakl's Life

Quiet voice,
In the midst of those blazing
Howitzers in blossom.
Their fire
Is a vacancy.

What do those stuttering machines
Have to do
With the solitude?

Guns make no sound.
Only the quiet voice
Speaks from the body of the deer
To the body of the woman.

My own body swims in a silent pool,
And I make silence.

They both hear me.
Hear me,
Father of my sound,
My poor son.

A Centenary Ode: Inscribed to Little Crow, Leader of the Sioux Rebellion in Minnesota, 1862

I had nothing to do with it. I was not here.
I was not born.
In 1862, when your hotheads
Raised hell from here to South Dakota,
My own fathers scattered into West Virginia
And southern Ohio.
My family fought the Confederacy
And fought the Union.
None of them got killed.
But for all that, it was not my fathers
Who murdered you.
Not much.

I don't know
Where the fathers of Minneapolis finalized
Your flayed carcass.
Little Crow, true father
Of my dark America,
When I close my eyes I lose you among
Old lonelinesses.
My family were a lot of singing drunks and good carpenters.
We had brothers who loved one another no matter what they did.
And they did plenty.

I think they would have run like hell from your Sioux.
And when you caught them you all would have run like hell
From the Confederacy and from the Union
Into the hills and hunted for a few things,
Some bull-cat under the stones, a gar maybe,
If you were hungry, and if you were happy,
Sunfish and corn.

If only I knew where to mourn you,
I would surely mourn.

But I don't know.

I did not come here only to grieve
For my people's defeat.
The troops of the Union, who won,
Still outnumber us.
Old Paddy Beck, my great-uncle, is dead
At the old soldiers' home near Tiffen, Ohio.
He got away with every last stitch
Of his uniform, save only
The dress trousers.

Oh all around us,
The hobo jungles of America grow wild again.
The pick handles bloom like your skinned spine.
I don't even know where
My own grave is.

Red Jacket's Grave

I have a deep identity
With something under
The bare stones, the
Variety of firemen,
In Buffalo, N.Y.,
Early nineteen something.

Their stones look all
Alike, the beefy faces, a few granite, sand, a little rich marble.
Somebody played with his callouses,
Then gouged down to find
Black hands. What name?
I am lonely among the black hands that are forgotten.
And lonely among the members of the Buffalo
Fire Department who
Died in World War I.
They are not alone.

And neither is Red Jacket,
Whose noble face rises

At the entrance of the
Grave grass.

I don't know who dug
The graves of the firemen,
I don't believe Red Jacket
Would have given his left
Hand to leave his body there,
Though his name is there.

Somebody
Dug the graves.
Somebody, for maybe a dollar an hour,
Hugged the seventy-five stones,
Into the ground.

And who dug the graves?
And who wasted his black hands away among the beautiful
Roots of the elms?
And who hugged the stones
Into the ground?

To the August Fallen

Below me, a pool gathers
Old wings and one leaf still shining
With a few jewels
And this light.
Only the feathers are heavy, and they drag
The skeleton down now, but tomorrow at dawn
Will float and rise up toward Canada.
I breathe
The waters poured out by snow hills
That are gone.

A thousand years ago,
Last night, on other huge prairies,
The Tartars of North China abandoned their rough-coated ponies
For the wind to blister, and blundered themselves off.

They groped in the snow for the shifting terraces of the moon.
They chased one another's footprints, staggering, drunk
On the fermented milk of lost mares.
They ran up the stairs of snow towers that vanished.
They huddled down between drifts,
Crying with famine.

Below me, already waterlogged,
The old leaves and the bright wing sink down between
The white hills of the south that loom now into shades,
To the fallen.

A Secret Gratitude

Eugen Boissevain died in the autumn of 1949. I had wondered already, at the time of our visit, what would happen to Edna [Millay] if he should die first.

—Edmund Wilson

1

She cleaned house, and then lay down long
On the long stair.

On one of those cold white wings
That the strange fowl provide for us like one hillside of the sea,
That cautery of snow that blinds us,
Pitiless light,
One winter afternoon
Fair near the place where she sank down with one wing broken,
Three friends and I were caught
Stalk still in the light.

Five of the lights. Why should they care for our eyes?
Five deer stood there.
They looked back, a good minute.
They knew us, all right:
Four chemical accidents of horror pausing
Between one suicide or another
On the passing wing

Of an angel that cared no more for our biology, our pity, and our
    pain
Than we care.

Why should any mere multitude of the angels care
To lay one blind white plume down
On this outermost limit of something that is probably no more
Than an aphid,
An aphid which is one of the angels whose wings toss the black
    pears
Of tears down on the secret shores
Of the seas in the corner
Of a poet's closed eye.
Why should five deer
Gaze back at us?
They gazed back at us.
Afraid, and yet they stood there,
More alive than we four, in their terror,
In their good time.

We had a dog.
We could have got other dogs.
Two or three dogs could have taken turns running and dragging
    down
Those fleet lights, whose tails must look as mysterious as the
Stars in Los Angeles.
We are men.
It doesn't even satisfy us
To kill one another.
We are a smear of obscenity
On the lake whose only peace
Is a hole where the moon
Abandoned us, that poor
Girl who can't leave us alone.

If I were the moon I would shrink into a sand grain
In the corner of the poet's eye,
While there's still room.

We are men.
We are capable of anything.
We could have killed every one of those deer.

The very moon of lovers tore herself with the agony of a
　　　wounded tigress
Out of our side.
We can kill anything.
We can kill our own bodies.
Those deer on the hillside have no idea what in hell
We are except murderers.
They know that much, and don't think
They don't.
Man's heart is the rotten yolk of a blacksnake egg
Corroding, as it is just born, in a pile of dead
Horse dung.
I have no use for the human creature.
He subtly extracts pain awake in his own kind.
I am born one, out of an accidental hump of chemistry.
I have no use.

　　2
But
We didn't set dogs on the deer,
Even though we know,
As well as you know,
We could have got away with it,
Because
Who cares?

　　3
Boissevain, who was he?
Was he human? I doubt it,
From what I know
Of men.

Who was he,
Hobbling with his dry eyes
Along in the rain?

I think he must have fallen down like the plumes of new snow,
I think he must have fallen into the grass, I think he
Must surely have grown around
Her wings, gathering and being gathered,
Leaf, string, anything she could use

To build her still home of songs
Within sound of water.

4

By God, come to that, I would have married her too,
If I'd got the chance, and she'd let me.
Think of that. Being alive with a girl
Who could turn into a laurel tree
Whenever she felt like it.
Think of that.

5

Outside my window just now
I can hear a small waterfall rippling antiphonally down over
The stones of my poem.

So She Said

"I'd rather not. I'm confused."

I did not plow her darknesses,
Only because I'd rather not
Flop rampant on the secrecies.
They are easy enough to violate.
Easy enough. As when my hand
Exploded my fantastic self
I did not know nor understand
The beauty of my lonely life.

She knew me lonely so she took
My bare body into her bed,
Yet could not bear to let me look
Her over, naked. For she said
She did not know if she could bear
Two hundred pounds of the blind sky,
A man, a rock that breathes a woman's hair.
Neither did I.

And when I lay me down to die
Let me call back I might have used

The woman of a girl who loved me
Enough to let me let her lie
Alone in her own loneliness,
And mind her own good business.

I love for what I will become
In my good time when I go home
Back to my skull, that is our face.

Trouble

Well, look, honey, where I come from, when a girl says
she's in trouble, she's in trouble.

—Judy Holliday

Leering across Pearl Street,
Crum Anderson yipped:
"Hey Pugh!
I see your sister
Been rid bareback.
She swallow a watermelon?
Fred Gordon! Fred Gordon! Fred Gordon!"
"Wayya mean? She can get fat, can't she?"

Fat? Willow and lonesome Roberta, running
Alone down Pearl Street in the rain the last time
I ever saw her, smiling a smile
Crum Anderson will never know,
Wondering at her body.

Sixteen years, and
All that time she thought she was nothing
But skin and bones.

Humming a Tune for
an Old Lady in West Virginia

dummy-dummy-dummy-dummy-day:
gran'ma's pretty baby . . .

More than other song,
Your song, all yours.
You cast line in the water
A long time ago.
You plumbed it down, down,
Down to the fish-heads,
Stones, closed windows,
The sludge black snow.

More than other song,
Yours wakes the catfish.
No other, not even
The splintering of ice.
Not even squeal and grind
Of chain on cold chisel
On a rust-rotten girder,
The terminal bridge.

More than other song,
Yours. I sit and listen
To the soft floppy whisper
A drowned boy made.
He rose in two pieces
A mile down the river,
One cord round his pecker
And one shoulder blade.

Now you're lost over water.
All the gouging and dragging,
Searching, finding,
Now, a mile down,
And into the other river,
I hear you still singing.
I don't die, I'm not deaf.
I scare, I go on.

Dummy-dummy comes round
Like the old blind mailman
Delivering bills that
Nobody can pay.
Black widow's the madam
Stone broke in the cat house,
And the girl with the best song
Can't sell it today,
So she gives it away.

To a Dead Drunk

How carefully, fastidiously,
You lounged beside the hollow lute.
The cold aristocrats that die
Left you alone in your defeat.
Nibbling in loneliness you ground
Bitter between your outraged teeth
Early Eliot and late Pound,
Before you drank yourself to death.

Oh, plenty will remember them.
Maybe the Cyclades will not,
Nor the frail Irishmen who scream
Into our century and rot.
But someone whose triumphant name
Is Lyndon Fink Jane Adam Smith
Will pounce on your forgotten name
To write a dissertation with.

God help me too, defeated poet.
You walked with me one afternoon
Of blind stone and Ohio soot,
To visit a great lonely man.
Never you mind. Today I bought
Collected poems of Ralph Hodgson.
Now you are dead. I am not yet.
Hodgson is now. I will be soon.

Still, in Minerva, he had still
A white tree, a white miracle
Beyond a little mound of coal
(Listen, what rhymes with miracle?)
We sang all afternoon, we tossed
A willing honey under the tongue.
I must have seemed a silly ghost.
Pity me now. I was just young.

Small Frogs Killed on the Highway

Still,
I would leap too
Into the light,
If I had the chance.
It is everything, the wet green stalk of the field
On the other side of the road.
They crouch there, too, faltering in terror
And take strange wing. Many
Of the dead never moved, but many
Of the dead are alive forever in the split second
Auto headlights more sudden
Than their drivers know.
The drivers burrow backward into dank pools
Where nothing begets
Nothing.

Across the road, tadpoles are dancing
On the quarter thumbnail
Of the moon. They can't see,
Not yet.

A Way to Make a Living
From an epigram by Plato

When I was a boy, a relative
Asked for me a job
At the Weeks Cemetery.

Think of all I could
Have raised that summer,
That money, and me
Living at home,
Fattening and getting
Ready to live my life
Out on my knees, humming,
Kneading up docks
And sumac from
Those flawless clerks-at-court, those beautiful
Grocers and judges, the polished
Dead of whom we make
So much.

I could have stayed there with them.
Cheap, too.
Imagine, never
To have turned
Wholly away from the classic
Cold, the hill, so laid
Out, measure by seemly measure clipped
And mown by old man Albright
The sexton. That would have been a hell of
A way to make a living.

Thank you, no.
I am going to take my last nourishment
Of measure from a dark blue
Ripple on swell on ripple that makes
Its own garlands.
My dead are the secret wine jars
Of Tyrian commercial travelers.
Their happiness is a lost beginning, their graves
Drift in and out of the Mediterranean.

One of these days
The immortals, clinging to a beam of sunlight
Under water, delighted by delicate crustaceans,
Will dance up thirty-foot walls of radiance,
And waken,
The sea shining on their shoulders, the fresh
Wine in their arms. Their ships have drifted away.

They are stars and snowflakes floating down
Into your hands, love.

A Summer Memory in the Crowded City

to Garnie Braxton

She came crying down to me
Out of the dim heaven
That I had been praying
Against all afternoon.
And I cannot say
That I loved the earth much
With its hay dust
That swaled my eyes closed.
And her voice did not have
The clear sweetness
We listen to
In the books of our childhood.
Shrill, nagging, beyond pity
Or anything like it,
She lashed down, just dying
To peck my eyes out.
Oh the darling,
She would have loved to get

Her hook in me.
She coiled back into a secret
Corner of the sky
And glared down,
A mere barn swift.

Well you can't stand there.
I threw my forearms around
My face and bent forward,
Hunched into the barn
With Dave Woods
And his boy Slim Carter.
Did you see that bird, Dave?
Yes. Never mind. Look here,

Look at these pups.
They don't eat anything but milk foam.
And look how fat they keep.

Somewhere a black woman
In absolute despair
Is cursing me blind
Gnashing jaw bone on shrunk
Gums. Dave, Slim, and I
Tossed her nightmare away.
We plodded into the barn.
We clattered the dung forks
Beneath the dank joists
Where surely, somewhere,
The nest curled over the blue
Veins of somebody's
Throat and wings.

We didn't look at each other.
What the hell are we supposed to do with these birds?
They clutter the whole barn,
They spend their days flailing the pinnacles of heaven
Where the angels do nothing
But pray and sing. Faugh!
We stabbed our forks
Into the cold cow pies
And shoveled them out.

A Poem by Garnie Braxton

"Garnie, I wish I was a seagull."

"Yeah, me too.
And when you want to get warm
All you got to do
Is put on your feathers
And fly away to the south.

I been there once."

Written in a Copy of Swift's Poems, for Wayne Burns

I promised once if I got hold of
This book, I'd send it on to you.
These are the songs that Roethke told of,
The curious music loved by few.
I think of lanes in Laracor
Where Brinsley MacNamara wrote
His lovely elegy, before
The Yahoos got the Dean by rote.

Only, when Swift-men are all gone
Back to their chosen fields by train
And the drunk Chairman snores alone,
Swift is alive in secret, Wayne:
Singing for Stella's happiest day,
Charming a charming man, John Gay,
And greeting, now their bones are lost,
Pope's beautiful, electric ghost.

Here are some songs he lived in, kept
Secret from almost everyone
And laid away, while Stella slept,
Before he slept, and died, alone.
Gently, listen, the great shade passes,
Magnificent, who still can bear,
Beyond the range of horses' asses,
Nobilities, light, light and air.

Eclogue at Nash's Grove

Cui dono lepidum novum libellum?

This is just one more
Of them, you can find them all over
America, just outside of town,
If you walk far enough.

It looks virgin, a sigh
Of maple and box-elder leaves so long held back and now
     mourning,
And the sun seeming kindly to the nibblings of rats at last,
As though by a change of heart.

I walked down this path, believing it.
No doubt the name belonged to some soft-eyed, sympathetic
Son of a bitch banker who stamped a Norwegian
Out of his money, this green place.

Virgin America, all right.
I wonder how much they cost, these cheap
Stones blackened in a short century.
No need to worry about standing on the dead.

The whole place is a grave, a virgin
Whose belly is black stone.
Not even the granary rats come out here any more.
Just me.

A man whom I never saw told me
The best days are the first
To flee away. I softly following
His elegy edge down the gully a little further.

He sang of war and the young prince
Far away from north Europe.
Since his day rose, I loved
The old mourner, and I wish he could mourn

For the granary rats gone home long ago.
For the Norwegians who worked this green place and cowered
     till the winter
Wind made them nervous wrecks.
For Nash, whether he was a land gouger
Or not. For my sons, who sound as unhappy as the old poet

Sometimes. For the lives who are eaten away
By the plump rats of brief years.
Whatever is left of them, it will sag into the salt cloud
When the sea comes back. And for me.

There was another with curls that clouded
His temples lonely as rich marble
And the black cement here
In Nash's Grove.

He killed his heart for the sake of living
Forever. But they do not live there, whoever
They are, and wherever forever is. This poem is a little
Darkness for them, where they do not have to weep.
Not for me, anyway.

In Memory of the Horse David, Who Ate One of My Poems

Larry

I remember a fight
In a snow fall.
I never saw it,
But I remember.

Ed told me, angry with me
For something else.

You and some little bastard
Caught you drunk,
Nagged you outside,
And cut you up with his fists.

Down, and down, and down, in the seven
Corners of snow.

Ed explained to me
That the little son of bitches
(He has several mothers, though few)
Cut you down.

Ed knew.
If you'd lost the fight
You'd have wakened
Next morning dead.
So he didn't step in.

You rose, out of the snow.
Burly, you rose,
Knowing.

You beat him out of lament and snow blindness.

There is a little sort of
Man who drifts obscenely
Soberly into the seven corners
Of Hell, 14, Minnesota:
He selects the big good drunk man,
And cuts him down.

The giant killer is
A dirty little bastard.

I, drunk then, awake now, remember
The angel crying, as one winged sufferer to another:
Hafiz, what in hell
Are you doing in this gutter?
Where have you fallen from? With your warm voice?
And Hafiz answering the angel out of the gutter
And the north gone blind:

Watch your step, oh beloved and beyond beautiful
Bearer of the cup.
The sickle moon has torn a star from my arms.
In this wheat field, watch your step, don't whirl down
So fast. Don't walk on that ant. For she too
Loves her life. Let go, Larry.
Let go.
Let go.

The Offense

1

All I have is the moment of my life. You
Took a moment away. Delighted, laughing,
You and I lonely by the Mississippi
        Wondered what hell was.

Hell to me was a girl whose lonely body
Needed me, somewhere, to be lonely with her.
Hell to you was the difficult, the dazzling
        Hendecasyllabic.

How in hell that we live in can we write it?
Long bones, was the phrase that I suggested.
No, you said, the bones of our lives are longer.
        What is our life, then?

We Americans, loneliness of body,
Puritans, sick at the beauty of the body,
Men and women we leave each other, lonely.
        Ray, you said lonely.

What is life? says the drunk in Sean O'Casey.
What is eternity? says Saint Augustine.
Where are you, Ray? I ask, and what the hell good does
        It do me the meter's breaking?

2

The buds shrink under the swelling moon.
We grow smaller as the moon grows.
The young men fall down on their faces.
The rain falls down on its face,
And the girls rise.
It still looks like the lashing of winter from the ocean.
I pull my hat down. I say the hell with it, mainly because I know
That this is spring.
The wing coils all over what I can see of New Jersey,
And somebody is weeping in a darkness that I cannot see
        through.
I want.

3

Listen, you didn't give
Me time enough to live
The true life that I care
To live. Even the air
That I still have to breathe
Is not my only death.
I have two. Which is which?

4

        And another thing. I still owe you that five dollars you gave
me that evening in St. Paul.
        Why did you do it, Ray?

        I wasn't even hungry.

To a Friendly Dun

1

A man owes me two hundred and fifty dollars.
And I would rather be dead than ask him
To pay me back.

2

He knows
Who he is. One afternoon in
Minneapolis, I slogged over the Tenth
Avenue bridge, I slogged upstairs
At Seven Corners, I had money enough
To climb the bitter dead
In the black snow.

3

The snow rotted down
The black river, the love
Died in my heart as I
Slogged up the rotten
Stair. My friend said all
I got is relief meat and maybe a little more
Bean soup and
Let's go see, because
I'm hungry too.

4

And so was I.
I drank, I ate.
I had some three hundred dollars in the bank.
At that time, all I knew
Was the rotting slit of my body.
I was dying, and my friend was hungry.
I took that fifty bucks left over
And got the hell
Out.

5

Now three years have gone, and I have succeeded in deluding
My real body into believing it will not die.
Cold, cold, and the snow blackens into the veins

Of my city, my love, my dark city, the ocean of
Darkness, where we are all
Lonely together. My veins
Gag in my body, I love my body
As my brothers love their own
Veins gagging into the loneliness that is
Only my own life: not much, I guess,
But it is all alone, and I love it.
It may go drifting face down down the Hudson,
Dead in its own darkness, but it will go drifting dead
In its own darkness. This morning I shared
Ten dollars with a man.
Not my loneliness, which I cannot share.
Just ten bucks, which I hope he will never fear
He has to pay me back.

6
A man who charges his brother money to save his brother's soul
Is scum.
You are scum.
I paid you.

7
I wash my hands.

To Harvey,
Who Traced the Circulation

Who is that blue
Dark, dreamer dreaming
Of me?

One afternoon I lonely found
Home when a lonely
Girl slipped her quick
Shelter down.

I love her, she is brave, she knew the moon was blooming
Under the horizon.

She said, give me my own lonely
Heart, so I can hear my heart
Beat in my left wrist.

I kissed her long
Left wrist.

Long ago the poor lonely
Brontosaurus lay down, face down, in his own
Place, death, ferns
Covered his face, secret
Body of the most delicate
Oil, the secret of steel,
The living creature who long ago smoothed
My bones into my love's lazily
Giving bones. Harvey,

There is nothing between us
But the strumming of my pulse yearning
Toward the sea. We
Are both blue.

Has any eye seen the body's eye gazing down in a daze below
The right wrist?
The blood is blue, there.

I walked once headlong into the water, longing
Or risking, if you want to risk the road,
The word road.

Just at the moment the moon
Sank into
Junk, my love rose,
I rose, and

The moon rose.

I tremble along the river.
I love breasts,
But I love most one soft
Wing of the vein.

Katydid

1

I was a good child,
So I am
A good man. Put that
In your pipe.

Something fell down between
Me and me,
One afternoon,
Long ago.

Uncle Shorty came home to live living in our house.
The man next door, laboring twelve hours
A day, came home.
Terrified white, he hated niggers,
And his human face, frightened with smoke,
Glared delighted in his pain through the open place
In the fence, the open place
Where I crept, sometimes,
Afraid of both.
My Uncle Shorty ran screaming back into the ruthless
House of his father, screaming
Dago! Dago!

And now my mother has told me the man next door
Walked weeping back home.

2

Shorty the lonely is
Dead with the
Black sooted and cold mined
Man next door.

3

I thought I was lonely, I thought I was lonely, so
I took my ghosts with me.
Whorehouse. Put
That in your pipe.
Shorty, he wanted to open a package store

Before the moon came down and the blue
Hands of the sea
Come back to gather him
And me with the black face
Of oil and grease in that place,
South Ohio, where the white man in his darkness
Scared Shorty home.

4

I had the measles. I snuck out,
When my mother was gone, alone, and my father was gone,
        laboring
I found you, katydid, alone, between the two yards.
My doctor told me I looked like a tomato, and to me you looked
Into my eyes as I knelt. You were utterly silent in daylight.

5

Annie and I have heard you sing in the dark moon
On the far side of Lake Minnewaska.
Utterly still green wings, song, moon darkly beginning,
You are she.
As for me, I have a white face
Of dark green.

Many of Our Waters: Variations on a Poem by a Black Child

Delivered as the Phi Beta Kappa poem, College of William and Mary, December 5, 1969

to my brother Jack

1

from my journal, March 8, 1969: Garnie's whisper to me, while we were watching a construction operation near Radio City. The operation had reached that early stage at which the workmen had dug extremely deep into the intended foundation of the building, obviously therefore to be a new skyscraper. As Garnie watched the working men, they were far below, and, to his eyes, as to mine, they

appeared very small. About a third of them were Negroes. And this
is exactly what he whispered to me. It has to, and it can—only it
can—speak for itself:

You know,
if a blind boy
ride his bicycle
down there
he might fall into that water
I think it's water
but I don't know
they call it acid
and if that poor boy
drive his poor blind bicycle
into that acid
he drown
he die
and then
they bury him
up

   2

to the Ohio

Along Aetnaville, where I was born,
I want to spend my eternity
In hell with you.
And the moment I'm off, I'm off
Back home to my own river.

My rotted Ohio,
It was only a little while ago
That I learned the meaning of your name.
The Winnebago gave you your name, Ohio,
And Ohio means beautiful river.

In this final dawn
Of my life,
I think of two lines by the unhappy and half-forgotten
American poet H. Phelps Putnam.

He was writing about a lonely girl's lovely place.

He cried out, "That reeking slit, wide, soft, and lecherous,
From which we bleed, and into which we drown."

Oh, my secret and lovely place, up shore from the railroad,
My bareass beach,
This is not a poem.
This is not an apology to the Muse.
This is the cold-blooded plea of a homesick vampire
To his brother and friend.
If you do not care one way or another about
The preceding lines,
Please do not go on listening
On any account of mine.
Please leave the poem.
Thank you.

Oh my back-broken beloved Ohio.
I, too, was beautiful, once,
Just like you.
We were both still a little
Young, then.
Now, all I am is a poet,
Just like you.
This morning I feel like that old child
You gathered so often
Into your rinsing arms,
And bathed, and healed.
I feel lonesome,
And sick at heart,
Frightened,
And I don't know
Why.

help.

3

learning from MacDiarmid

The kind of poetry I want to write is
    The poetry of a grown man.
The young poets of New York come to me with
Their mangled figures of speech,

But they have little pity
For the pure clear word.

I know something about the pure clear word,
Though I am not yet a grown man.
And who is he?

The long body of his dream is the beginning of a dark
Hair under an illiterate
Girl's ear.

And everybody goes on explaining to us
The difference between a nutmeg and a squirrel,
The grown man plows down.

He longs for the long body of his dream.
He works slowly day by long day.
He gets up in the morning and curses himself
Into black silence.
He has got his guts kicked in,
And he says
Nothing. (Reader, I am a liar. He says plenty.)
He shuts up.
He dies.
He grows.

4
This morning
My beloved rose, before I did,
And came back again.

The kind of poetry I want is my love
Who comes back with the rain. Oh I
Would love to lie down long days long, the long
Down slipping the gown from her shoulders.

But
I got to go to work.

Work be damned, the kind
Of poetry I want
Is to lie down with my love.

All she is
Is a little ripple of rain
On a small waterfall.

What do you want from me?

5

on the way to the planetarium

That bright black boy whom I love
Came out of the grocery
On the other side of the street.

If you don't know that street,
84th and Amsterdam,
Be proud and true to yourself if you go there.
Otherwise, get through it
Fast,
Fast,
Fast as you can.
He'll catch you.
He's the gingerbread man.

That lithe white girl whom I love
Stood on the one side of 84th
And Amsterdam.

That bright black boy whom she loves
Yelled from the other side of the street:

Can Kinny come too?
Kinny's my brother.

I yelled: Garnie,
The light's changing.
Get the HELL over here.

Can Kinny come too?
I ain't got nothing but my brother.

Garnie, you and Kinny get the hell over here.

I ain't got nothing but my brother.

Neither have I, get the hell over here.

And then my lithe proud love, a little darker
Than Kinny, lifted
The baby Gemela into her long and lonely arms,
And left her back home because
Outside it was raining.

6

Gemela

Small fawn edging through the underbrush,
Small fawn secret,
My love, my love's
Secret fawn
Fell asleep on my love's white shoulder because
It was raining,
And she couldn't go with us
To raise cain on the way to the planetarium
And brood on the stars there.

Gemela face down the Hudson River
Where even the rats drift
Belly up.
Aren't they cute little pickaninny fawns
Drifting face down the Hudson with the rats
Belly up?

7

A Message from the Mountain Pool
Where the Deer Come Down

My love and I went swimming naked one afternoon
When mother and daughter came down and watched us and went
        away
In their own good time.
For once in our lives we did not frighten
The creation. It never occurred to them
What we might be.

I have a little time left, Jack.
I don't know what you want.
But I know what I want.
I want to live my life.

And how can I live my life
Unless you live yours?

All this time I've been slicking into my own words
The beautiful language of my friends.
I have to use my own, now.
That's why this scattering poem sounds the way it does.
You're my brother at last,
And I don't have anything
Except my brother
And many of our waters in our native country,
When they break.
And when they break,
They break in a woman's body,
They break in your man's heart,
And they break in mine:

Pity so old and alone, it is not alone, yours, or mine,
The pity of rivers and children, the pity of brothers, the pity
Of our country, which is our lives.

A Moral Poem Freely Accepted
from Sappho

for the marriage of Frances Seltzer and Philip Mendlow

I would like to sleep with deer.
Then she emerges.
I sleep with both.
This poem is a deer with a dream in it.
I have stepped across its rock.
The three wings coiling out of that black stone in my breast
Jut up slashing the other two
Sides of the sky.
Let the dead rise.
Let us two die
Down with the two deer.
I believe that love among us
And those two animals
Has its place in the

Brilliance of the sun that is
More gold than gold,
And in virtue.

Northern Pike

All right. Try this,
Then. Every body
I know and care for,
And every body
Else is going
To die in a loneliness
I can't imagine and a pain
I don't know. We had
To go on living. We
Untangled the net, we slit
The body of this fish
Open from the hinge of the tail
To a place beneath the chin
I wish I could sing of.
I would just as soon we let
The living go on living.
An old poet whom we believe in
Said the same thing, and so
We paused among the dark cattails and prayed
For the muskrats,
For the ripples below their tails,
For the little movements that we knew the crawdads were making
        under water,
For the right-hand wrist of my cousin who is a policeman.
We prayed for the game warden's blindness.
We prayed for the road home.
We ate the fish.
There must be something very beautiful in my body,
I am so happy.

Bleibe, bleibe bei mir,
Holder Fremdling, süsse Liebe,
Holde süsse Liebe,
Und verlasse die Seele nicht!
Ach, wie anders, wie schön
Lebt der Himmel, lebt die Erde,
Ach, wie fühl ich, wie fühl ich
Dieses Leben zum erstenmal!

—Goethe

Two Citizens

For Annie, my wife,
and for Rae Tufts,
our steadfast friend

"Well, bright boy," Max said, looking into the mirror, "why don't you say something?"

"What's it all about?"

"Hey, Al," Max called, "bright boy wants to know what it's all about."

"Why don't you tell him?" Al's voice came from the kitchen.

"What do you think it's all about?"

"I don't know."

"What do you think?"

—Hemingway, "The Killers"

Ars Poetica: Some Recent Criticism

1

I loved my country,
When I was a little boy.
Agnes is my aunt,
And she doesn't even know
If I love any thing
On this God's
Green little apple.

I have no idea why Uncle Sherman
Who is dead
Fell in with her.
He wasn't all that drunk.
He longed all life long
To open a package store,
And he never did anything,
But he fell in with Agnes.
She is no more to me
Than my mind is,
Which I bless. She was a homely woman
In the snow, alone.

Sherman sang bad,
But he could sing.
I too have fallen in
With a luminous woman.

There must be something.

The only bright thing
Agnes ever did
That I know of
Was to get hurt and angry.
When Sherman met my other uncle
Emerson Buchanan, who thinks he is not dead,

At the wedding of Agnes
Uncle Emerson smirked:

"What's the use buying a cow,
When you can get the milk free?"

She didn't weep.
She got mad.
Mad means something.
"You guys are makin' fun
Out of me."

    2
She stank.
Her house stank.
I went down to see Uncle Sherman
One evening.
I had a lonely furlough
Out of the army.
He must have been
One of the heroes
Of love, because he lay down
With my Aunt Agnes
Twice at least.
Listen, lay down there,
Even when she went crazy.
She wept two weeping daughters,
But she did not cry.
I think she was too lonely
To weep for herself.

    3
I gather my Aunt Agnes
Into my veins.
I could tell you,
If you have read this far,
That the nut house in Cambridge
Where Agnes is dying
Is no more Harvard
Than you could ever be.
And I want to gather you back to my Ohio.
You could understand Aunt Agnes,
Sick, her eyes blackened,
Her one love dead.

4

Why do I care for her,
That slob,
So fat and stupid?
One afternoon,
At Aetnaville, Ohio,
A broken goat escaped
From a carnival,
One of the hooch dances
They used to hold
Down by my river.
Scrawny the goat panicked
Down Agnes's alley,
Which is my country,
If you haven't noticed,
America,
Which I loved when I was young.

5

That goat ran down the alley,
And many boys giggled
While they tried to stone our fellow
Goat to death.
And my Aunt Agnes,
Who stank and lied,
Threw stones back at the boys
And gathered the goat,
Nuts as she was,
Into her sloppy arms.

6

Reader,
We had a lovely language,
We would not listen.

I don't believe in your god.
I don't believe my Aunt Agnes is a saint.
I don't believe the little boys
Who stoned the poor
Son of a bitch goat
Are charming Tom Sawyers.

I don't believe in the goat either.

7

When I was a boy
I loved my country.

Ense petit placidam
Sub libertate quietem.

Hell, I ain't got nothing.
Ah, you bastards,

How I hate you.

Son of Judas

The last time I prayed to escape from my body,
You threw me down into a tangle of roots.
Out of them I clambered up to the elbows
Of a sycamore tree, in Ohio, a place
I tried to visit.
I got within maybe a hundred and fifty yards
Of the strip mine.
I don't damn Mark Hanna or anyone else
In hell.
I have crawled along the edges of plenty
Of scars.
All I wanted to do
Was get out.

Now I've discovered my body that was alive
After all, I prayed to get back
Into my own.
I was perfectly willing to accept your world,
Where Mark Hanna and every other plant
Gatherer of the grain and gouging son
Of a God whonks his doodle in the
United States government of his hand.

Now, sure enough,
You came down and answered both my prayers.

I rose out of my body so high into
That sycamore tree that it became
The only tree that ever loved me.

And when I came back down into my own body
Some Hanna among the angels
Strip-mined it.

Now hovering between the dead sycamore,
That tree I made my secret love to,
And the edge of a wound I paid for by God,

I have bought your world.
I don't want it.
And I don't want all your money
I got sucked into making
Either.

I'm getting out, this time.
Out of that body I prayed to get out of,
Out of that soul that only existed
In the Jenny sycamore that is now the one wing,
The only wing.
It had little shadows of mark on it
That looked like feathers.
I never peeled off a single one.
You did.

Here's your money.
I didn't even count it.

Damn your own son,
And leave us go.

Prayer to the Good Poet

Quintus Horatius Flaccus, my good secret,
Now my father, a good man in Ohio,
Lies alone in pain and I scarcely
Know where to turn now.

Fifty years he worked in that bitter factory.
He learned how to love what I found so ugly.
Ugliness. What is it? A bitter
Taste of one body.

Now, if I ask anything, I would ask you
How to gather my father to your bosom.
He knew, after all, how to love Italians.
Others said dagoes.

One good friend of mine, Bennie Capaletti,
Told me how in a basketball game, one person
Called him a dirty guinea, and Bennie
Did not even slug him.

Quintus Horatius Flaccus, my good secret,
Bennie Capaletti had the fastest
Hands in that fast Ohio Valley.
He could have killed him.

More than love, my father knew how to bear love,
One quick woman a dark river of labor.
He led me and my two good brothers
To gather and swim there.

I still love the fine beauty of his body.
He could pitch a very good Sunday baseball.
One afternoon he shifted to left hand
And struck out three men.

Every time I go back home to Ohio,
He sits down and tells me he loves Italians.
How can I tell you why he loves you,
Quintus Horatius?

I worked once in the factory that he worked in.
Now I work in that factory that you live in.
Some people think poetry is easy,
But you two didn't.

Easy, easy, I ask you, easy, easy.
Early, evening, by Tiber, by Ohio,
Give the gift to each lovely other.
I would be happy.

Now my son is another poet, fathers,
I can go on living. I was afraid once
Four loving fathers meeting together
Would be a cold day in hell.

Quintus Horatius Flaccus, my good father,
You were just the beginning, you quick and lonely
Metrical crystals of February.
It is just snow.

The Last Drunk

Whatever kills my life,
All that I have to lose
With a knife in my back,
It won't be booze.

You, you, if you read this,
I wouldn't have you think
I would give up the kiss
Of strong drink,

My secret root, my own
Jackhammer that blew off
The dead trees of my spine.
Hooch was enough.

For everybody else
Who couldn't take what I

Can take through many hells
Before I die.

I sired a bitter son.
I have no daughter.
When I at last get done,
I will die by water.

She, what she might have been,
Her shoulder's secret gold,
Thin as her mother is thin.
I could have grown old!

Love in a Warm Room in Winter

The trouble with you is
You think all I want to do
Is get you into bed
And make love with you.

And that's not true!

I was just trying to make friends.
All I wanted to do
Was get into bed
With you and make

Love with you.

Who was that little bird we saw towering upside down
This afternoon on that pine cone, on the edge of a cliff,
In the snow? Wasn't he charming? Yes, he was, now,
Now, now,
Just take it easy.

Aha!

The Young Good Man

1

The young good man walked out savoring
His own tongue instead of the lips
Of the wild crab apple.
You will believe this,

But there used to be places just on the other side
Of Cadiz, Ohio, where you could slip in
Without anybody knowing,
And find them sweet.

Everybody I knew, loved, and respected,
Like Charlie Duff, my cousin Dave,
George Ellis, Gene Turner from Bellaire
Who tackled me twice, and even I swear to Christ
John Shunk, the one man all the way from Pittsburgh
To Cincinnati who knew how to use
A diving suit and who got his name
In the newspapers all the time for
Dragging up the drowned boys,

Said leave them crab apples alone,
They taste so bitter you pucker
Two days at least. You bite one,
You'll be sorry.

2

I don't know why,
One evening in August something illuminated my body
And I got sick of laying my cold
Hands on myself.
I lied to my family I was going for a walk uptown.
When I got to that hill,
Which now, I hear, Bluehart has sold to the Hanna
Strip Mine Company, it was no trouble at all to me.
Within fifteen yards of his charged fence I found me
A wild crab apple.

I licked it all over.
You are going to believe this.
It tasted sweet.

I know what would have happened to my tongue
If I had bitten. The people who love me
Are sure as hell no fools.

3
You and I could not have been simple married lovers.
There are so many reasons I can't count them,
But here are some few:
You are much more intelligent and learned than I am.
I have a very quick felicity of tongue.
Sooner or later I would have bitten your heart
With some snide witty remark or other.
And you wouldn't stand for it.
Our lives being what we are,
We didn't have a chance.

I wish we had had.
I have written this poem to you before I die.
And I don't mean to die
For some good time yet.

Afternoon and Evening at Ohrid

1
I walked with a browned woman in a time that grieved her,
The end of summer, above blue water, and the weeds
Came out wondering to her
About their names.

There was no one there to tell her in Serbo-Croatian
The name of that small flower song, and so we had to keep
Our own words in the vastness of that place,

And the dimness of mountains across the huge water,
And my grieving love wondering about being alone in the world,
And my love's clear face.

How could I tell her about their clear names?
I did not know them. I had to hold her.
That was all I had.

So I began. This one is the sun-blooded eye
Of a man who drifted weeping
Downhill into water, gathering, gathering

The awake woman. How are young lovers going
To take their way, and talk together?

Well,
For the first time in my life,
I shut up and listened.

2

Those little birds are singing
In a language that is strange to you and me.
So our love for them is a silly
Love, a sooth gathering and ringing
In a coil of snail shells.

The one thing that I most longed for to meet in the wildness
Here was a spider. I already know
My friends the spiders. They are mountains.
Every spider in America is the shadow
Of a beautiful woman.
Shy, marveling at the architecture
Of my own eyes, I found the best
Spider here. She spoke the best language.
And it spins her face.

3

She wandered ahead of me, muttering to herself
That language of grief, the mountains and water that are always
A strange face, browned at the end of summer.
Ahead of me on the mountain path, my browned love told me
    clearly:
Come to me and love me clearly with the thinning shadow of the
    turtle.

I missed the turtle, the first time
I caught up with my love,
So we walked on.
Then we walked back. Oh, you should have seen her,
My love said to me, she was just going home
Between one road and another, and we don't even know
In Serbo-Croatian. What is your name,
I said.
I love you,
She said.

Ohio Valley Swains

The granddaddy longlegs did twilight
And light.

Oh here comes Johnny Gumball.

Guido?
Bernoose got Lilly deVecchis.
Guido don't give a diddly damn.

Up on my side of the river
The cocksmen ramp loose.

The bad bastards are fishing.
They catch condoms.

What are you doing here, boy,
In cherry lane?

Leave her alone. I love her.

They knocked me down.

So I walked on up the river,
Outside the Jesus Jumpers' tent,

Oh God our help in ages past,
Our hope for years to come.

Here comes Johnny Gumball.

It took me many years to understand
Just what happened to her that evening.

I walked, stiff and lonely, up the long river.
The railroad dick asked me
Very politely what
I was doing there.

They're hurting a girl down there, I said.
Well, he said, you go on home,
And get out of this.

Johnny Gumball,
You and your gang caught up with my brother,
And beat him up. But that was no terror of mine.
My brother has his own life.

But I heard you and Guido cackling down below
That tent where the insane Jesus Jumpers
Spoke in their blind tongues,
And you laughed and laughed.

You thought that was funny, didn't you, to mock a girl?
I loved her only in my dreams,
But my dreams meant something
And so did she,
You son of a bitch,
And if I ever see you again, so help me in the sight of God,
I'll kill you.

I Wish I May Never Hear of the United States Again

The ringing and sagging of blue flowers,
And the spider shedding her diamond shadow down

On the turtle's body,
The old woman's hair lock golden spinning a web out of her
    clothes,
And the girls who have no trouble worrying
About the length of their dresses,
As they stroll slowly, vanishing into their own twilight
Beside the slim shoulders of the donkeys:

I can be silent among these.

One afternoon in northern California,
Which is a Jack London nut house,
I almost found my own country.
At the edge of a field
I gathered the neck of a buckskin into
My arms and whispered: Where were you
All this time?

Alone all this time, and bored with being alone,
I have been walking all afternoon at the edge
Of a town where the language is only to me
The music of mountain people.

In Yugoslavia I am learning the words
For greeting and goodbye.
Everything else is the language
Of the silent woman who walks beside me.

I want the mountains to be builded golden,
And my love wants the cathedrals to be builded
By time's love back to their gray, as the gray
Woman grows old, that gray woman who gave us
Some cheese and whispered her affectionate sound
To my love and me wandering silent in the breeze
Of a strange language, at home with each other.
Saying nothing, listening

To a new word for mountain, to a new
Word for cathedral, to a new word for
Cheese, to a word beyond words for
Cathedrals and homes.

The Old WPA Swimming Pool
in Martins Ferry, Ohio

I am almost afraid to write down
This thing. I must have been,
Say, seven years old. That afternoon,
The families of the WPA had come out
To have a good time celebrating
A long gouge in the ground,
That the fierce husbands
Had filled with concrete.

We knew even then the Ohio
River was dying.
Most of the good men who lived along that shore
Wanted to be in love and give good love
To beautiful women, who weren't pretty,
And to small children like me who wondered,
What the hell is this?

When people don't have quite enough to eat
In August, and the river,
That is supposed to be some holiness,
Starts dying,

They swim in the earth. Uncle Sherman,
Uncle Willie, Uncle Emerson, and my father
Helped dig that hole in the ground.

I had seen by that time two or three
Holes in the ground,
And you know what they were.

But this one was not the usual, cheap
Economics, it was not the solitary
Scar on a poor man's face, that respectable
Hole in the ground you used to be able to buy
After you died for seventy-five dollars and
Your wages tached for six months by the Heslop
Brothers.

Brothers, dear God.

No, this hole was filled with water,
And suddenly I flung myself into the water.
All I had on was a jockstrap my brother stole
From a miserable football team.

Oh never mind, Jesus Christ, my father
And my uncles dug a hole in the ground,
No grave for once. It is going to be hard
For you to believe: when I rose from that water,

A little girl who belonged to somebody else,
A face thin and haunted appeared
Over my left shoulder, and whispered, Take care now,
Be patient, and live.

I have loved you all this time,
And didn't even know
I am alive.

Paul

Plenty of times
I ran around in the streets in that small
Place. I didn't know what in hell
Was happening to me.

I had a pretty good idea
It was hell.
What else are you going to get
When you ain't got nothing?

You are going to get your friends who love paw-paws
Under a black street-light which will go damned if it blow.

You are going to wish you could be in love, and you are going
To die, and if you have anything in you that matters, you are
      going
To care for the man who picked you up on the street.

If I care for anything, I care
For the man who picked me up on the street.
Don't you remember? You said to me, Come on,
Get in, and we drove down to Brookside.

I remember your fury because I got a stuck piece of
Coal in my eye.

Come on, Paul, said your friend,
Rattling the tipple.
You told him to go to hell.
Because I had a speck of coal
In my eye.

You were making less than twenty dollars a week.
You drove that cracked truck down to Brookside lovelier and
    friendlier
Than Alcaeus loving Sappho.

You wouldn't even know what I'm talking about.

I wouldn't even know what you're talking about.

By God, I know this much:
When a fine young man is true to his true love
And can face out a fine deep shock on his jaw
(That scar so low off, that true scar of love),
And when a man can stand up in the middle of America
(That brutal and savage place whom I still love),

Never mind your harangues about religion.
Anybody could pick me up out of the street
Is good to me, I would like to be good

To you, too, good man.

In Memory of Charles Coffin

What was that cold and ugly thing
That snuck into your brain and killed

My love and your love. I would bring
The best of what I understand
In hand to you, were you alive.
I still care knowing you believe
In the body a soul can give.
You heard the soul rave and you send
A lonely echo of good Mars.
In that black summer when I worked
At the Mount Vernon, Ohio, Bridge
Company, I came damn near
Killing a man, and going blind.
All right, you said: Ben Jonson said
Give Salathiel Pavy one
More chance, and give yourself one more.
No, I have no idea where
You lie in Mary's ground alone.
I know, well, you would approve
Of this intricate sound I make.
It has three beats, though your heart break,

My loving teacher, whom I love,
It is almost too late to live.

At the Grave

All I am doing is walking here alone.
I am not among the English poets.
I am not even going to be among
The English poets after my death.
You loved them the best.
And you liked me, fine. It is still raining
This morning, this November morning.
And I am not even standing at your grave.
I am fiddling with a notebook in New York,
Wondering about Ohio where now at this moment
A leaf hangs on a locust thorn shredding
Its form into the rain.
John Keats, coughing his lungs out,
John Clare, crazy,
And Geoffrey Chaucer the only one.

And Edward Thomas, who got killed, the only
Soldier in this century who was sane.
If these lines get published, I will hear
From some God damned deaf moron who knows
Everything. The dead are nothing.
And he will be right.
The living giggle in the dark all night,
And the dead are nothing. I nearly got
My knees smashed at the Mount Vernon, Ohio, Bridge Company
That summer when I worked among the swinging girders,
To make enough money so I could write a good essay
For you. The essay wasn't all that good, but you loved it,
And you loved me. Steubenville,
Ohio, is a hell of a place to be buried.
But there are some lovely places to be buried.
Like Rome. Listen. So help me sweet leaping
Christ, it is going to be a cold day
In hell when any Johnny Bull knows
What I am saying to you:
I have found a woman who lives, and so
I am going to Rome with her
For a long time yet.
It is raining today in Steubenville.
Blessed be the dead whom the rain rains upon.
And damned the living who have their few days.
And blessed your thorned face,
Your shragged November,
Your leaf,
Lost.

Hotel Lenox

And she loved loving
So she woke and bloomed
And she rose.

And many men had been there
To drowse awake and go downstairs
Lonely for coffee and bread.

But she drowsed awake lonely
For coffee and bread.

And went upstairs
With me, and we had
Coffee and bread.

And then we were so happy to see the lovely
Mother who had been her mother a long time.

In this city broken on the wheel

We went back to the warm caterpillar of our hotel.

And the wings took.

Oh lovely place,

Oh tree.

We climbed into the branches
Of the lady's tree.

We birds sang.

And the lemon light flew out over the river.

The Streets Grow Young

1

One first summer evening in Paris my love and I strolled among
The young students, studying the cathedrals
In one another's faces.
No rain there.
Inside an alley behind our own green bones
A peaked woman of fifty years, I guess,
Darted straight down at me in the darkness
And bluntly asked for a coin.

2
A while later,
Hare Krishna, his cigar, his piano, and his orchestra
Forgave me for giving them cancer.

3
The shrewd angel, the abandoner of his own solitude,
The native country of his hand,
Clambering from pit to scar up his mother's
Dugless chest. He has no woman,
But he has found how
To make a good thing out of hell.
No moss grows on those horny wings,
Even in Paris.

While he was forgiving me, the skinny whore staggered past,
Gnawing her spit-soggy
Claw of bread.

Okay. I accept your forgiveness.
I started the Reichstag fire.
I invented the ball-point pen.
I ate the British governor of Rhodesia.

(But that was a long time ago,
And I thought he was assorted fruits and chicken sauce.
Still, all the same.)

Okay now, hit the road, and leave me
And my girl alone.

4
The amused Parisians snickered
While a retarded fat man on the corner
Shook a rubber rat in the faces
Of passing women.
The poor bastard needs money to die with,
And he can't even beg.

The Old Man Said Tomorrow

When we come back to these
    black currants
And roses reeling heavily,
    blearily over
The green cress of rain,

He will be gone.

We will have to go all the way back
To Chartres, where he reels
    lightly, scarcely
Able to keep his wings folded,

As he rises into the honey stone that
    gathers
The gray rain of evening.

How can he keep wing with one
    flittering swallow?
When we come back, love,

He will be gone.

                    St. Benoît-sur-Loire

The Last Pietà,
in Florence

The whole city
Is stone, even
Where stone
Doesn't belong.
What is that old
Man's public face
Doing sorrowing,
Secretly a little,
A little above and
A little back from

A limp arm?
What is that stone
Doing sorrowing
Where stone
Doesn't belong?

The Old Dog in the Ruins of
the Graves at Arles

I have heard tell somewhere,
Or read, I forget which,
That animals tumble along in a forever,
A little dream, a quick longing
For every fine haunch that passes,
As the young bitches glitter in their own light.

I find their freedom from lonely wisdom
Hard to believe.
No matter the brief skull fails to contain,
The old bones know something.

Almost indistinguishable from the dust,
They seek shadow, they limp among the tombs.
One stray mutt, long since out of patience,
Rises up, as the sunlight happens to strike,
And snaps at his right foreleg.

When the hurrying shadow returns
He lies down in peace again,
Between the still perfectly formed sarcophagi
That have been empty of Romans or anybody
Longer than anybody remembers.
Graves last longer than men. Nobody can tell me
The old dogs don't know.

Voices Between Waking and Sleeping
in the Mountains

All afternoon you went walking,
Just you, all alone,
And what you went wondering about
I still don't know.

I was trying to find something in that mountain snow,
And I couldn't find it by walking,
So I lay asleep
For three good hours.
There is something in you that is able to discover the crystal.
Somewhere in me there is a crystal that I cannot find
Alone, the wing that I used to think was a poor
Blindness I had to live with with the dead.

But it was not that I was dying when I went asleep
When you walked into the snow.
There was something I was trying to find
In that dream. When I finally fought my way
Down to the bottom of the stairs
I got trapped, I kept yelling
Help, help, the savage woman
With two heads loaded me, the one
Face broken and savage, the other,
The face dead.

Two hands gathered my two.

And you sang: Why, what have you been dreaming?

I don't know, I said.
Where were you?

You said you just took a walk.

Annie, it has taken me a long time to live.
And to take a long time to live is to take a long time
To understand that your life is your own life.

What you found on that long rise of mountain in the snow
Is your secret. But I can tell you at last:

There used to be a sycamore just
Outside Martins Ferry,
Where I used to go.
I had no friends there.
Maybe the tree was no woman,
But when I sat there, I gathered
That branch into my arms.
It was the first time I ever rose.

If only I knew how to tell you.
Some day I may know how.

Meantime your hand gathered me awake
Out of my good dream, and I pray to gather
My hands into your hands in your good dream.

What did you find in your long wandering in the snow?
I love your secret. By God I will never violate the wings
Of the snow you found rising in the wind.
Give them, keep them, love.

On the Liberation of Woman

In the middle of my age I walked down
Toward a cold bloom.
I don't give a damn if you care,
But it half-rhymes with blossom.
And no body was ever so kind to me
As one woman, and begins spring
In the secret of winter, and that is why

I love you best.

I have a pretty good idea you won't believe
In your life. I don't deny our life is lost.
By God I want to live, and so do you.

I was too much a small boy to love
The cold trees you know.

Forgive and gather
My man's broken arms
Beneath them. This evening
The ice in New York City is bleeding.
What warms you?
What gathers beneath the cold wing, the west
Shoulder of heaven?

What is going to happen when we both die?

I love you best.

Bologna: A Poem about Gold

Give me this time, my first and severe
Italian, a poem about gold,
The left corners of eyes, and the heavy
Night of the locomotives that brought me here,
And the heavy wine in the old green body,
The glass that so many have drunk from.
I have brought my bottle back home every day
To the cool cave, and come forth
Golden on the left corner
Of a cathedral's wing:

White wine of Bologna,
And the knowing golden shadows
At the left corners of Mary Magdalene's eyes,
While St. Cecilia stands
Smirking in the center of a blank wall,
The saint letting her silly pipes wilt down,
Adoring
Herself, while the lowly and richest of all women eyes
Me the beholder, with a knowing sympathy, her love
For the golden body of the earth, she knows me,
Her halo faintly askew,

And no despair in her gold
That drags thrones down
And then makes them pay for it.

Oh,
She may look sorry to Cecilia
And
The right-hand saint on the tree,
But
She didn't look sorry to Raphael,
And
I bet she didn't look sorry to Jesus,
And
She doesn't look sorry to me.
(Who would?)
She doesn't look sorry to me.

She looks like only the heavy deep gold
That drags thrones down
All day long on the vine.
Mary in Bologna, sunlight I gathered all morning
And pressed in my hands all afternoon
And drank all day with my golden-breasted

Love in my arms.

A Poem of Towers

I am becoming one
Of the old men.
I wonder about them,
And how they became
So happy. Tonight
The trees in the Carl Schurz
Park by the East River
Had no need of electricity
To light their boughs, for the moon
And my love were enough.
More than enough the garbage

Scow plunging, the front hoof
Of a mule gone so wild through the water,
No need to flee. Who pities
You tonight, white-haired
Lu Yu? Wise and foolish
Both are gone, and my love
Leans on my shoulder precise
As the flute notes
Of the snow, with songs
And poems scattered
Over Shu, over the East River
That loves them and drowns them.

To You, Out There (Mars? Jupiter?)

I believe I can appreciate the nobility of your dreams.
Some first thing, perhaps
Floating softly out of the dewrise of sulphur
Astonished to find yourself awake, life
Floating delightedly, flimsy to be so sudden
Between the one hand of a sard mountain
And the other locked sea-light of two chalcedony moons.

And then,
After the thousands, the years of gazing,
Fondling through lenses the tiny
Charming blue smoke-haze, spinning, a secret
Beyond all the moons.
It must look lovely,
So far off.
I wonder what you call it.

Look there! Look there!
Shift your great lenses aside slightly.
They are not all dining dreamily over minced hirsute puppy
And *moo moo gai pan.*
They are not forever drifting lazily in a cool evening across
Those turquoise niplets of shores, those cerulean
Inlets forever clustered with just the right number

Of clever and handsome black creatures
Who love to serve them.

No.
Shift your lenses aside a little,
Look there. Look there.

They are standing for hours in a line, huddling
Alone in the griped cold, hopelessly longing
To pray to someone whose name
Is Streisand.
They are smiling underground in the evening, storing
Long exquisitely sharp blades so that soon
They may touch each other's bodies.
They are sneaking aside to finger little bones
Which they call money.
They are carefully selecting their children, to slit open
Their pubes and inner arms.

To you out there,
Oh no, oh no, don't look here.
Sure, you will find a great plenty of things
On this tiny smoke-haze.
You will not find God.

The Art of the Fugue: A Prayer

Radiant silence in Fiesole
And the long climb up a hill which is only one feather
Of the sky, and to set out within the sky,
As the dark happy Florentine would surely gather
All that he had to gather and every night set forth
And enter the pearl.

Florence below our hands, the city that yielded
Up the last secret of Hell.
Fiesole below me and around me and the wings
Of the invisible musician Brother Esposito folded
Around me and my girl.

And the organ
Silent in its longing for the only love.
And Bach and Dante meeting and praying
Before the music began.

And a little bell ringing halfway down the hill.

And me there a long way from the cold dream of Hell.
Me, there, alone, at last,
At last with the dust of my dust,
As far away as I will ever get from dying,
And the two great poets of God in the silence
Meeting together.

And Esposito the organist waiting to begin.
And the little bell halfway down delicately drifting off.

And Florence down there darkening, waiting to begin.

And me there alone at last with my only love,
Waiting to begin.

Whoever you are, ambling past my grave,
My name worn thin as the shawl of the lovely hill town
Fiesole, the radiance and silence of the sky,
Listen to me:

Though love can be scarcely imaginable Hell,
By God, it is not a lie.

Names Scarred at the Entrance to Chartres

to Marsh and his music

P. Dolan and A. Doyle
Have scrawled their names here.
You other stupid angels,
They have no wings
Here. Here all they have
Are squalling babies and the leaves

Of the wild strawberries you can still gather
Beside wet roads.

The cracked song
Of my own body limps into the body
Of this living place. I have nobody
To go in with
But my love who is a woman,
And my crude dead, my sea,
My sea, my sepulcher, the crude
Rhythm of my time.

This cracking blossom is my second America.
And though my first
Shatters itself cold with hatred, though
I might have given my leaves here
A long time ago,

P. Dolan and A. Doyle are the faint names
I enter with.

We have no home in the local strawberry leaves,
The wild peas' reverence, the living faces of men.

I have no way to go in
Except only
In the company of two vulgars,
Furies too dumb to remember
Death, our bodies' mother, whose genius it is
To remember our death on the wet
Roads of Chartres, America, and to forget
Our names. The wild strawberry leaf
Does not need to bother with remembering
Its own name, and Doyle, Dolan, and me.

All three Americans, drunk on our lonely women.

In our own way we hewed the town mayor
Among the several damned.
We sat up all night,
Rocking some frail accident of love who became
A secret of blossoms we had no business

To understand, only to remember.
Nameless builder of strawberry leaves,
So true to me in my lonely praying, so common
To the French builders who sing among lettuce
And proud tongue singing the clearest
Stone song.

God, I don't know who sat up all one night
Wishing in the name of sweet leaping Christ
He could get the kid to sleep before first light,
So he could get a couple hours to lie half-waking
And gathering the wild strawberry leaves,

That true woman.

I remember her name, but I won't tell.
I remember the names of Doyle and Dolan,
Who had their own ugly way to hack
Their names on this prayer.

These hideous wanderers hate life, they
Love, sullen, bitter, sitting
Up all night, waking beside women, waking
With leaves in their hands.

Who built this place?

Emerson Buchanan

Emerson Buchanan, gun on his arm.
Uncle Willy the lone, Shorty the drunk.
All I wanted to do. That was the wrong
Place to be dead. All that we have,
Death, is Ohio. Franklin Pierce will scan.
Nobody else will scan, Allen the love,
Allen the lovely song, these are my friends.
Reader, alone, die. Die in the cold.
Publius Vergilius Maro scans.

Emerson talked too much. One time
On Christmas Eve I yelled out that he should keep
His mouth shut.

Shorty is dead, mewling,
Shorty is puke in the ground.
Uncle Willy is following
Two dead women out of sound,
Franklin Pierce was a single friend.
Once Nathaniel Hawthorne died with him.

Emerson Buchanan, who talked too much,
Shut up, and now he is one half-hendecasyllabic,

And almost an amphibrach.

I try and try to hear them, and all I get

Is a blind dial tone.

The Snail's Road

A snail on Max Jacob's grave
At Fleury-sur-Loire.

A tiny whorl of colors,
Black and pale bronze.

Little whorls toiling out of
The poet's right toe.

I was in love with a girl who found
This grave for me.

We placed some wild morning-glories over
The sun-warmed granite of the poet's forehead.

We stood for a long time, watching
Rain fall straight down on the western horizon.

I love this poet, and I could not have found him
Without the girl whom I love. Too late be damned.

The snail beneath the right foot,
The toe pointing toward thunderclouds.

My right hand forgot Jerusalem,
And I forgot my cunning.

The snail remembered the Jerusalem of the Loire
And I knelt with my hat off.

The creature began the spinning path of his long journey,
While the bronze Jew snail of the rain bloomed.

We walked, holding hands, coil within coil, both looking
For love Max Jacob in the rain. We found him. We found our
    hands.

The sun came out long enough,
And too late be damned.

You and I Saw Hawks
Exchanging the Prey

They did the deed of darkness
In their own mid-light.

He plucked a gray field mouse
Suddenly in the wind.

The small dead fly alive
Helplessly in his beak,

His cold pride, helpless.
All she receives is life.

They are terrified. They touch.
Life is too much.

She flies away sorrowing.
Sorrowing, she goes alone.

Then her small falcon, gone,
Will not rise here again.

Smaller than she, he goes
Claw beneath claw beneath
Needles and leaning boughs,

While she, the lovelier
Of these brief differing two,
Floats away sorrowing,

Tall as my love for you,

And almost lonelier.

Delighted in the delighting,
I love you in mid-air,
I love myself the ground.

The great wings sing nothing
Lightly. Lightly fall.

Well, What Are You Going to Do?

I took a nap one afternoon in Ohio
At the end of a pasture,
Just at the good moment when Pet our poor lovely
Lay moaning and gave birth to Marian my calf.

What was I going to do? All I could do
Was wake and stand there.
I don't know anything about the problem
Of beautiful women.
I was afraid to run two hundred yards
To call my mother
And ask her what to do

With a beautiful woman.
Besides, she wouldn't know either.

Two hours.
Two whole hours.
While Pet lay mumbling among the Grimes Golden apples
That fell from time to time.
I ate two or three, maybe.
What was I supposed to do there
But eat the apples while Marian's face
Peeked out slowly?

I ate the apples,
And when Marian was born
I helped her come out.
I had been in love with a lot of girls, but that was my first time
To clasp the woman beneath her chin
And whisper, Come out to me,
Come on, come on, and you can be Marian.

I led Marian out of her mother's belly
Down in the cold
Autumn thorns,
And there was a pile of horse manure
I couldn't evade, and so by God
I did not even try.
All I could do was fall
From time to time.
Marian's face was all right, speckled with rust
And more white than snow.
The one I was the more in love with
Was Pet, the exhausted.

I lay down beside her, she snuffled, she smelled like a Grimes
Golden apple.
Then I carried Marian two hundred yards down the pasture.
She delicately sprayed the insides of her beginning body
All over my work shirt.

I don't know that I belonged
In that beautiful place. But

What are you going to do? Be kind? Kill?
Die?

October Ghosts

Jenny cold, Jenny darkness,
They are coming back again.
We came so early,
But now we are shoveled down
The long slide.
We carry a blackened crocus
In either hand.

I will walk with you and Callimachus
Into the gorges
Of Ohio, where the miners
Are dead with us.

They carry one another
In their arms, still alive.
What do I know of them? I know
Uncle Charlie prowling along the cold shores of their lives,
His meters broken,
And your voice the only living voice, the only
Wind the wind
Of this autumn.

I knew a beautiful woman when I was young.
She wept over me as one who could hardly care.
Diphtheria starred her earlobes,
And she wailed all night.
That time is gone when the young women died
Astounded to hear black veins in their bodies
Coil round one another all night.

Jenny, fat blossoming grandmother of the dead,
We were both young, and I nearly found you, young.
I could not find you. I prowled into my head,
The cold ghost of October that is my skull.

There is a god's plenty of lovers there,
The dead, the dying, and the beautiful.

But where are we,
Jenny darkness, Jenny cold?
Are we so old?
We came so early, we thought to stay so long.
But it is already midnight, and we are gone.
I have nothing at all against that song,
That minor bird I hear from the great frost,
My robin's song, the ancient nothingness.

Friends, I have stolen this line from Robinson,
From Jenny, and from springtime, and from bone,
And from the quick nuthatch, the blooming of wing upon the sky.

Now I know nothing, I can die alone.

She's Awake

My slim, high-strung
Beauty cannot sleep
On nights like this, and I wish I could follow
And soothe her where she goes.

I have an idea the road she walks on
Is a blue secret smoothed over
A long time now.

Wound after wound, I look for
The tree by the waters where
She lay somehow naked,
Somehow still alive.

Lying myself awake,
I imagine everything terrible in my own life,
The hitchhiking drunk, the shame of knowing
My self a fool.
Bad friend to me.

There was a mean kid I knocked down because I was weak.
There was a mongrel bitch I saw whose backside
Was set fire with kerosene and a firecracker.
I fought the son of a bitch who did it,
And I lost.

I bawled like an idiot
And crawled home, ashamed.

I try to imagine myself killing somebody,
My enemies the rats, the snakes, the
Drunk Indians, the
Bad men from the graveyard, hail,
They ruin everything, you give them a wing,
And they fly.

For God's sake, wake up, how in hell am I going to die?

It was easy.
All I had to do was delete the words lonely and shadow,
Dispose of the dactylic hexameters into amphibrachs

Gather your lovely life into my life,
And love your life.

To the Creature of
the Creation

Lonely as my desire is,
I have no daughter.
I will not die by fire, I
Shall die by water.

Water is fire, the wand
Some body wandering near,
Limping to understand,
If only he somewhere

Could find that lonely thing
That fears him, yet comes out
To look through him and sing.

He cannot do without.

Without the moon, and me.
And who is she?
This poem frightens me
So secretly, so much,
It makes me hard to touch
Your body's secret places.
We are each other's faces.

No, I ain't much.
The one tongue I can write in
Is my Ohioan.
There, most people are poor.
I thought I could not stand it
To go home any more,
Yet I go home, every year,
To calm down my wild mother,
And talk long with my brother.

What have I got to do?
The sky is shattering,
The plain sky grows so blue.
Some day I have to die,
As everyone must do
Alone, alone, alone,
Peaceful as peaceful stone.
You are the earth's body.
I will die on the wing.
To me, you are everything
That matters, chickadee.
You live so much in me.
Chickadees sing in the snow.
I will die on the wing,
I love you so.

Selected Prose Pieces

Magnificence

They tell me that the Arena in Verona is the most beautifully preserved Roman amphitheatre in Italy, and I believe them. Twenty thousand people could sit in it comfortably. On a sunlit day its pink and white marbles glow from within, and they glow from within when it is raining.

The Arena is magnificent. It means that it is greatly made. It must be twenty-five hundred years old. The Romans, like Octavius and Cicero, were sometimes as noble as Ortega in his intelligent anguish could hope for; and even his hopes were harsh and critically severe.

In this setting, whose grandeur consists in its uncluttered purity and simplicity of design, Verdi's Requiem emerged with exquisite gentleness, tenderness, and sadness. Of course, the trumpets were played high at the rim of the Arena. No human Director could have resisted that opportunity. But the great Veronese musicians were so masterful in their understanding of the music, its shapeliness as fully as its clear depth of stillness all the more passionate for its revelations of silence, that during one brief passage while orchestra, chorus, and soloists were all singing lucidly and quietly together, we heard a cricket singing in the darkness at the farthest rim of the Arena.

His song was not extraordinarily melodious. He was evening. He was not trying to compete with Verdi. I think he was just trying to sing himself to sleep among the warm darkened stones.

It was characteristic of the Veronese company that the Director of the chorus had concealed himself head and shoulders behind a discreetly colored screen behind the soloists.

Only occasionally, at some moment of absolute necessity for the evocation of the chorus, we could see his beautiful hands fluttering with perfect precision above the screen, like the wings of a happy yet teetotalling cabbage-white butterfly.

For some reason known possibly to God in His more responsive moments of attentiveness, one of the softest passages of the Requiem was joined from the rear end of the Arena by an extremely coarse whistle of the sort that New York delicatessen managers make when they catch small children in the act of snitching candy placed by an oversight near the entrance to the store. I do pray our cousins from Jersey go elsewhere for their vacations.

The musicians paid no attention whatever, and softly though they sang, their music rose above his cacophony, as Verdi himself, a human artist whose soul had the shape and sound of something greatly made, was present among us at once in time and beyond time, almost beyond sound, at the same moment and in the same space on one of the earth's loveliest places, both diminutive and vast, very like the city of Verona itself.

Very, very like.

Verona

The Legions of Caesar

Today, on the Feast of the Assumption, the Congress of the United States has required the President to order a cessation of bombing in Cambodia. Three men are standing below me on the shore of Lake Garda. They poise on the rocks, trailing their fishing lines in the clear water. Now and again a man draws in his line. Each carries a clear plastic bag perhaps one-third filled with piccolini. The glittering silver creatures have been living in this water surely since Catullus was a boy. The year he was born, the legions of Julius Caesar attempted to invade Britain, and failed. The year he died, thirty years later, they tried again, and more or less succeeded. A Roman temple once stood in Britain, in Dorchester, Dorset, and now it is the site of the Church of St. Peter's and All Saints.

In front of that church this morning, far away on that northern island, cut off long ago from all other human beings while a poet grieved for his first days, the statue of William Barnes turns slowly greener as he looks down the West High Street towards the King's Arms Hotel. There, once only, there stood in the front doorway the most beautiful girl he had ever seen or was ever to see in his life. He lived a long time, and so did she. Below me on the olive-silver pebbles of the Garda shore, some small boys are scampering in search of an escaped piccolino. They are serious, hurrying, before the little fish stops struggling back towards the water and turns to stone. I don't know what time it is in Cambodia. I wonder if there is ever any silence there. Where is it, hiding from the invaders? The sunlight once glinted off William Barnes's coffin. From a hill so far away it seemed the other side of the earth, his friend Thomas Hardy wrote down the sunlight as a signal. He knew his friend was opening a hand, saying goodbye.

Torri del Benaco

The Language of the Present Moment

Off the shore of Gargnano the mountains in this summer mist look barren. Tall and short mountains stand still beside me as I drift past on Lake Garda. They throw their own flowers on the water. It is warmer than the oldest olive.

A few miles up the lake a town called Limone long ago gave up hope of surviving. The lemons of Sicily, quicker and more numerous, banish the town I will see, back to its own shadow that lies in the Garda water like a garland.

Limone, wreath of the Garda mountains, the stone villa of Catullus still stands down at the far southern end of the lake. I hope you are in blossom when his ghost comes home.

Gargnano

Saying Dante Aloud

You can feel the muscles and veins rippling in widening and rising circles, like a bird in flight under your tongue.

Verona

A Letter to Franz Wright

Twice when I was young, I stood on the side of Fujiyama. I have drifted down the Seine in a boat while the summer rain turned gray; and, along the Seine in late twilight, I glimpsed quite adequate shadows of several rats undoubtedly descended from the fellow-fugitives of François Villon, who learned where he could learn it. At the Volksoper in Vienna I have looked down from the balcony and seen a trumpeter crouch over and hand a glass of wine to a violinist right in the middle of a performance of *Die Zigeunerbaron*. And once I spent an entire day of my life (my life!) talking with Pablo Neruda and looking into his face.

But I have never, anywhere, anytime, seen anything so appallingly beyond accounting for as a place in Tuscany in late autumn. I have come, and not for the first time, to the limits of my own language.

All I have with me at this moment is the memory of a time so recent that I can't yet bear to free it to live its own life in the "just city and free land" of the past. But, come to think of it, the memory is not all I have. There are these fragments of words I picked up on the hither side of my limits. I am sending them to you, because you will love them. Consequently, you will know to piece them together into a vision of your own design. Your imagination is not mine. How could it be? Who would want it to be? I wouldn't. You wouldn't. But I love both, so I trust yours. Here are some fragments of my hammer that broke against a wall of jewels.

Darkness fell suddenly one evening as Annie and Janie and I descended from the fortress of Volterra, which still broods suspiciously over the small valleys of Tuscany. The fortress by dusk looks like a paranoid Dragon, or except for the city's severe dark beauty, like Nixon keeping watch over uncurtained windows where some voluptuous young woman or man has just slipped off the National Security and stretches naked by the window before turning out the light.

We drove for a while, and even got lost, and found our way again at a tiny little bar-restaurant at the edge of a village. An almost absurdly beautiful girl greeted us, gave us some coffee and grappa, spread out a huge map of Tuscany on the table, and sped us on our way with God. We finally found the sign we needed: SAN GIMIGNANO. Then we drove up, and up, and around, and up, and around, and up again, till we found ourselves picking our way in semi-darkness. (The headlights burned out in our rented Fiat.) It was almost like being in Ohio, and I felt a momentary convulsion of homesickness.

Then we emerged on a town square, not a very large one as piazzas go, and checked in at a hotel over in the corner. The town seemed pleasant enough. We were road-weary and hungry. We stepped a few doors down the street to a trattoria for a small late meal, and went back to bed.

The next morning Annie rose first, opened the curtained doors to bright sunlight, and went out on the balcony. I thought I heard her gasp. When she came back into the room again, she looked a little pale, and said, "I don't believe it."

San Gimignano is poised hundreds of feet in the air. The city is comparatively small, and it is perfectly formed. We felt ourselves strange in that presence, that city glittering there in the lucid Tuscan morning, like a perfectly cut little brilliant sparkling on the pinnacle of a stalagmite. Far below us we could look almost straight down into vineyards and fields where people, whole families, even small children, had evidently been at work for hours. In all directions below us were valleys whose villages were just beginning to appear out of the mist, a splinter of a church here, an olive grove there. It was a life in itself.

The wall is still standing.

San Gimignano

A Lament for the Martyrs

I am sitting in an outdoor cafe across the street from the Colosseum. The noon is so brilliant that I have to wear my dark glasses. You would think a Roman noon could lay even the Colosseum wide open.

But darknesses still foul the place and its hateful grandeur. The Roman Chamber of Commerce and Betelgeuse in combine could gut the Colosseum by day or by night till the ghost of Mussolini and the ghost of God turned blue in the face, and light wouldn't mean a thing in that darkness. Cities are times of day. Once Rome was noon. To take a slow lazy walk with Quintus Horatius Flaccus at four o'clock in the night was to become light. If you don't believe me, I offer you a method of scientific verification. I lay you eight to five that you will go blind if you take a walk at high noon with the President of the United States. I love my country for its light. I love Rome because Horace lived there. I am afraid of the dark. I am game to live with intelligent sinners. Sometimes these days the Romans say that whatever the Barbarians left behind was later sacked and raped by the Barberinis, the noble family who needed the remnant marble for their country palaces. I find them fair enough for me. When I was a boy, the mayors of five towns in the Ohio River Valley solved the practical problems of prohibition by picking the purest and most perfect bootlegger between Pittsburgh and Cincinnati to become Chairman of the Committee for Liquor Control. I think it would be wicked for me to wonder what the five mayors did with their cut in private. All I know is that within a year after Milber's public appointment to a legal office, a symphony orchestra mysteriously appeared in one town, two spacious football stadiums appeared in two other towns, the madame of the cathouse in Wheeling was appointed a dollar-a-year man by the Federal Government, and I lost an essay-contest whose subject was the life and work of William Dean Howells, an American author who was born in Martins Ferry, Ohio, for Christ's sake, and whose books I had never even heard of, much less read. (As I look back over the shadow of the years, I confess that I have read two of his novels. But I like him. He was a good friend of Mark Twain.)

But right now the Roman noon is so brilliant that it hurts my eyes. I sip my cappuccino at a wobbly sidewalk table and ponder the antiquities of my childhood: the beautiful river, that black ditch of horror, and the streetcars. Where have they gone now, with their wicker seats that seemed to rattle behind the dull headlights in the slow dusk, in summer where everything in Ohio ran down and yet never quite stopped?

Now, the Romans and the discovered Americans stroll blinded in the Colosseum deaf to the shadows the place never loses, even at noon in Rome, that was for a little while one of the few noons.

Some archaeologist gouged out the smooth dust floor of the Colosseum to make it clean. The floor now is a careful revelation. It is an intricate and intelligent series of ditches, and the sun cannot reach them. They are the shadows of starved people who did not even want to die. They were not even Jews.

There is no way to get rid of the shadows of human beings who could find God only in that last welcome of the creation, the maws of tortured animals.

Is that last best surest way to heaven the throat of the hungry? If it is, God is very beautiful, if not very bright.

Who are the hungry? What color is a hungry shadow?

Even the noon sunlight in the Colosseum is the golden shadow of a starved lion, the most beautiful of God's creatures except maybe horses.

Rome

The Lambs on the Boulder

I hear that the Commune di Padova has an exhibition of master-pieces from Giotto to Mantegna. Giotto is the master of angels, and Mantegna is the master of the dead Christ, one of the few human beings who seems to have understood that Christ did indeed come down from the cross after all, in response to the famous jeering invitation, and that the Christ who came down was a cadaver. Mantegna's dead Christ looks exactly like a skidroad bum fished by the cops out of the Mississippi in autumn just before daylight and hurried off in a tarpaulin-shrouded garbage truck and deposited in another tangle of suicides and befuddled drunkards at the rear entrance to the University of Minnesota medical school. Eternity is a vast space of distances as well as a curving infinity of time.

No doubt the exhibition in noble Padova will be a glory to behold.

But there is a littler glory that I love best. It is a story, which so intensely ought to be real that it is real.

One afternoon the mature medieval master Cimabue was taking a walk in the countryside and paused in the shade to watch a shepherd boy. The child was trying to scratch sketches of his lambs on a boulder at the edge of the field. He used nothing, for he could find nothing, but a little sharp pebble.

Cimabue took the shepherd boy home with him and gave him some parchment and a nail or a crayon or something or other, and began to show him how to draw and form lines into the grandeur of faces other than the sweet faces of sheep.

The shepherd boy was Giotto, and he learned how to draw and form lines into the grandeur of faces other than the sweet faces of sheep. I don't give a damn whether you believe this story or not. I do. I have seen faces of angels drawn by Giotto. If angels do not look like Giotto's angels, they have been neglecting their health behind God's back.

One of my idle wishes is to find that field where Cimabue stood in the shade and watched the boy Giotto scratching his stone with his pebble.

I would not be so foolish as to prefer the faces of the boy's lambs to the faces of his angels. One has to act his age sooner or later.

Still, this little planet of rocks and grass is all we have to start with. How pretty it would be, the sweet faces of the boy Giotto's lambs gouged, with infinite and still uncertain and painful care, on the side of a boulder at the edge of a country field.

I wonder how long Cimabue stood watching before he said anything. I'll bet he watched for a very long time. He was Cimabue.

I wonder how long Giotto worked before he noticed that he was being watched. I'll bet he worked a very long time. He was Giotto.

He probably paused every so often to take a drink of water and tend to the needs of his sheep, and then returned patiently to his patient boulder, before he heard over his shoulder in the twilight the courtesy of the Italian good evening from the countryside man who stood, certainly out of the little daylight left to the shepherd and his sheep alike.

I wonder where that boulder is. I wonder if the sweet faces of the lambs are still scratched on its sunlit side.

By God I know this much. Worse men than Giotto have lived longer than Giotto lived.

And uglier things than Giotto's wobbly scratches on a coarse boulder at the edge of a grassy field are rotting and toppling into decay at this very moment. By the time I reach Padova at fifteen minutes past four this afternoon, I wouldn't be a bit surprised to hear that Rockefeller's Mall in Albany, New York, had begun to sag and ooze its grandiose slime all over the surrounding city of the plain, and it will stink in the nostrils of God Almighty like the incense burned and offered up as a putrid gift on the altars of the Lord, while the King Jeroboam the Second imprisoned the righteous for silver and sold the poor for the buckles on a pair of shoes.

Giotto's boyish hand scratched the sweet faces of lambs on a coarse stone.

I wonder where the stone is. I will never live to see it.

I lived to see the Mall in Albany, though.

In one of the mature Giotto's greatest glories, a huge choir of his unutterably beautiful angels are lifting their faces and are becoming the sons of the morning, singing out of pure happiness the praises of God.

Far back in the angelic choir, a slightly smaller angel has folded his wings. He has turned slightly away from the light and lifted his hands. You cannot even see his face. I don't know why he is weeping. But I love him best.

I think he must be wondering how long it will take Giotto to remember him, give him a drink of water, and take him back home to the fold before it gets dark and shepherd and sheep alike lose their way in the darkness of the countryside.

Padua

Bari, Old and Young

The old women of Bari near the sea sit in the small shadows of open doors. Their faces are beautifully darkened in the sunlight. Their hair is gray enough. They have seen the wars. They have known the young Germans blundering and falling out of the sky like poisoned moths. The young men in Bari today swagger and smirk as though no one had ever lived before, as though no one had ever died. Forever titivating their lank hair in the Adriatic breeze, voluptuously caressing their own armpits, they love to be told they are the lost youth, unemployed and betrayed by The System. Their motorcycles whinny insanely along the dark streets, and they are interested in women only to frighten them. They are too mindless to be skillful thieves. But the old women of Bari in their open doors know that young men will find something else to do, and I walk in this city as frightened as an old sea woman startled by moths.

Once the old city of Bari rose and gathered its companions out of the sea. But the new city, a growth of our present desperate century, squats a little inland, companionless. It is no place for solitude. Already the stone faces of new tall buildings are beginning to crumble.

On my last day here, I will walk carefully through the barren places and find the past again, the old city where I can stand solitary beside the noble churches. And beyond the old city, even beyond the past, there is the sea itself, the ancient freshness of the natural world that God, stirring in His loneliness and unapproached in His light, breathed upon. The fragrance of the water moves heavily and slowly with mussel shells and the sighs of drowned men. There is nothing so heavy with earth as the sea's breath and the breath of fresh wilderness, the camomilla fields along the shore. I would like to stand among them and breathe their air, one more day of my life, before I have to turn around and make my way back to this present century, back through the ugliness of vicious young faces who will leave no churches behind them in the fullness of their age, but only the blind scars of motorcycle tires, the wrinkles of panic on women's faces, and an echo of brutal laughter at the edge of the sea.

The Brief Season

As we rode the train south from Florence, through the slow green castled countryside, I began to fancy that Italy had gone back to the original grass for good. The dark ilex and the luminous double-cherry rose everywhere by the rivers, and the rivers, too, rose, though here they posed no danger to any human place, for all the towns were pinnacles, more or less. Orvieto alone, set delicately at the top of four rising natural walls, seemed defenseless against flood from the river. It is no use objecting that Orvieto stands above all the rivers of the earth. The shepherds who live there have all of them long ago drowned in green light, and two of them a moment ago have risen for the brief season, to stand on the cliff and wave to us as we hurry past.

A First Day in Paris

Some twenty years ago I was still a young man. I did not know anything more about Paris than a small black-haired sea tern knows about inland mountain gardens on the first day of his life. All he does is gaze around him, puzzled at the solitary distances of the ocean. How many mountains I have flown across, how many nests I have lain down in and abandoned between the big American cities. Now I walk in the gardens of the Tuileries. Here, a song tells me, some twenty years ago the chestnut buds in April were too heavy to bear themselves any longer. When a late frost fell on them, they suddenly shuddered in the night, and the next morning they opened, green as before, in spite of everything. The startled frost ran off and vanished, and the open blossoms turned white in their own good time. In Paris the natural world, alert and welcome in a moment to its own loveliness, offers a strange new face, as though God were creating it for the first time. Sometimes the women in the Tuileries grow so old they outlive death, and their shadows lie on chestnut leaves like sunlight.

In Memory of Hubert Robert

A Hillside in Fiesole

An ancient city is the only place where the ancient creatures have room to become new. This wild rabbit has allowed her children to scamper among the tough green weeds near the ruins. Delicately fluffy and light as the parachutes of milkweed, the children would be young and ignorant in any case, so I let them go by. But she is the one I love to look on, she is the youthful one, in spite of the winter she has somehow got through. Her muscular hind legs are terrible weapons of defense and flight, but her forepaws in repose are gentle, as her long wiry whiskers flick precisely above them, branches ready for blossom in the green twilight.

Poppies in Trajan's Market

For once among the centuries, it is not human blood, this scattering of a wild thing among the stones of a splendid human place. As far as I know, not even the emperor ordered men to be disposed of here, his friends, his enemies, or the strange kings of Africa too hopelessly proud to cut and bear stones on their shoulders or wrestle in the arena with starved orangutans or race the fleet ostriches in irregular circles. And today, for once, in Rome, a whole week has gone by, and I have not heard of a single recent murder. No. The brilliant scattering of scarlet petals here belongs in a field near the sea, and the stone belongs deep in a hill. Both stone and flower stand homeless beside each other here, strangers among the bewildering Romans.

The Cross

It is one of the longest afternoons of the world, an afternoon long past one of our wars. On the ruined wall of the mayor's house in Anghiari, some soldier, wandering up and down the city and exploring it, paused long enough to stitch a cross precisely with bullets. He must have done it for love of his art, for no Christ hangs there now. Somehow a seed from the field of wild dill blossoms paused in its own wandering and exploring flight, halfway up the mountain city, and I can see the solitary long stem and the golden crown, and the root in the crevice, the root also wandering and exploring the elegant cross on the wall stone, the machine-gunned cross. By this time the soldier is scattered farther away than the seed of the dill.

The Aristocrat

All over Apulia, currents of sea air snarl among winds from the landwise mountains. I can see thistle seeds tumbling everywhere, but I lose their pathways, they are so many. Flowers of every color flock up and down the walls of white ruin and beyond, between the snaggles of useless rock and the sea, poppies and camomilla clustered together like brilliant sheep. But somehow the thistle, disdainful in the general flight of seeds, ends up alone in the mob of wildflowers. Its bloom is so wealthy it would become scarlet, but scarlet is not the name. Scarlet is the shadow the poppies already wear. The thistle pauses all alone, elegant in its tatters, too proud to name itself, too aloof to accept any name I might give.

The Sunlight Falling at Peace in Moret-sur-Loing

At ten o'clock on this midsummer morning the wings of summer mosquitoes appear in the sunlight across the water. Sudden and brief, they flash into sight and out again. They move in the light, deep in its summer life, exposed and defenseless. I am too far away to glimpse their real bodies, but I know they are there because of the light they give. I remember a man long ago who could not bear to look on the face of God, and who fell to his knees in prayer at the sight of a beloved human face. The mosquitoes move again, deep in the light. They are like the blue veins that girls do their best to hide on the backs of their hands for fear somebody will catch their blood in the act and remind them that they too will grow old. But the obscene calamity of gray faces and cynical knowingness is a despair that the mosquitoes are likely to escape. The swallows resting under the stone bridge are waiting for twilight and its hungers, but the mosquitoes neither know nor care.

The river, the Loing, moves so lightly it seems adrift from its reeds. Fish nuzzle the surface into ripples that lie there a long time before they slide over to the marges. Two small boys chatter like finches and sway at the ends of their fishing poles. Their voices nuzzle the surface of the sky, and lie there a long time before they slide over to the roof of the church, lost finally in the voice of the old bell. The river, the Loing, moves so lightly it seems forever still. I would rather forget it is moving. I would rather forget that its fate guides it, with its small boys and fish and fishermen, downstream, to enter the dark red waters of the Marne.

Flowering Olives

It is futile to pretend I am looking at something else. In fact, I am doing my best to gaze as deeply as I can into the crevice of a single olive blossom. There must be hundreds of thousands of these tiny flowers, falling all over themselves among the silver leaves of a single small tree. Too many for one tree to bear, they gather in heaps beneath the twisted branches, clusters so thick on the top of the low stone wall, all the breeze can do is blow them back and forth across each other, the way a larger wind can do no more with sand than allow it to build and dissolve and rebuild itself into dunes. I have a single olive flower in my palm. I mean I had one. Now the breeze has it, and I will never catch another. The whole mile of this mountain road high above tiny golden Gargnano gleams right now in a momentary noon of olive flowers, and I am the only darkness alive in the Alps.

The Gift of Change

Of all the creatures, they seem to know best the art of sunning themselves. Without brooding unhappily, they understand where the best shades are. It is next to impossible to catch them and imprison them in the usual human ways, because they live in perpetual surrender: They love to become whatever it is that gazes upon them or holds them. They can turn as precisely green as the faintest hint of moss-shadow thirty seconds after noon, or a little gray knitted into silver of drying algae buoyed up ashore and abandoned there to the random wind of children's feet in flight.

But the lizard lying beside me now has gone too far. Wholly abandoning himself to his gift of change, he lifts his head above the edge of a linden blossom freshly fallen and alone. His exquisite hands have given up clinging to anything. They lie open. The leaf on the flower is so smooth, a light wind could blow him away. I wonder if he knows. If he knows, I wonder that my breath doesn't blow him away. I am that close to him, and he that close to me. He has gone too far into the world to turn back now. His tail has become a spot on the sun, the delicate crease between his shoulder blades, the fold in a linden leaf, his tongue finer and purer than a wild hair in my nostril, his hands opener than my hands. It is too late to turn back into himself. I can't even faintly begin to understand what is happening behind his serene face, but to me he looks like the happiest creature alive in Italy.

Beside the Tour Magne in Nîmes

The tower is a long way up, and though I am no one to search out difficult valleyways to climb, I have strained up here freely, and now I have got what I came for. A breathing space. One thing I love about the stones here, even beyond their tottering and ramshackle balance, is their namelessness. Not even the doctors of history, with their fine hands sifting the skeletons of ancient leaves away from the branches of lost children's hands, can find on the great tower the slightest scar that can tell who built it here and left it for someone finally to approach and leave alone. Nearly every stone the Romans laid on it has long since rolled back down the hill. I am delighted to leave the tower alone, to lie down beside it on the high grass, feeling only a little less young and silly than a Roman, alive and at peace with the purposes of men's names I bless and will never know, names I will never have to be sorry that I knew.

Goodnight

By the Seine in the evening on the right-hand shore north of the Pont Alexandre, gangs of workmen have left a tangle of canvas and boards. A ditch opens there on the other side of the sycamores. I imagine by daylight the place must look like a wound. But the trees have been shedding their bark at the end of August, and their new skin, a peculiar golden, welcomes the lamplight thrown lightly from the ancient bridge, as well as whatever moonlight can find its way down the river. The trees might cling to the light forever, but they hold on for a moment only, and shed whatever lamplights and moons they have all over the torn ground, the lumber, the dirty canvas, and the four eyes of rats hurrying from the shadow beside the river to the strange new light on the other side of the trees. Soundless behind them, François Villon waves goodnight to his kinsmen.

A Snail at Assisi

The snail shell has lain up here all summer along, I suppose. It is smaller than my thumbnail, where it rests now, but it casts its light shadow huge on the ground, and my shadow is there, following very carefully. Already the light has taken my shadow into the air and laid it down the slope below me, where it grows longer and longer, always moving, yet hardly to be seen moving. The air is dry far up here on the highest hill in Assisi, on the far side of the fortress wall where the earth falls nearly straight down. Even as I squint in the sun and try to bear it alive, I wonder how the tiny snail was alive and climbed and climbed and made it all the way up to this pinnacle, the armed building and the arrow-skewered wall. The great hollow skeleton of this fortress is empty now, its back turned away from Francis's solitary hill, its face still set grimly toward Perugia. The snail is long gone, maybe lifted high into sunlight, devoured by songbirds between one fortress and another. By this time, one more long summer afternoon is nearly over. My shadow and the shadow of the snail shell are one and the same.

Epistle from the Amphitheatre

Dear, I have gone through a long slow summer and an autumn which is hard for me to understand. Italy is a new country, a country I never knew. Italy is so old. Here in Verona the Romans built an amphitheatre of pink marble nearly a thousand years before Amerigo Vespucci was born. Yet today the Arena stands still, nearly flawless. Its shape holds so fine a balance between the ground and the sky that its very stones are a meeting and an intermingling of light and shadow. At noon, even the fierce Italian sunlight cannot force a glare out of the amphitheatre's gentleness. In late twilight the Arena can hold twenty-two thousand people who still have plenty of room to hold their breath. If some person, welcome and yet alien to this place, is foolish enough to applaud the musicians in the Arena while they are still singing, some Veronese lover of the music will briefly, decisively hush up the stranger. The Veronese hush in defense of the music is a kind of indrawn breath. It sounds as though silence itself had spoken. And yet you can hear it from one end of the enormous Arena to the other, a clear whisper to the inner ear of the stranger: Shut up and listen. Be still. Be glorified. Or be damned.

Still, I wonder why it is hard for me to understand this Italian autumn. I think it is because the warmth has lasted so long. Verona is a city older than the Romans, and out of its old age it moved something in the sleep of those sparkling and victorious young engineers. I myself was once in an army, an excellent army as armies go, and I know it is almost immoral for a soldier to get out of bed in the morning until some barbaric Draco from West Virginia blasts him out of sleep with a whistle. Nick Bottom has nothing on me. I have a reasonably good ear for music, and when I am alone, I can hear voices that spoke to me twenty years ago more clearly than I can hear the oratorical squalls of Mario Proccacino. (Dear, you don't know his name. Never mind. It is enough for you to know that he is not a Veronese. He is not even an Italian. He is an American. An American statesman. He has a certain voice. His voice is a mistake; but it is unmistakable.) The young Roman soldiers who rose before daybreak in Verona were not moralists. They were pious men. The pious man, sang Vergil, does his duty with love. The restless young Roman legionaries stationed in Verona rose out of bed without being screamed at, and they found they had been given what in the American army today is still called good duty. Disciplined, intelligent young masters of roads and walls, those young Romans gazed full-face into their first daylight. Having slept dreamless, they dreamed by molding and lifting in place this new Arena, a comely body whose very stones give a new shape to the air that people breathe, hush, whisper, and listen to.

Those engineers were so young. Deep in the Alps, minerals hard enough to cut perfect diamonds had already been crumbling, a handful of grains every thousand years or so, and flowing downhill as the ice melted into the river Adige. And the young Romans woke beside the Adige.

Today, in the middle of my own life, I woke beside the Adige. We hurried through breakfast for once, because the sun was splendid, and we wanted to enter the Arena and to walk all the way around it. We climbed and stood as far away from each other as we could get without falling off the rim, as Amerigo Vespucci might have done. Far away I could see her, tiny and blazing in her golden skin, her wide-brimmed straw hat fluttering, one feather of one wing, still ascending. Instantly, we came home. I was impatient to write to you, because I do not want to waste time.

To a Blossoming Pear Tree

For my friends
Helen McNeely Sheriff
and
John Logan

I forget when it was that I heard the news that San Gemi-
gnano had been destroyed or partially destroyed in that war
on Italian territory which was merely one more of the crimi-
nal stupidities of this decade. It came along with so many
other useless disasters that one's feeling of dismay was dulled
by incredulity. It seemed impossible that the tangible homes
of so many personal memories—towns and landscapes,
buildings and works of art—had vanished utterly or were so
mangled that what little being they retained was almost worse
than complete destruction. It was something like the shock of
incredulous pain and dismay parents feel at the loss of a
child—I had expected to die and leave Europe, not that Eu-
rope would die and leave me. . . . But I will not weary the
reader with useless enthusiasms for obliterated pictures or
smashed churches or shattered towers and palaces or rubble-
choked streets. If they are gone, they are gone; and there is
no use in making people unhappy by saying that they have
forever lost beautiful things. Still, not everything that came
out of San Gemignano was destroyed by the brutal guns.

—Richard Aldington, *A Wreath for San Gemignano*, 1945

No one knew that I knelt in the mud beneath the bridge
In the city of Chicago . . .
And then, you see, it was spring,
And soft sunlight came through the cracks of the bridge.
I had been long alone in a strange place where no gods came.

—Sherwood Anderson, "American Spring Song"

Redwings

It turns out
You can kill them.
It turns out
You can make the earth absolutely clean.

My nephew has given my younger brother
A scientific report while they both flew
In my older brother's small airplane
Over the Kokosing River, that looks

Secret, it looks like the open
Scar turning gray on the small
Of your spine.

Can you hear me?

It was only in the evening I saw a few redwings
Come out and dip their brilliant yellow
Bills in their scarlet shoulders.
Ohio was already going to hell.
But sometimes they would sit down on the creosote
Soaked pasture fence posts.
They used to be few, they used to be willowy and thin.

One afternoon, along the Ohio, where the sewer
Poured out, I found a nest,
The way they build their nests in the reeds,
So beautiful,
Redwings and solitaries.
The skinny girl I fell in love with down home
In late autumn married
A strip miner in late autumn.
Her five children are still alive,
Floating near the river.

Somebody is on the wing, somebody
Is wondering right at this moment
How to get rid of us, while we sleep.

Together among the dead gorges
Of highway construction, we flare
Across highways and drive
Motorists crazy, we fly
Down home to the river.

There, one summer evening, a dirty man
Gave me a nickel and a potato
And fell asleep by a fire.

One Last Look at the Adige:
Verona in the Rain

Some crumbling of igneous
Far off in the coverts
Of my orplidean country,
Where tall men
Are faintly bearded
Pines, now, the slow stalagmon
Gathers downward
Stone, milk of mineral
Below my graying face.
This is another river
I can still see flow by.

The Ohio must have looked
Something like this
To the people who loved it
Long before I was born.
They called the three
Slim islands of willow and poplar
Above Steubenville,
They, they, they
Called
The three slim islands
Our Sisters.

Steubenville is a black crust, America is
A shallow hell where evil

Is an easy joke, forgotten
In a week.

Oh, stay with me a little longer in the rain,
Adige.

Now, Adige, flow on.
Adige, river on earth,
Only you can hear
A half-witted angel drawling Ohioan
In the warm Italian rain.

In the middle of my own life
I woke up and found myself
Dying, fair enough, still
Alive in the friendly city
Of my body, my secret Verona,
Milky and green,
My moving jewel, the last
Pure vein left to me.

The unrighteous heathen,
Valerio Catullo,
Was born in Verona,
And you held him in the curve of your arm.
He couldn't stand it.
He left home and went straight
To hell in Rome.
Io factum male io miselle
Adige, the lights
Have gone out on the stone bridge,
Where I stand, alone,
A dark city on one shore,
And, on the other,
A dark forest.

Hell

I had no idea
How far down I was.

I stood there, nothing.
A dead fact.
I heard no howls.
I listened for the hollows
Of ice.
My bones cast their emerald shadow
On the glittering fangs.

Then I heard the tiny
Rustling, the wings.
Here they come,
I thought.

But nobody came
Except a delicate little mosquito.
And I gave him all I had left
To drink, to live.

The Wheeling Gospel Tabernacle

Homer Rhodeheaver, who was the evangelist Billy Sunday's psalm-odist and shill at the offertory, did something in the year of Our Lord 1925 that made both of my parents almost ecstatic with happiness all the rest of their lives, until they died within a few months of each other in 1973.

Just as the Reverend Doctor Sunday was admonishing the congregation in congress assembled with his customary warning that they warn't no virtue in the clinking of shekels, a wicked sound; just as the Reverend Doctor was in full oratorical blossoming cry in praise of each silken soft certain rustle of one twenty-dollar bill against another in the wicker collection plate; just as the former semi-professional baseball player of the Lord God Almighty Lord of Hosts was advising how as "Bruthern, a twenty don't take up no more room in that there plate than a wun"—it happened.

One of Doctor Sunday's locally hired ushers glided to the minister's side and with ghostly discretion reported to the evangelical ear that the cops from Pittsburgh had just left Weirton, West Virginia, and were hurtling down the West Virginia Route 40 in their Prohibition-style armored Cord cars, bound to catch Homer Rhodeheaver in full song. He was wanted in Pittsburgh on a paternity charge.

By the time the Pittsburgh cops burst into the Wheeling Gospel Tabernacle, it was as empty and dark as the waiting room of a speakeasy. Where had the brethren gone? Some thought that Doctor Sunday ascended. I lean toward the opinion that the two laborers in the vineyards of the Lord skinned the populace of Benwood down the river the next day, and that possibly Homer had time between hymns to make some lonely widow happy.

The year was 1925. My mother and father got one of their chances to laugh like hell for the sheer joy of laughter before the Great Depression began.

They were younger than I am this year. I was born two years after Homer Rhodeheaver and Billy Sunday appeared to run up their crusading flag near the blast furnace down the Ohio River for what was surely a one-night stand.

For all I know, my mother and father loved each other in 1925. For all I know, Homer Rhodeheaver is still in full flight from the Paternity Squad of the Pittsburgh Police Department. For all I know, Homer Rhodeheaver really was a glorious singer of the great hymns down home. For all I know, he carried a better tune than he knew. Women heard him in Pittsburgh. Maybe women heard him in the Wheeling Gospel Tabernacle. Maybe Jehovah was drowsing, and Eros heard the prayer and figured that love after all was love, no matter what language a man sang it in, so what the hell.

Little I know. I can pitch a pretty fair tune myself, for all I know.

A Lament for the Shadows in the Ditches

Right now the Roman noon is so brilliant it hurts my eyes. I sip my cappuccino at a wobbly sidewalk table and ponder the antiquities of my childhood: the beautiful river, that black ditch of horror where a strange boy drowned; and the streetcars. Where have they gone now, with their wicker seats that seemed to rattle behind the dull headlights in the slow dusk, in summer, when everything in Ohio ran down and yet never quite stopped?

The Romans and the discovered Americans stroll blinded in the Colosseum to make it clean across the street. The floor there now is a careful revelation. It is an intricate and intelligent series of ditches, and the sun cannot reach them. They are the shadows of starved people who did not even want to die. They were not even Jews.

There is no way to get rid of the shadows of human beings who could find God only in that last welcome of the creation, the maws of tortured animals. Is that last best surest way to heaven the throat of the hungry?

What color is a hungry shadow? Even the noon sunlight in the Colosseum is the golden shadow of a starved lion, the most beautiful of God's creatures except maybe horses.

By the Ruins of a Gun Emplacement: Saint-Benoît

Behind us, the haystack rustles
Into the summer dusk, and the limber girl's knees
Alone are barely visible among the rust
Of grape leaves. We are one face
Gazing into another, dim.

What shall we do if the round moon comes down
The river alone,
And strolls up out of the Loire
To make once more his command of these pastures,
Orchards, and the many bypaths for wandering,
Takes them for his own once more, his own
Paternal fields?

As the lovers scuffle
In the drying coins of the dewfall behind us,
I can close my eyes and see the tall young
Noble the moon, pausing
A mile or so down the river, inland
Maybe three quarters of a mile
By the sandpit pond. There, no one at nightfall
Pauses alone with his wine. There, no one
At dewrise but only the moon
Lifting deliberately, between the long slim

Fingers, the startling faces
Of night creatures. Who are they?

I met a snail on a stone at Fleury,
Where, now, Max Jacob walks happily among the candles
Of his brothers, but I still do not know
The snail's secret.
I do not even know
What we shall do if the round moon comes down
The river and strolls up
Out of the Loire
To take once more your startling face up
Among his drowsed swans,
All three, whose names,
Dewfall and Nightrise and Basilica,
Napoleon stole from Spanish horses
A dusk long ago, before the last time

Somebody gouged a trench along the Loire.

The Flying Eagles of Troop 62

Ralph Neal was the Scoutmaster. He was still a young man. He
liked us.

I have no doubt he knew perfectly well we were each of us
masturbating unhappily in secret caves and shores.

The soul of patience, he waited while we smirked behind each
other's backs, mocking and parodying the Scout Law, trying to imitate
the oratorical rotundities of Winston Churchill in a Southern Ohio
accent:

"Ay scout is trusswortha, loll, hailpful, frenly, curtchuss, kand,
abaydent, chairful, thrifta, dapraved, clane, and letcherass."

Ralph Neal knew all about the pain of the aching stones in our
twelve-year-old groins, the lava swollen halfway between our peck-
ers and our nuts that were still green and sour as half-ripe apples
two full months before the football season began.

Socrates loved his friend the traitor Alcibiades for his beauty and
for what he might become.

I think Ralph Neal loved us for our scrawniness, our acne, our fear; but mostly for his knowledge of what would probably become of us. He was not a fool. He knew he would never himself get out of that slime hole of a river valley, and maybe he didn't want to. The Vedantas illustrate the most sublime of ethical ideals by describing a saint who, having endured through a thousand lives every half-assed mistake and unendurable suffering possible to humanity from birth to death, refused at the last moment to enter Nirvana because he realized that his scruffy dog, suppurating at the nostrils and half mad with rabies, could not accompany him into perfect peace.

Some of us wanted to get out, and some of us wanted to and didn't.

The last I heard, Dickey Beck, a three-time loser at housebreaking, was doing life at the State Pen in Columbus.

The last I heard, Dale Headley was driving one of those milk trucks where the driver has to stand up all day and rattle his spine over the jagged street-bricks.

The last I heard from my brother-in-law, Hub Snodgrass was still dragging himself home every evening down by the river to shine, shower, shave, and spend a good hour still trying to scrape the Laughlin steel dust out of his pale skin. He never tanned much, he just burned or stayed out of the river.

The last I heard, Mike Kottelos was making book in Wheeling.

I have never gone back there down home to see Ralph Neal. My portrait hangs on one of the walls of the Martins Ferry Public Library. Ralph Neal would think I've become something. And no doubt I have, though I don't know just what. Scribbling my name in books. Christ have mercy on me alive; and after I'm dead, as Pietro Aretino of Florence requested of the priest after he had received extreme unction on his deathbed, "Now that I've been oiled, keep me from the rats."

When I think of Ralph Neal's name, I feel some kind of ice breaking open in me. I feel a garfish escaping into a hill spring where the crawdads burrow down to the pure bottom in hot weather to get the cool. I feel a rush of long fondness for that good man Ralph Neal, that good man who knew us dreadful and utterly vulnerable little bastards better than we knew ourselves, who took care of us better than we took care of ourselves, and who loved us, I reckon, because he knew damned well what would become of most of us, and it sure did, and he knew it, and he loved us anyway. The very name of America often makes me sick, and yet Ralph Neal was an American. The country is enough to drive you crazy.

What Does the Bobwhite Mean?

to Jimmie East

I don't know
Yet. I, too, have walked down there
In that place where the green
Acacias get dark before your eyes.
That place: wherever it is,
Only you know.

As for me, as for mine,
We have held each other's hands alone, each alone,
And felt the green dew turn dark gold, brilliants
In the darkness outside
A town called Fiesole.
What can the name of Fiesole mean to you?
What does the bobwhite mean?

I have heard the katydid counting out syllables
Over and over on the side of mountain water
In the darkness outside
Minnewaska. Minnewaska?
What will your loneliness mean to me?
What does the bobwhite mean? I don't know
Yet, but I have
A pretty good twilight.

And around you a twilight is gathering in good faith
The solitary armadillos together in Florida,
Where you have your life.
And what dim angel weaves through the long moss there,
And what does it mean there,
South of my darkness? You know.
Go, listen.

With the Shell of a Hermit Crab

Lugete, O Veneres Cupidinesque
— Catullus

This lovely little life whose toes
Touched the white sand from side to side,
How delicately no one knows,
Crept from his loneliness, and died.

From deep waters long miles away
He wandered, looking for his name,
And all he found was you and me,
A quick life and a candle flame.

Today, you happen to be gone.
I sit here in the raging hell,
The city of the dead, alone,
Holding a little empty shell.

I peer into his tiny face.
It looms too huge for me to bear.
Two blocks away the sea gives place
To river. Both are everywhere.

I reach out and flick out the light.
Darkly I touch his fragile scars,
So far away, so delicate,
Stars in a wilderness of stars.

Neruda

Trees that are not trees easily,
The little leaves
That are trees in secret.

Under one bough,
One vein of one leaf,
One side of the sea
Sang for a thousand inches

Uphill, as though
The tree in the leaf
Were sorry for being human
And wanted to run back
Across a river
In the center of America
Into the arms of an old beard,
Architect of spiders
Climbing up the long
Hill to gain
The crumbling pinnacle and spin
One strand of his body to join
The earth to one star anyway,
And save it, maybe.

The leaves of the little
Secret trees are fallen,
And where the earth goes on spinning,
I don't know.

In Defense of Late Summer

I have called up this every
Variety of green foliage
To hide me from the gray,
The vast ocean that changes
From color to color so often
It will not stand and stay.
Like a dry swamp, endless
Wherever I look, it offers me
A million dead leaves, only
Occasionally fluttering
Against the shore out of reach.
I turn shoreward to find
Every variety of living green,
Only half a mile off I find one
Copper beech, nearly as maple
As a Japanese girl far from home.

Lighting a Candle for W. H. Auden

At the Church of Maria am Gestade, Vienna

The poet kept his promise
To the earth before he died.
He sleeps now in Kirchstetten
Some twenty miles from here.
I did not go to mourn him,
Although I could have gone
And found him among beeches.
Best to leave him alone.

Maria am Gestade,
Mary on the shore,
The loud gouge of the subway
Scuttles my silences.
If I come here to laud a
Wise shadow, I restore
The first light in my hallway,
A strange forgiving grace.

Twenty miles west, Vienna
Scrambles to keep its trees.
Since 1957
The poet, shragged and wise,
Sang in an Austrian choir,
A sudden holiness
Behind the crag-faced fire,
The prayer, the good man's prayers.

I happen now to be
Within his twenty miles.
Kindly as Thomas Hardy,
Whose dream the towpath fills,
The poet Auden lies down
His twenty miles from here.
His perfect love is limestone,
Maria on the shore.

What have I got to do
With a kind poet's death?

One day he wrote to me
I had a book to give.
I gave my book, Maria,
While Auden was awake.
I give you my small candle
For the large master's sake.

To the Saguaro Cactus Tree
in the Desert Rain

I had no idea the elf owl
Crept into you in the secret
Of night.

I have torn myself out of many bitter places
In America, that seemed
Tall and green-rooted in mid-noon.
I wish I were the spare shadow
Of the roadrunner, I wish I were
The honest lover of the diamondback
And the tear the tarantula weeps.

I had no idea you were so tall
And blond in moonlight.

I got thirsty in the factories,
And I hated the brutal dry suns there,
So I quit.

You were the shadow
Of a hallway
In me.

I have never gone through that door,
But the elf owl's face
Is inside me.

Saguaro,
You are not one of the gods.

Your green arms lower and gather me.
I am an elf owl's shadow, a secret
Member of your family.

Discoveries in Arizona

All my life so far
I have been afraid
Of cactus,
Spiders,
Rattlesnakes.

The tall fourteen-year-old boy
    who led me through
The desert whispered, Come over
    this way.
Picking my steps carefully over
    an earth strangely familiar,
I found four small holes large
    enough
For a root that might have been
    torn out
Or a blacksnake hole in Ohio,
    that I hated.
What is it, I said, some cute
    prairie dog,
Or an abandoned posthole,
    maybe?
No, he said, she's down there
    with her children.
She doesn't hate you, she's not
    afraid,
She's probably asleep, she's
    probably keeping warm
With something I don't know about,
And all I know is sometimes in
    sunlight
Two brown legs reach out.
It is hard to get a look at
    her face.

Even in the museum she turns away.
I don't know where she is looking.

I have lived all my life in
      terror
Of a tarantula,
And yet I have never even seen
A tarantula turn her face
Away from me.

That's all right, said the boy.
Maybe she's never seen you either.

Simon

I am spending my whole life turning
My face away.
My best moment of wakefulness
Rises
When I gather to me
A huge gross dog.
We slobber all over each other's faces.
Simon
Carries in his fur
The thick blossoms of black spring mud
Even in winter.

He sits down with me on a Christmas evening.
We sing out of key.
He vanishes
And comes home, alone,
The cockleburs snarled in his ears.
Ah, what a mess!

Simon,
Where are you gone?
Some shaggy burdocks in Minnesota
Owe their lives to you,
Somewhere.

The Moorhen and Her Eight Young

They are little balls of charcoal-gray mallow among drifting lily stems, as though the flower had escaped from the garden of the waters behind the hangman's cottage and chosen to blossom at night. Yet here they drift in the daylight behind their mother. Herself so dark, she almost threatens to blaze into another color entirely. She stays in whatever leaf shadow she can find. Only her beak reveals her sometimes. It is red as valerian rising from a night lily.

What Does the King of the Jungle Truly Do?

What is the true love of a lion?

In Serengeti, the huge grassy plain of central Africa, a Belgian father and son saw, and photographed, a male lion lying on his back awake and fondling the cubs, while his female, clearly her own person, drowsed under a shade tree and, when she felt like waking, yawned, skipping her beauty, loins and all golden, lovely as his long mane, rippled together in the sunlight.

Small wonder Jesus wept at a human city.

In Exile

I kneel above a single rail of the Baltimore and Ohio track. The little green snake lies there blazing on the steel. It is almost perfect noon. He has no shadow to cast anywhere. But even if it were twilight, he would have slight shade to cast. What can I do to join him? His face seems turned toward the fireweed along the track. I too turn my face and gaze at the fireweed along the track. The roots must be healthy. I sit back on the rail and see it burn. The garter snake does not seem troubled. He may not be gazing at the fireweed at all. We may be praying the same prayer. I hope not. I draw his face close to me, and he looks a little mournful, but not old, and not alone.

Young Don't Want to Be Born

I know just how you feel. There was a time when your feet touched bottom. Then the sea polyps tangle themselves around one ankle, and a wave deep under the surface, that looks so smooth to all the idle strollers a mile behind you on the sunlit sands, knocks both feet out from under you, and you cling, desperate and terrified, to the tail of a giant sting-ray.

God is alone again. You are supposed to be some kind of a perfect beginning, for once. And just look at you. Well, just look at God and His own children.

Miles and miles down in the darkness of the waters, you grip with extravagant ferocity to the slime of the sting-ray's tail. He is going somewhere. But where? All you know is he is not going back to that shore ever again.

Thinking himself free and alone, the giant sting-ray relaxes in his flight and allows himself to be lifted slowly up on a long swell that rises from some depth God alone knows how far down. The giant thrashes and dances for miles on miles near the surface, from what seems one sea to another.

One afternoon he feels himself growing hungry. It is getting on toward evening. Your hands can't hold on any longer. He lets himself float idly on the surface. His eyes quicken to find something simple and not too much trouble to eat. You try to drift off a few yards in the deepening and thickening sea dusk joining the fog. The sting-ray hasn't seen you yet.

Hurry.

Has he seen you yet?

Oh, my poor brother, gather your strength if you have any.

Hurry off.

On a Phrase from Southern Ohio

for Etheridge Knight

A long time's gone.
Now all I recall for sure
Is a long shattering of jackhammers that stripped
Away the whole one side of one foothill of one
Appalachian mountain

Across the river from me where I was born.
It is summer chilblain, it is blowtorch, it is not
Maiden and morning on the way up that cliff.
Not where I come from.

It is a slab of concrete that for all I know
Is beginning to crumble.

Once,
Lazy and thieving toward the dark of an afternoon,
Shamba, Dick, Crum, Apie, Beanie, Bernardo,
And I got hold of a skiff,
And crawled all the way over to West Virginia
To the narrow hot mud shore, the foot
Of the scarred mountain.

Then from the bottom
Of that absolutely
Smooth dead
Face
We
Climbed
Straight up
And white

To a garden of bloodroots, tangled there, a vicious secret
Of trilliums, the dark purple silk sliding its hands deep down
In the gorges of those savage flowers, the only
Beauty we found, outraged in that naked hell.

Well, we found two black boys up there
In the wild cliff garden.

Well, we beat the hell out of one
And chased out the other.

And still in my dreams I sway like one fainting strand
Of spiderweb, glittering and vanishing and frail
Above the river.
What were those purple shadows doing
Under the ear
Of the woman who was weeping along the Ohio
River the woman?
Damned if you know;
I don't.

Little Marble Boy

Little marble boy
on the font of holy water,
lifting your hand,
your half hand,
to snatch at a white fish,
are you lonely when they shut the cathedral?
Are you cold
in the winter
with only your marble body
sitting above the water?
Little marble boy
on the font of holy water,
lifting your hand,
your half hand,
in an everlasting gesture
to catch a white fish.

Annie Wright
Lucca, 1963

Piccolini

Looming and almost molten and slowly moving its gold down the hill just behind my back is the summer villa of the poet, the Grotte de Catullo.

But I care more now for the poetry of the present moment. An easy thousand of silver, almost transparent piccolini are skimming the surface of the long slab of volcanic stone. They swim through a very tiny channel at the very rim of the lake. They tickle the skin of my ankles, smaller than Latin diminutives.

Catullus, grieving over his Lesbia's sparrow, turned *misere* from harsh *wretched* into *miselle*, poor and little and lovely and gone, all in one word.

But those tiny fish that tickle the skin of my ankles are already so diminutive that they would have dissolved altogether into droplets of mist at a mere touch of Catullus's fingertip. I reckon that is why he never wrote of them by name, but left them tiny and happy in their lives in the waters, where they still have their lives and seem to enjoy tickling the skin of my ankles.

Sirmione

The Secret of Light

I am sitting contented and alone in a little park near the Palazzo Scaligere in Verona, glimpsing the mists of early autumn as they shift and fade among the pines and city battlements on the hills above the river Adige.

The river has recovered from this morning's rainfall. It is now restoring to its shapely body its own secret light, a color of faintly cloudy green and pearl.

Directly in front of my bench, perhaps thirty yards away from me, there is a startling woman. Her hair is black as the inmost secret of light in a perfectly cut diamond, a perilous black, a secret light that must have been studied for many years before the anxious and disciplined craftsman could achieve the necessary balance between courage and skill to stroke the strange stone and take the one chance he would ever have to bring that secret to light.

While I was trying to compose the preceding sentence, the woman rose from her park bench and walked away. I am afraid her secret might never come to light in my lifetime. But my lifetime is not the only one. I will never see her again. I hope she brings some other man's secret face to light, as somebody brought mine. I am startled to discover that I am not afraid. I am free to give a blessing out of my silence into that woman's black hair. I trust her to go on living. I believe in her black hair, her diamond that is still asleep. I would close my eyes to daydream about her. But those silent companions who watch over me from the insides of my eyelids are too brilliant for me to meet face to face.

The very emptiness of the park bench just in front of mine is what makes me happy. Somewhere else in Verona at just this moment, a woman is sitting or walking or standing still upright. Surely two careful and accurate hands, total strangers to me, measure the invisible idea of the secret vein in her hair. They are waiting patiently until they know what they alone can ever know: that time when her life will pause in mid-flight for a split second. The hands will touch her black hair very gently. A wind off the river Adige will flutter past her. She will turn around, smile a welcome, and place a flawless and fully formed Italian daybreak into the hands.

I don't have any idea what his face will look like. The light still hidden inside his body is no business of mine. I am happy enough to sit in this park alone now. I turn my own face toward the river Adige. A little wind flutters off the water and brushes past me and returns.

It is all right with me to know that my life is only one life. I feel like the light of the river Adige.

By this time, we are both an open secret.

Verona

A Small Grove in Torri del Benaco

Outside our window we have a small willow, and a little beyond it a fig tree, and then a stone shed. Beyond the stone the separate trees suddenly become a grove: a lemon, a mimosa, an oleander, a pine, one of the tall slender cypresses that a poet here once called candles of darkness that ought to be put out in winter, another willow, and a pine.

She stands among them in her flowered green clothes. Her skin is darker gold than the olives in the morning sun. Two hours ago we got up and bathed in the lake. It was like swimming in a vein. Everything that can blossom is blossoming around her now. She is the eye of the grove, the eye of mimosa and willow. The cypress behind her catches fire.

Torri del Benaco

Written on a Big Cheap Postcard from Verona

Here they are on the balcony,
Garish, burned harsh into color.
In the city of Pisanello and Stefano,
Who lightly touched the Madonna's hair into wings,
I can buy this romantical junk for fifty lire
And send vulgarity home. Romeo, Giulietta,
How do you survive? Not even Shakespeare
Could kill you once and for all, lavishing
So much clear genius on his fierce cold play:
First, his thugs on the streets, held back
From cutting each other's throats only
By threats of a flat thwack on the skull;
Then families hating each other,
The trysts after dark,
One pointless murder after another,
The questionable marriage the world
Would have hushed up and broken anyway.
And the absolutely final death, ridiculous,
Brutal, a cheap loss, a death cruel
And stupid as yours or mine.

Yet not even Shakespeare could kill them
Once and for all. If you don't believe me,
Just mention the names to anyone,
A stranger on the street: Romeo, Juliet.
And all that the stranger will remember
Is a radiance in the dusk,
A light wing fluttering in a vine,
Hands shocked by touching,
Strange and forbidden,

A bomb, and no chance
To live long.

Oh, I know:
It's nothing after all
But a prosaic clutter:
Shakespeare, in a hurry,
Stole the plot of *Romeo and Juliet*
From a mediocre narrative poem
Written in fourteeners by Arthur Brooke.
And I know:
He probably lifted at least part of the plot
Of *As You Like It*
From an English translation of an Italian novella
By Robert Greene,
Who bad-mouthed the young Shakespeare
For stealing scenes from his betters,
As Greene, defeated and debt-ridden,
Lay whining penances
On his own dirty deathbed.
I know:
The citizens of Verona once called
Their ruler a crazy dog.
I know:
The heavens blossoming above this ravishing
And beautiful city blackened with wings
Of bombing planes,
And children scampering like mice
Into the cracks of the vast marble Arena,
All hell broken loose.
Oh, I know
All I'm giving you is a cheap, chintzy
Picture postcard, a gross and messy imitation
Of a poet's dream of something hopeless
That didn't have a chance in this world.
What chance do we have?
We are nothing but a poet's dream
Of lovers who chose to live.
Not a chance.

Oh, I know:
I know, I know, I know,

How can I forget?
This world is a mess,
A sinking menace of loveliness and danger.
Fumbling to touch hands in the dark,
Their hands fluttered into flames.
I know, and yet—
Just mention their names
To any stranger,
Anyone at all.
He will recall,
Not the strange menace of their loveliness,
But only the lovers.

Two Moments in Rome

I. How Spring Arrives

The very last snow, gritty and cruel as the wrinkles scarred in the corners of a fanatic's mouth, has disappeared overnight. Eternal winter was merely yesterday. True, high on the Borghese cliffs these gardens are still crowded with dead branches. The gross limb of a pine, torn from the body by some blind night wind, shoulders some tiny bushes out of its way. An entire oleander, uprooted weeks ago, turns harder with decay. Slouched on a stone bench, it casts a sneering shadow. The dead loiter indecently here in the fresh sunlight, bound and determined to get revenge on somebody if it's the last thing they ever do.

Three girls are coming up the path. They are so excited they can't keep their feet still. They are not running. But they touch the ground so quickly, they scarcely touch it at all. All three shake out their black hair. One after another they take off their sweaters. At each end of the stone bench, they pluck up the dead oleander as though it weighed nothing at all, and toss it out of the stream, with birds nesting all round it.

They, too, must have slept all night with their eyes open.

II. Reflections

At noon on a horizon the Colosseum poises in mid-flight, a crumbling moon of gibbous gold. It catches an ancient light, and gives form to that light. Gazing at the Colosseum from a spot two miles away, I feel as though I had just caught a quick glimpse of a girl's face. Young and alone, she is sitting high up on the stone, glancing about for her friends. Bored, she ignores that tangle of skinny mumblers far below her in the arena. She is waiting for the entrance of the animals.

Now, beyond the Colosseum, another moon, a day moon, appears in the sky. Even its little scars are ghosts.

Winter, Bassano del Grappa

Underground, the hair
Of the old man is growing
Golden again.
By noon, the barren
Sheaf along the
River leans down,
And the ten thousand
Austrians loom white
On the dim mountain.
I can't stand to hear Italians screaming across
This valley.
But the evening
Shows the old
Man a moment, casting
Light on a girl's face.
She carries a little
Basket of willow
Slowly home.

Two Moments in Venice

I. *Under the Canals*

Venice is a deep city, yet filmy and fragile at times. I don't mean merely its physical appearance, although the outline of roofs and towers in the early morning light can be a light and spidery thing, and the shadows among the few passages and stone streets after dark can assume almost the solidity of stone. I mean that the city can change its character, its appearance and mood, at any given moment, even in broad daylight. Consequently, it is very easy to get lost here.

Yet all one needs to do is follow the sound of water, and the things and persons of the water, to find one's way home again, wherever home may be.

We saw a very old man appear suddenly around a corner. He entered the square very slowly, for all his quick appearance, an apparition of a kind. He carried a middle-sized wooden ladder on his shoulder, and a small curious net in one hand. A chimney sweep, Annie said. Perhaps he was. With his coat elbows and his crushed hat scuffled enough, he could have prowled his way up and down the insides of these silvery, rotten walls.

But I am sure I noticed the green moon-slime on his shoes, and, until I hear otherwise, I will half-believe that he had just climbed up some of those odd stairs out of a nearby narrow canal. How can I know what he was doing under water? I can't forget it. But he was doing something. This, after all, is Venice; the very streets of the city are water; and what magnificent and unseemly things must sway underneath its roads; a lost Madonna and Child frantically flung away by a harried thief last year; the perfect skeleton of a haughty cat, his bone-tail curled around his ribs and crushed with salt three centuries ago; the right hand of a disloyal artisan in spun glass, the blood long gone back to the sea; some reflection of the moon caught and kept there, snaggled between the teeth of a Turkish sailor; or the sailor himself, headless, a scimitar in one hand and a Coca-Cola in the other; a snide note from Byron; an empty American Express folder; even a chimney, swept free, till this hour passes, of all the webs they weave so stoutly down there, the dark green spiders under the water who have more than all the time they need.

There he was: a chimney sweep in warm summer weather? Hardly. A sweeper of sea-stairs.

II. City of Evenings

The word evening has always seemed beautiful to me, and surely Venice is the city of evenings. It is renowned everywhere for its dawns, when the cathedrals and basilicas take solid shape out of the milky pearl. But their solidity is stone, even the finest of stone, the delicate sea-washed rippled marble floated here from Constantinople. It is only the evenings that give the city the shape of light;

they make the darkness frail and they give substance to the light.

It is still too early for evening, and the smoke of early September is gathering on the waves of the Giudecca Canal outside my room. Steamers, motorboats, trash-scows are moving past in large numbers, and gondolas are going home. In a little while we too will meet the twilight and move through it on a vaporetto toward the Lido, the seaward island with its long beach and its immense hotel, its memories of Aschenbach and his harrowing vision of perfection, of Byron on horseback in the moonlight, and the muted shadows of old Venetians drifting as silently as possible in flight from the barbarians, drifting as far away as the island of Torcello, taking refuge as Ruskin said like the Israelites of old, a refuge from the sword in the paths of the sea. Maybe Torcello was nothing much for the princess of the sea to find, but the old Venetians discovered the true shape of evening, and now it is almost evening.

The Silent Angel

As I sat down by the bus window in the gate of Verona, I looked over my left shoulder. A man was standing in one of the pink marble arches at the base of the great Roman Arena. He smiled at me, a gesture of the utmost sweetness, such as a human face can rarely manage to shine with, even a beloved face that loves you in return.

He seemed dressed like a musician, as well he might have been, emerging for a moment into the sunlight from one of the secluded and cool rehearsal chambers of the upper tiers of the Arena.

As the bus driver powered his motor and drew us slowly around the great public square, the Piazza Bra, the man in the half-golden rose shadow of the Arena kept his gaze on my face. He waved goodbye to me, his knowing eyes never leaving me as long as he could still see any of me at all, though how long that was I don't precisely know.

He raised his hand at the last moment to wave me out of Verona as kindly as he could. He held in his right hand what seemed to be a baton, and it hung suspended for a long instant in the vast petals of rose shadows cast down by the marble walls. Even after he had vanished back into the archway I could still see his baton.

Oh, I know it was not a baton. I was far away now, and all I could see behind me were the diminishing cicadas, lindens, and slim cedars rising, one feather folding upwards into another, into the spaces of evergreen and gold beyond the Roman Arena, beyond the river and the hills beyond the river, the beginning of everlasting change, Saint Martin's summer. All those trees, the durable and the momentary confused with one another into the eternity of Saint Augustine's despair of time. They will still be rising there long after even the Giusti Gardens, where Goethe walked, have run back to weeds, a few of my beloved lizards left to make company with them perhaps, a spider or two still designing for days and then patiently building the most delicate of ruins.

I could not afford to let myself think of the river Adige any longer, because I loved it too much. The wings of the smiling musician are folded. His baton, grown cool again by this time, rests on his knees. I can imagine that all the other musicians have risen into the riverside hills for the night, and my musician, who meant me no harm and only wanted to wave me away as gently as possible out of the beautiful space he guarded, is himself asleep with the late crickets along the river.

I turned at last away from the city, gritted my teeth, two of which are broken and snaggled, fingered the shred of pink marble in my jacket pocket, and forced my face toward Milano with its factories, London with its fear and hopelessness, and beyond that, the final place, New York, America, hell on earth.

I felt fallen. But not very happy. Nor lucky either.

The musician had not played me a single tune, he had not sung me a single song. He just waved me as gently as he could on the way out, the way that is my own, the lost way.

I suppose I asked for it. And he did his best, I suppose. He owns that heavenly city no more than I do. He may be fallen, as I am. But from a greater height, unless I miss my guess.

Verona

The Best Days

Optima dies prima fugit

First, the two men stand pondering
The square stone block sunk in the earth.
It must weigh five hundred pounds. The best

Days are the first
To flee. The taller man has gray hair
And long thin arms, the other
Squat with young shoulders, his legs
Slightly bowed already, a laborer
With the years, like a tree.

One works the edge
Of his steel claw subtly
Between the stones.
The other waits for the right instant,
A dazzle of balance, and slips the blade
Of his cold chisel into the crack.

Balancing the great weight of this enormous
And beautiful floorstone laid by the Romans,
Holding a quarter ton of stone lightly
Between earth and air,
The tall man with the gray hair reaches
Around the corner of stone
And most delicately eases
A steel pipe beneath.
The best days are the first
To flee. Now both men
Can stand upright, then gradually,
Their fine hands sure, they can ease
The stone from its place.

I look beneath.
It does not look like a grave
Of anybody, anybody at all,
Not even a Roman
Legionary or slave.
It is just under the stone.
The earth smells fresh, like the breath
Of a calf just born in Ohio
With me.

When I look up,
The tall old man with the slender arms, the young man
With the frail bulging shoulders
Are gone for some wine. Work hard, and give

The body its due of rest, even at noon.
The best days are the first to flee,
And the underside of the stone
Is pink marble
From Verona. The poet found, in Verona,
The friendship of daylight,
And a little peace.

The First Days

Optima dies prima fugit

The first thing I saw in the morning
Was a huge golden bee ploughing
His burly right shoulder into the belly
Of a sleek yellow pear
Low on a bough.
Before he could find that sudden black honey
That squirms around in there
Inside the seed, the tree could not bear any more.
The pear fell to the ground,
With the bee still half alive
Inside its body.
He would have died if I hadn't knelt down
And sliced the pear gently
A little more open.
The bee shuddered, and returned.
Maybe I should have left him alone there,
Drowning in his own delight.
The best days are the first
To flee, sang the lovely
Musician born in this town
So like my own.
I let the bee go
Among the gasworks at the edge of Mantua.

Names in Monterchi: To Rachel

We woke early
Because we had to wake.
What is that country
To me?

The spider in Anghiari is a brilliant
In the dust. I am going to find my way
To Anghiari, because on the way
The earth is a warm diamond.
Anghiari is a true place on the earth.
But that is one last true name I will tell.

On the way to Anghiari
We mounted the true frightening
Mountains, and there
The slim bus driver, the messenger,
Set us down and said,
Go find her.

I hurried you and my beloved
(Both you beloved)
To a secret place.

In the little graveyard there,
We are buried, Rachel, Annie, Leopoldo, Marshall,
The spider, the dust, the brilliant, the wind.

The Fruits of the Season

It is a fresh morning of late August in Padova. After the night's rain, the sun is emerging just enough so far to begin warming the grapes, melons, peaches, nectarines, and the other fruits that will soon fill this vast square. Women and children in bright flower print dresses are already beginning to amble from stall to stall.

At the very far end of the square I can see the azure and golden face of the town clock on the Torre dall'Orologio.

A baker with white flour sprinkled all over his boots just drifted across the extreme right corner of my eye.

It is all commonplace, ordinary, the firm shaping of the morning in an Italian city of middling size.

And yet—to my left I can see the entire front length of the Palazzo della Ragione, on whose second floor the community has arranged a huge exhibit of paintings, the enduring fruits of five hundred years.

And spread below the faces of those peculiarly tender and fierce angels, the men and women and their children are still arriving from the countryside, arranging for our slow ambling choice the heaps of grapes, melons, peaches, nectarines, and all the other fruits of the season in a glory that will not last too long.

But they will last long enough. I would rather live my life than not live it. The grapes in a smallish stall are as huge and purple as smoke. I have just eaten one. I have eaten the first fruit of the season, and I am in love.

Padua

With a Sliver of Marble from Carrara

Old men beneath the mountain
Stand in its shadow, unemployed.
They do not talk much about
Michelangelo.

They know

A man's hand worked the face.

You are out of work
At ten o'clock in the morning
At Carrara, a working town
North of Florence, where

The holiest human face
Among all Christ's mothers
Knew very well it dreamed:
Why did I wake? Whose
Face is this, weeping

Suddenly awake out of my coarse
And distant body
Behind Carrara that only
A lonely God made?

And a lonely man there
Wept for the faces of the prisoners in Florence.
Even he could not finish.
Even he
Could not live long enough.

Hook

I was only a young man
In those days. On that evening
The cold was so God damned
Bitter there was nothing.
Nothing. I was in trouble
With a woman, and there was nothing
There but me and dead snow.

I stood on the street corner
In Minneapolis, lashed
This way and that.
Wind rose from some pit,
Hunting me.
Another bus to Saint Paul
Would arrive in three hours,
If I was lucky.

Then the young Sioux
Loomed beside me, his scars
Were just my age.

Ain't got no bus here
A long time, he said.
You got enough money
To get home on?

What did they do
To your hand? I answered.
He raised up his hook into the terrible starlight
And slashed the wind.

Oh, that? he said.
I had a bad time with a woman. Here,
You take this.

Did you ever feel a man hold
Sixty-five cents
In a hook,
And place it
Gently
In your freezing hand?

I took it.
It wasn't the money I needed.
But I took it.

To a Blossoming Pear Tree

Beautiful natural blossoms,
Pure delicate body,
You stand without trembling.
Little mist of fallen starlight,
Perfect, beyond my reach,
How I envy you.
For if you could only listen,
I would tell you something,
Something human.

An old man
Appeared to me once
In the unendurable snow.
He had a singe of white
Beard on his face.
He paused on a street in Minneapolis
And stroked my face.

Give it to me, he begged.
I'll pay you anything.

I flinched. Both terrified,
We slunk away,
Each in his own way dodging
The cruel darts of the cold.

Beautiful natural blossoms,
How could you possibly
Worry or bother or care
About the ashamed, hopeless
Old man? He was so near death
He was willing to take
Any love he could get,
Even at the risk
Of some mocking policeman
Or some cute young wiseacre
Smashing his dentures,
Perhaps leading him on
To a dark place and there
Kicking him in his dead groin
Just for the fun of it.

Young tree, unburdened
By anything but your beautiful natural blossoms
And dew, the dark
Blood in my body drags me
Down with my brother.

Beautiful Ohio

Those old Winnebago men
Knew what they were singing.
All summer long and all alone,
I had found a way
To sit on a railroad tie
Above the sewer main.
It spilled a shining waterfall out of a pipe

Somebody had gouged through the slanted earth.
Sixteen thousand and five hundred more or less people
In Martins Ferry, my home, my native country,
Quickened the river
With the speed of light.
And the light caught there
The solid speed of their lives
In the instant of that waterfall.
I know what we call it
Most of the time.
But I have my own song for it,
And sometimes, even today,
I call it beauty.

This Journey

To the city of Fano,
Where we got well,
From Annie and me

Entering the Temple in Nîmes

As long as this evening lasts,
I am going to walk all through and around
The Temple of Diana.
I hope to pay my reverence to the goddess there
Whom the young Romans loved.
Though they learned her name from the dark rock
Among bearded Greeks,
It was here in the south of Gaul they found her true
To her own solitude.
For here surely the young women of Gaul
Glanced back thoughtfully over their bare
White shoulders and hurried away
Out of sight and then rose, reappearing
As vines and the pale inner hands of sycamores
In the green places.
This evening, in winter,
I pray for the stone-eyed legions of the rain
To put off their armor.
Allow me to walk between the tall pillars
And find the beginning of one vine leaf there,
Though I arrive too late for the last spring
And the rain still mounts its guard.

This and That

I am not going to share
Those high, those delicate
Cheekbones with her.
Nor the light feet I saw
Walking beneath the long
Stems, lovely of youth.

I am not going to name
The place where usual men
Pronounced on her
A heavy ritual stone.
They were all right, those men.
They didn't know.

In a panic once, she blurted
She loved me, and I had
Too much to say.
If I had only shared
The silences, she would
Have been all right.

But, no, I had to intone
A long harangue about
The this, the that.
Now this and that are gone,
And the high delicate
Bones are gone.

Light feet I saw walking
Bewildered by long stems,
She walked away.
And still I sit here talking.
And I still have, it seems,
The east wind to say.

Come, Look Quietly

The bird on the terrace has his own name in French, but I don't know it. He may be a nuthatch, only he doesn't eat upside down.

He has a perfectly round small purple cap on his crown and a slender long mask from his ears to his eyes all the way across. Come, look quietly. All the way across Paris. Far behind the bird, the globes of Sacré Coeur form out of the rain and fade again, all by themselves. The daylight all across the city is taking its own time.

The plump Parisian wild bird is scoring a light breakfast at the end of December. He has found the last seeds left in tiny cones on the outcast Christmas tree that blows on the terrace.

Old Bud

Old Bud Romick weighed three hundred pounds if he weighed an ounce, and he weighed an ounce. He used to sit on his front porch swing, enraged and helpless, while his two tiny grandchildren, hilarious and hellish little boys, scampered just out of his reach and yelled hideously, "Hell on you, Grandpa." His unbelievable Adam's apple purpled and shone like the burl on the root of a white oak, and he sang his God Damns in despair.

Old Bud Romick has fallen asleep as the twilight comes down Pearl Street in Martins Ferry, Ohio. The window shutters close here and there, and the flowing streetcars glow past into silence, their wicker seats empty, for the factory whistles have all blown down, and the widows all gone home. Empty, too, are the cinder alleys, smelling of warm summer asphalt. The streetlight columns, faintly golden, fill with the cracked mirrors of June bugs' wings. Old Bud Romick sags still on the porch swing. The rusty chains do their best for his body in the dark.

The dark turns around him, a stain like the bruise on a plum somebody somehow missed and left under a leaf. His two hellions have long since giggled their way upstairs. Old Bud Romick is talking lightly in his sleep, and an evening shower brings him a sticky new sycamore leaf in his sleep.

Whether or not he is aware of leaves, I don't know. I don't know whether or not he is aware of anything touching his face. Whether or not he dreams of how slender sycamores are, how slender young women are when they walk beneath the trees without caring how green they are, how lucky a plum might be if it dies without being eaten, I don't know.

The Turtle Overnight

I remember him last twilight in his comeliness. When it began to rain, he appeared in his accustomed place and emerged from his shell as far as he could reach—feet, legs, tail, head. He seemed to enjoy the rain, the sweet-tasting rain that blew all the way across lake water to him from the mountains, the Alto Adige. It was as near as I've ever come to seeing a turtle take a pleasant bath in his natural altogether. All the legendary faces of broken old age disappeared from my mind, the thickened muscles under the chins, the nostrils brutal with hatred, the murdering eyes. He filled my mind with a sweet-tasting mountain rain, his youthfulness, his modesty as he washed himself all alone, his religious face.

For a long time now this morning, I have been sitting at this window and watching the grass below me. A moment ago there was no one there. But now his brindle shell sighs slowly up and down in the midst of the green sunlight. A black watchdog snuffles asleep just beyond him, but I trust that neither is afraid of the other. I can see him lifting his face. It is a raising of eyebrows toward the light, an almost imperceptible turning of the chin, an ancient pleasure, an eagerness.

Along his throat there are small folds, dark yellow as pollen shaken across a field of camomilla. The lines on his face suggest only a relaxation, a delicacy in the understanding of the grass, like the careful tenderness I saw once on the face of a hobo in Ohio as he waved greeting to an empty wheat field from the flatcar of a freight train.

But now the train is gone, and the turtle has left his circle of empty grass. I look a long time where he was, and I can't find a footprint in the empty grass. So much air left, so much sunlight, and still he is gone.

The Sumac in Ohio

Toward the end of May, the air in Southern Ohio is filling with fragrances, and I am a long way from home. A great place lies open in the earth there in Martins Ferry near the river, and to this day I don't know how it came to be. Maybe the old fathers of my town, their white hair lost long since into the coal smoke and the snow, gathered in their hundreds along the hither side of the B&O railroad track, presented whatever blades and bull tongues they could spare, and tore the earth open. Or maybe the gully appeared there on its own, long before the white-haired fathers came, and the Ohio changed its direction, and the glacier went away.

But now toward the end of May, the sumac trees on the slopes of the gully are opening their brindle buds, and suddenly, right before my eyes, the tough leaf branches turn a bewildering scarlet just at the place where they join the bough. You can strip the long leaves away already, but the leaf branch is more thoroughly rooted into the tree than the trunk itself is into the ground.

Before June begins, the sap and coal smoke and soot from Wheeling steel, wafted down the Ohio by some curious gentleness in the Appalachians, will gather all over the trunk. The skin will turn aside hatchets and knife blades. You cannot even carve a girl's name on the sumac. It is viciously determined to live and die alone, and you can go straight to hell.

Reading a 1979 Inscription on Belli's Monument

It is not only the Romans who are gone.
Belli, unhappy a century ago,
Won from the world his fashionable stone.
Where it stands now, he doesn't even know.
Across the Tiber, near Trastevere,
His top hat teetered on his head with care,
Brushed like a gentleman, he cannot see
The latest Romans who succeed him there.

One of them bravely climbed his pedestal
And sprayed a scarlet MERDA on his shawl.
This afternoon, I pray his hidden grave
Lies nameless somewhere in the hills, while rain
Fusses and frets to rinse away the stain.
Rain might erase when marble cannot save.

Contemplating the Front Steps of the Cathedral in Florence as the Century Dies

Once, in some hill trees long ago,
A red-tailed hawk paused
Long enough to look me over

Halfway down the air.
He held still, and plainly
Said, go.
It was no time
For singing about the beauties of nature,
And I went fast.
I stubbed my toe
On a rock hidden by the big wing-shadows,
But the small wound
Was worth paying for.
I got one glimpse of him,
Alive, before I die.
And that is all I know
About his body.

It would be easy
To touch the snaggle of infected meat
In front of me now.
But the blowflies
Have got to it first.
The maggots have burrowed
Up one collapsing thigh.
The body, even in death,
Flinches and hides one wing
Behind it, but already
A mass of slick green beetles
Have crawled around there.
I do not want to join them, I want
To leave the last wing
Alone to the beetles and the maggots.
Let them have Giotto's long wing stretched out in the terrible
        sunlight.
Maybe they will rend one another
And explode.

Wherever Home Is

Leonardo da Vinci, haggard in basalt stone,
Will soon be gone,

A frivolous face lost in wisteria flowers.
They are turning gray and dying
All over his body.
Subtlest of all wanderers
Who live beautifully by living on other lives,
They cannot find a warm vein
In Leonardo, and Leonardo
Himself will soon
Be gone.

Good riddance a little while to the insane.
Although the wisteria gets nowhere
And the sea wind crumbles Leonardo down,
A new lizard frolics in the cold sunlight
Between Leonardo's thumb and his palette.
One brief lizard
Lavishes on Leonardo and on me
The whole spring.

Goodbye to Leonardo, good riddance
To decaying madmen who cannot keep alive
The wanderers among trees.
I am going home with the lizard,
Wherever home is,
And lie beside him unguarded
In the clear sunlight.
We will lift our faces even if it rains.
We will both turn green.

A Dark Moor Bird

A dark moor bird has come down from the mountains
To test the season.
He flies low across the Adige and seines
The brilliant web of his shadow behind him.
Slender and sure,
His wings give him the nobility
Of a small swan.
But his voice

Ruins it, he has seen me and he can't
Shut up about it.
He sounds
Like a plump chicken nagging a raccoon
Who is trying to get out of the henhouse
With a little dignity.

I wonder why the beautiful moor bird
Won't leave me alone.
All I am doing is standing here,
Turning to stone,
Believing he will build a strong nest
Along the Adige, hoping
He will never die.

Notes of a Pastoralist

In a field outside of Pisa, I saw a shepherd
Keeping warm from a late autumn day.
Blown a little
To one side by the cooling sunlight,
He leaned as though a good tree were holding
His body upright.
But the nearest cypresses
Were standing a long way off,
And it seemed that only his green umbrella
Held him there.
His sheep did not flock together
As they do in Spenser and Theocritus.
They ambled all over the slope
Too old to care
Or too young to know they were posing
For the notes
Of a jaded pastoralist.
If the shepherd had a tune,
I stood too far away to hear it.
I hope he sang to himself. I didn't feel
Like paying him to sing.

The Vestal in the Forum

This morning I do not despair
For the impersonal hatred that the cold
Wind seems to feel
When it slips fingers into the flaws
Of lovely things men made,
The shoulders of a stone girl
Pitted by winter.
Not a spring passes but the roses
Grow stronger in their support of the wind,
And now they are conquerors,
Not garlands any more,
Of this one face:
Dimming,
Clearer to me than most living faces.
The slow wind and the slow roses
Are ruining an eyebrow here, a mole there.
But in this little while
Before she is gone, her very haggardness
Amazes me. A dissolving
Stone, she seems to change from stone to something
Frail, to someone I can know, someone
I can almost name.

In View of the Protestant Cemetery in Rome

It is idle to say
The wind will blow your fingers all away
And scatter small blue knucklebones upon
The ground from hell to breakfast and beyond.
You will sit listening till I am gone
To seed among the pear trees. For my voice
Sprinkles a few light petals on this pond,
And you nod sagely, saying I am wise.
Your fingers toss their white cocoons and rise
Lightly and lightly brush against my face:
Alive still, in this violated place,

Idle as any deed that Cestius did,
Vanished beneath his perfect pyramid.

Above San Fermo

Somehow I have never lost
That feeling of astonished flight,
When the breath of my body suddenly
Becomes visible.

I might be standing beside a black snowdrift
in Ohio, where the railroad gravel
And the mill smoke that gets everything in the end
Reveal the true colors
Of a bewildered winter.
When I lit a match and breathed there,
A solitary batwing sailed out of my mouth
And hovered, fluttering.
All the way over to West Virginia
And beyond.

Even now,
Abandoned beside the abandoned battlements
Above the Adige, above
San Fermo, a hand waves over my lungs.
The demon leaps out
And takes off his hand-me-down jacket.
He strolls downhill
In the warm Italian sunlight, as though
He didn't care to choose between winter and spring.
But spring will do him all right,
For the time being.

A Reply to Matthew Arnold on My Fifth Day in Fano

*"In harmony with Nature? Restless fool . . . Nature and man
can never be fast friends. . . ."*

It is idle to speak of five mere days in Fano, or five long days, or five years. As I prepare to leave, I seem to have just arrived. To carefully split yet another infinitive, I seem to have been here forever or longer, longer than the sea's lifetime and the lifetimes of all the creatures of the sea, than all the new churches among the hill pastures and all the old shells wandering about bodiless just off the clear shore. Briefly in harmony with nature before I die, I welcome the old curse:

a restless fool and a fast friend to Fano, I have brought this wild chive flower down from a hill pasture. I offer it to the Adriatic. I am not about to claim that the sea does not care. It has its own way of receiving seeds, and today the sea may as well have a flowering one, with a poppy to float above it, and the Venetian navy underneath. Goodbye to the living place, and all I ask it to do is stay alive.

Petition to the Terns

I have lived long enough to see
Many wings fall
And many others broken and driven
To stagger away on a slant
Of wind. It blows
Where it pleases to blow,
Or it poises,
Unaccountably,
At rest. Today, sails
Don't move.
In the water,
In front of my eyes,
The huge dull scarlet men-of-war loll, uncaring and slobbish,
And stain
All the shore shallows
That men might hope to become

Green among.
The sea
Is already unfriendly.
The terns of Rhode Island
Dart up out of the cattails, pounce on the sunlight,
Claim it,
And attack.
They must be getting their own back,
Against the wind. But the wind is no angrier
Than any wing it blows down,
And I wish the terns would give it
And me a break.

In Gallipoli

Gray as the sea moss wavering among the green shallows along
the shore, her hair blows shaggy. The sky holds. She lifts a cluster
of grapes, aloof and strangely sacred in their frost, and urges them
on me. Forty years ago, her young man, as gray and unaware as an
English butterfly blinded by fog, fluttered amazed across this ce-
rulean light, sagged, and exploded. I select two or three purple
grapes, and one of them bursts inside my mouth. But they are not
nearly enough for her to give, and she urges me on and on, till all
she holds in her fingers is the hulled branch of the vine. It sways
like a tree set on fire and thrown into water. She looks into the sky.
It holds. All her offerings are gone.

The Limpet in Otranto

These limpets have lain empty and bodiless for long years now.
Flecks of brown gold gather on their slopes like old flowers on hills
at the end of autumn. They shine, even when the sun has gone
down. Virgil approached them and listened inside them. But their
caves were too shallow and bright to contain any ghosts. Their bodies
were already gone a long time into the air. Cloud shadows and the
shadows of scarred headlands fell all over the old man's shoulders,
like oak leaves, the old everlasting bronzes of November, the tragic

sea-faces of the trees in North Carolina, that tremble and grow older all through the year, but never fall. Caressing the inner side of a limpet with one finger, Virgil turned back inland. The purple of thistles aristocratically brushed his knees aside. He heard a voice in a tree, crying in Greek, "Italy. Italy." He listened again to the limpet in his hand. It said nothing.

Apollo

A young man, his face dark
With the sea's fire,
Quickens his needle bone through webbing,
And passes away.
He moves out of my sight
And back again, as the moon
Braces its shoulders and disappears
And appears again. The young face
Begins to turn gray
In the evening light that cannot
Make up for loss.
It is morning and evening again, all over the water.
I know it is only moonlight that changes him, I know
It does not matter. The sea's fire
Is only the cold shadow of the moon's,
And the moon's
Fire itself only the cold
Shadow of the young
Fisherman's face:
The only home where now, alone in the evening,
The god stays alive.

May Morning

Deep into spring, winter is hanging on. Bitter and skillful in his hopelessness, he stays alive in every shady place, starving along the Mediterranean: angry to see the glittering sea-pale boulder alive with lizards green as Judas leaves. Winter is hanging on. He still believes. He tries to catch a lizard by the shoulder. One olive tree below Grottaglie welcomes the winter into noontime shade, and talks as softly as Pythagoras. Be still, be patient, I can hear him say, cradling in his arms the wounded head, letting the sunlight touch the savage face.

A True Voice

for Robert Bly

In northern Minnesota the floors of the earth are covered with white sand. Even after the sun has gone down beyond the pine trees and the moon has not yet come across the lake water, you can walk down white roads. The dark is a dark you can see beyond, into a deep place here and there. Whatever light there is left, it has room enough to move around in. The tall thick pines have all disappeared after the sun. That is why the small blue spruces look so friendly when your eyes feel at home in the dark. I never touched a blue spruce before the moon came, for fear it would say something in a false voice. You can only hear a spruce tree speak in its own silence.

Chilblain

My uncle Willy with his long lecherous face
Once told me wisely:
Over in France in them cathouses
In the big war,
They used to sell a salve,
That you squeezed on the inside
Of your forefinger knuckle,
And it spread all over.
Sure, it didn't cure chilblain.
But it stung so bad it took
Your mind off your troubles.

He snickered darkly, without sound,
The proud man's wisdom.

Willy the liar is buried in Colrain,
And every time in dreams I see him there
The violets and snowflakes run
Together, till all June
Earth smokes like slag.
Violets and snowflakes gather, gather
In a mock caress,
And Willy's stone clenches shut like a young man's hand
Frightened of France and winter.
Before I wake, the stone remembers
Where it is, where Ohio is,
Where violets last only a little.
Mill-smoke kills them halfway through spring,
And chilblain still stings
In June when earth smokes like slag.

Coming Home to Maui

It took her an hour to climb the green cliff here.
She rose as the light rose. Now,
On this small pinnacle, the long-legged brown girl,
American from Chicago, places
One glittering opihi shell,
Bony with light,
Into my pale hand.

One afternoon in the dark howling
Of ice off Lake Michigan,
She blundered into a bewildered young man,
A Hawaiian lost on State Street.
So she brought him home.

Now, as we stand here, the young man searches
Below us, down, into the ocean.
He is hunting for shellfish
Among the strange trees.
He brings the opihi home in the evening,
And she shines them.

He makes a living
Grounging under water before sunrise and after.
He turns home toward the woman,
He turns the dark creatures of his ocean
Over to the woman,
And soon they shine.

Years ago, far from home, I came to these islands.
I had rolled, puking in a dark shell,
A troopship, all of two nights.
Then, when I woke,
It was hard to believe the earth
Could be lived on at all, much less the beautiful

Home of this woman's hands, home of this light.
And yet here it is, this green cliff where she rose,
The home of this light.

Against Surrealism

There are some tiny obvious details in human life that survive the divine purpose of boring fools to death. In France, all the way down south in Avallon, people like to eat cake. The local bakers there spin up a little flour and chocolate into the shape of a penguin. We came back again and again to a certain window to admire a flock of them. But we never bought one.

We found ourselves wandering through Italy, homesick for penguins.

Then a terrible and savage fire of the dog-days roared all over the fourteenth arondissement: which is to say, it was August: and three chocolate penguins appeared behind a window near Place Denfert-Rochereau. We were afraid the Parisians would recognize them, so we bought them all and snuck them home under cover.

We set them out on a small table above half the rooftops of Paris. I reached out to brush a tiny obvious particle of dust from the tip of a beak. Suddenly the dust dropped an inch and hovered there. Then it rose to the beak again.

It was a blue spider.

If I were a blue spider, I would certainly ride on a train all the way from Avallon to Paris, and I would set up my house on the nose of a chocolate penguin. It's just a matter of common sense.

The Ice House

The house was really a cellar deep beneath the tower of the old Belmont Brewery. My father's big shoulders heaved open the door from the outside, and from within the big shoulders of the ice-man leaned and helped. The slow door gave. My brother and I walked in delighted by our fear, and laid our open palms on the wet yellow sawdust. Outside the sun blistered the paint on the corrugated roofs of the shacks by the railroad; but we stood and breathed the rising steam of that amazing winter, and carried away in our wagon the immense fifty-pound diamond, while the old man chipped us each a jagged little chunk and then walked behind us, his hands so calm they were trembling for us, trembling with exquisite care.

The Journey

Anghiari is medieval, a sleeve sloping down
A steep hill, suddenly sweeping out
To the edge of a cliff, and dwindling.
But far up the mountain, behind the town,
We too were swept out, out by the wind,
Alone with the Tuscan grass.

Wind had been blowing across the hills
For days, and everything now was graying gold
With dust, everything we saw, even
Some small children scampering along a road,
Twittering Italian to a small caged bird.

We sat beside them to rest in some brushwood,
And I leaned down to rinse the dust from my face.

I found the spider web there, whose hinges
Reeled heavily and crazily with the dust,
Whole mounds and cemeteries of it, sagging
And scattering shadows among shells and wings.
And then she stepped into the center of air
Slender and fastidious, the golden hair
Of daylight along her shoulders, she poised there,
While ruins crumbled on every side of her.
Free of the dust, as though a moment before
She had stepped inside the earth, to bathe herself.

I gazed, close to her, till at last she stepped
Away in her own good time.

Many men
Have searched all over Tuscany and never found
What I found there, the heart of the light
Itself shelled and leaved, balancing
On filaments themselves falling. The secret
Of this journey is to let the wind
Blow its dust all over your body,
To let it go on blowing, to step lightly, lightly
All the way through your ruins, and not to lose
Any sleep over the dead, who surely
Will bury their own, don't worry.

Young Women at Chartres

In memory of Jean Garrigue

> . . . like a thief I followed her
> Though my heart was so alive
> I thought it equal to that beauty.
> —"The Stranger"

ONE

Halfway through morning
Lisa, herself blossoming, strolls
Lazily beneath the eastern roses

In the shadow of Chartres.
She does not know
She is visible.
As she lifts her face
Toward the northwest,
Mothwings fall down and rest on her hair.
She darkens
Without knowing it, as the wind blows on down toward the river
Where the cathedral, last night,
Sank among reeds.

TWO

Fog
Rinses away for a little while the cold
Christs with their suffering faces.
Mist
Leaves to us solitary friends of the rain
The happy secret angel
On the north corner.

THREE

You lived so abounding with mist and wild strawberries,
So faithful with the angel in the rain,
You kept faith to a stranger.
Now, Jean, your musical name poises in the webs
Of wheatfield and mist,
And beneath the molded shadow of the local stones,
I hear you again, singing beneath the northwest
Angel who holds in her arms
Sunlight on sunlight.
She is equal
To you, to her own happy face, she is holding
A sundial in her arms. No wonder Christ was happy
Among women's faces.

To the Cicada

Anacreon

A few minutes ago
I got up out of the burlap rags somebody

Flung last night into the corner
Of the stone floor.

I am standing here in the field.
I have got my back turned on the whitewashed wall of the house.
The sunlight glances off it and flays
The back of my neck.

It's not yet noon,
But noon is gathering and solidifying,
Splotching my shoulders.
My eyelids weigh ten pounds. Nevertheless,
I lift them open with my fingers.
It's hard to bend the joints.

But there it is,
On the other side of the field,
The water barrel, the only real thing
Left in the shadow.
I can see the rust-stained bung dribbling
Its cold slaver down the curved slats,
Squiggling into black muck beneath
The barbed-wire fence.

Here, now,
Sick of the dry dirt, the southern barrenness,
The Ohio hillside twenty-five miles lost
Away from the river,
I feel my shoulders grow heavier and heavier,
And the dead corn-blades coiling,
Stinging my thighs.
Here,
Just as in the airless corner
Of the barn over the hill
The disinfected hooks stand arranged
Along one wall at head height,
Where the farmer has screwed them in;
Just there where he'd hung them after he'd finished
Dusting out the doorway, hopelessly scattering
Stray wheat beards, tiny dry blossoms of hay,
Mouse droppings, cow pies jagged and cruel
As old gravestones knocked down and scarred faceless;

And just as the meat hooks, gleaming softly, hold
Long sidemeat crusted with salt and the dull hams
Gone rigid with smoke,
And the hooks creak as the meat sags, just so
My bones sag and hold up
The flesh of my body.

Still, now, I hear you, singing,
A lightness beginning among the dark crevices,
In the underbark of the locust, beyond me,
The other edge of the field.
A lightness,
You begin tuning up for your time,
Twilight, that belongs to you, deeper and cooler beyond
The barbed wire of this field, even beyond
The Ohio River twenty-five miles away,
Where the Holy Rollers rage all afternoon
And all evening among the mud cracks,
The polluted shore, their voices splintering
Like beetles' wings in a hobo jungle fire,
Their voices heavy as blast furnace fumes, their brutal
Jesus risen but dumb.

But you, lightness,
Light flesh singing lightly,
Trembling in perfect balance on the underbark,
The locust tree of the southeast, you, friendly
To whatever sings in me as it climbs and holds on
Among the damp brambles:

You, lightness,
How were you born in this place, this heavy stone
Plummeting into the stars?
And still you are here. One morning
I found you asleep on a locust root, and carefully
I breathed on your silver body speckled with brown
And held you a while in my palm
And let you sleep.
You, lightness, kindlier than my human body,
Yet somehow friendly to the music in my body,
I let you sleep, one of the gods who will rise
Without being screamed at.

Lightning Bugs Asleep
in the Afternoon

These long-suffering and affectionate shadows,
These fluttering jewels, are trying to get
Some sleep in a dry shade beneath the cement
Joists of the railroad trestle.

I did not climb up here to find them.
It was only my ordinary solitude
I was following up here this afternoon.
Last evening I sat here with a girl.

It was a dangerous place to be a girl
And young. But she simply folded her silent
Skirt over bare knees, printed with the flowered cotton
Of a meal sack her mother had stitched for her.

Neither of us said anything to speak of.
These affectionate, these fluttering bodies
Signaled to one another under the bridge
While the B&O 40-and-8's rattled away.

Now ordinary and alone in the afternoon,
I find this little circle of insects
Common as soot, clustering on dim stone,
Together with their warm secrets.

I think I am going to leave them folded
And sleeping in their slight gray wings.
I think I am going to climb back down
And open my eyes and shine.

Greetings in New York City

A man walking alone, a stranger
In a strange forest,
Plucks his way carefully among brambles.
He ploughs the spider pits.

He is awake and lonely in the midday,
The jungle of the sun.

He steps out of the snaggle, naked.

A hundred yards away,
One more stranger steps out of the dank vines,
Into the clearing.

Nothing is alone any more.

Two alone, two hours, they poise there,
Afraid, gazing across.

Then,
The green masses behind one shoulder
Cluster their grapes together,
And they become night. And by night each stranger
Turns back into a tree and lies down,
A root, alone.

Sleepless by dawn,
One rises
And finds the other already awake,
Gazing.
Weary,
He lifts his hand and shades his eyes.

Startled,
He touches his chin.
The other stranger across the distance
Touches his chin.
He pauses, then leans down,
And lifts a stone.
The other stranger leans down
And lifts a stone.

All the long morning
They edge the clearing
With little patterns of stones.
Sometimes they balance
Three pebbles on boulders

Or patterns of stars.
Or they lay out new flowers
In circles
Or little gatherings of faces
That neither stranger
Had ever seen.

And then, when noon comes,
Each stranger
Has no room left in the light
Except for only his hands.
Here are mine. They are kind of skinny. May I have your
      lovely trees?

To the Silver Sword Shining on the Edge of the Crater

Strange leaves on Haleakala,
My torn home,
You have no family among orchids, African tulips.
Or plumeria and their children.

Yet you lift your face
Ten thousand feet above trees here, and trees here
Are also strange presences among the rest.
We rend one another.

Opening on one of the highest pinnacles
Of light we have left,
You look like a lonesomeness
From somewhere else.

I am not a stranger here.
I stand beside you and gaze over ninety miles of water.
Not long ago, many young men golden in the light of the human
      body
Killed one another so horribly

They bloated the azure ocean
Into a brilliant scarlet shadow.
O lovely stranger, sometimes in this place we do not even allow
The night to heal us.

Whoever you are,
Who may have made some kind gesture
To me on my earth, you are welcome
To me and mine.

Look, I bring you a wild thing,
A token of welcome, a withered thing,
A human hand. Sometimes the strange creatures
Ten thousand feet below us who somehow

Go on living near waters
Give these things to each other.
And sometimes things like these go searching
Along dark paths, and find trees there,

And blossoms in tall rain.

With the Gift of an Alabaster Tortoise

One afternoon, we stole
Away, we two, around
The whole wall of Arezzo,
A town of golden shadow.
Behind one wall, we found
One lizard, who was whole.

You led me to that place
Where I had never gone.
No, where I'd had no song
Nor prayer of anything.
You stood, still on the stone.
You touched my face.

I gazed at the green shoulder
And the golden long tail,
Magnificent, and quick.
I stood low in the thick
Pines of Arezzo, still
As Dante, and no older.

What the air sang me then
Was simple, and enough:
No, I would never find
How far God's terrible wind
Could whirl me out of love,
Across, or up, or down.

That lizard, green and gone,
Still lives his life among
Those crevices ago.
Would I have caught him? No.
I listened to the song
You sang, still on the stone.

I let time pass, and went
Alone up a long hill,
Volterra, the tawny city
Trembling above Tuscany,
Where the air hovered still
Like a dumb lament.

Behind your back, I found
A stone some girl had molded
And polished into this
Small alabaster tortoise;
I carried it, and folded
Your voice, and made no sound.

The living lizard stays
Far off in Arezzo,
While now this little stone
Waits for your hand alone
To warm its Casentino
And lift its face.

You will raise it above
That Casentino where
The air sings beyond song.
It will shine among
Your glittering hands in the air
And then it will move.

Small Wild Crabs
Delighting on Black Sand

Nearsighted, I feel a kinship
With these clear shadows.
They scatter, gather, scatter
All around my bare feet.

Two, who feel like two,
Sketch quick faces on my insteps.
Who are they? I don't want to know.
I want to see.

Why do these creatures come out to be
Family to me?
I am not in the water yet.
I wait a little.

Do they want to know me?
I have no more faces to give them
Than the moon has,
Scattering the eight fastidious feet of its light

Around the mountain behind my shoulder,
And now these small shoulders
And faces that seem
Not afraid of me.

Maybe they like to feel
Some warm voice
Singing out of my skin.
Why else would they touch me?

I don't know any language either.
But I hope
They can hear me, singing,
They owe me nothing.

But I believe them, I believe them:
These nearsighted gatherers of one another's flowers.
They touch my flinching instep, but now they float all the way
        across
The mauve mountain of the evening to rest on the little hill,
Your ankle. And now they are gone. And they do not laugh.

But you do,
My delight, whom I can see
In the dark.

Ohioan Pastoral

On the other side
Of Salt Creek, along the road, the barns topple
And snag among the orange rinds,
Oil cans, cold balloons of lovers.
One barn there
Sags, sags and oozes
Down one side of the copperous gully.
The limp whip of a sumac dangles
Gently against the body of a lost
Bathtub, while high in the flint-cracks
And the wild grimed trees, on the hill,
A buried gas main
Long ago tore a black gutter into the mines.
And now it hisses among the green rings
On fingers in coffins.

The Fox at Eype

   He knows that all dogs bounding here and there, from the little
vales all the way to the cliff-meadows and Thorncombe Beacon and

beyond, are domestically forbidden to kill him. So every evening just before the end of twilight he emerges softly from the hedge across the lane and sits elegantly till darkness, gazing, with a certain weary amusement, into the middle distance of the sea.

Fresh Wind in Venice

North of one island
Where the tall tenements of old Jews freed by Napoleon
Loom and grieve stubbornly,

I found the fine gauze of willow that gathers.
It is the sea's fragrance that gathers
Me, heavily, more and more.

Out of this city, a slippery gathering
Of cities left empty, I went up there
North of one island,

And it is no use to try to gather
Anything new out of Venice, even the sea,
Even the dark eyes of the faces.

The only thing new in it is the light gathers
Gauze on willow
North of one island.

North of the city where factories
Murder the sun and what is left of the city
I found the sea gathering.

I found the sea gathering
All that was left.

Butterfly Fish

Not five seconds ago, I saw him flutter so quick
And tremble with so mighty a trembling,

He was gone.
He left this clear depth of coral
Between his moments.
Now, he is here, back,
Slow and lazy.
He knows already he is so alive he can leave me alone,
Peering down, holding his empty mountains.
Happy in easy luxury, he grazes up his tall corals,
Slim as a stallion, serene on his far-off hillside,
His other world where I cannot see
His secret face.

Entering the Kingdom of the Moray Eel

There is no mystery in it so far
As I can see here.
Now the sun has gone down
Some little globules of mauve and beige still cling
Among coconuts and mangoes along the shore.
Over my right shoulder I glimpse a quick light.

I can believe in the moon stirring
Behind the hill at my back.
Before me, this small bay,
A beginning of the kingdom,
Opens its own half-moon.

Solitary,
Nearly naked, now,
I move in up to my knees.
Beneath the surface two shadows
Seem to move. But I know
They do not move.
They are only two small reefs of coral.

Some time this evening the moray eel will wake up
And swim from one reef to the other.
For now, this pathway of sand under water
Shines clear to me. I lift up my feet

And let the earth shift for itself.
Vicious, cold-blooded among his night branches,
The moray eel lets me
Shift for myself.
He is not going to visit his palaces
In my sight, he is not going to dance
Attention on the brief amazement of my life.
He is not going to surrender the spendid shadow
Of his throne. Not for my sake. Not even
To kill me.

At Peace with the Ocean
off Misquamicut

A million rootlets
Shifting their dunes
Quiver a little on the deep
Clavicles of some body,
Down there, awhile.
It is still asleep, it is the Atlantic,
A stingray drowsing his fill of sunlight, a molting angel
Breathing the grateful water,
Praying face downward to a god I am afraid
To imagine.
What will I do when the stingray
And the angel
Wake?
Whose mercy am I going to throw
Myself upon?
When even the Atlantic Ocean
Is nothing more than
My brother the stingray.

In Memory of Mayor Richard Daley

When you get down to it,
It, which is the edge of town,

You find a slab of gritstone
Face down in the burned stubble, the stinkweed,
The sumac, the elderberry.
Everything has gone out of the blossoms except the breath
Of rust from the railroad tracks.

And there in the river's graveyard
Nobody moves any more but you and me.
Ironweeds hunch up and live a long time, a strange forever.
They don't fall on the gravestones even in spring.
They don't fall in winter.
They go on living like the mystery
Of cancer.

One evening,
John Woods and somebody else and I
Killed the Chevy motor down home
There, just above the singed-out brambles.
The citizens of the United States called that place
The Mill Field, that desolation, because
Some rum-bum back in the Depression flung
His last Bugler into the dead
Sawdust there.

We were there to sing drunk.
But a Model T got
Between us and the B&O
And the Bareass Beach down the hill
And the river.

Halfway down the gouged bank
We found a flat gravestone
Nameless.
But we know the lost name.

When you get down to it,
It, on the edge of town,
You find this face.
It is a precious thing.
I took a good hard look at it
Before it was gone.
I can't get away from it.

This face fills me with grief as I sing to myself
In my sleep: Remember, remember
This is what you're up against.

Lament: Fishing with Richard Hugo

If John Updike had been
Ed Bedford, his wife
Zetta would have called
Goose Prairie something high-toned.
Swan Meadow? The Ironic
Byronic Paradox in two
Eleatic heuristic footnotes?
Ed's dank tavern might have become
The Puce Nook, featuring
A menu illuminated by Doris Day,
With Updike composing the prose
Of Howard Johnson, accompanying himself
On an oboe, singing of tender
Succulent golden
French fries.

But now, though the hills around Goose Prairie
Are full of voices, nobody echoes
The rasping hinge of Zetta's quick cackle
Nor the slow sighs of Ed Bedford
Breaking the wind at dusk.
And I miss the unhorned
Elk that drifted across
The other side of Goose Prairie
Into pines that evening so long ago:
When Ed Bedford charged double for beer,
The pink flesh of trout from the Bumping River
Turned into you, and Howard's prose
Rendered into fish fat
And drifted, drifted
Over white water.

Sheep in the Rain

In Burgundy, beyond Auxerre
And all the way down the river to Avallon,
The grass lies thick with sheep
Shorn only a couple of days ago.
They shine all over their plump bodies
In the June mist.

Sheep eat everything
All the way down to the roots.
And maybe that is why
These explorers of the rain
Seem so relaxed in their browsing.
Someone has freed them only a little while
Into the fields, and they have a good life of it
While it lasts.

Burgundian farmers will return
Some morning soon,
And flock the fat sheep down a wall
Into glittering rocks.
Then a boy will go alone back into the grass
And care for the grass.
The farmers are kind to the grass.
They have to be.

A Flower Passage

In memory of Joe Shank, the diver

Even if you were above the ground this year,
You would not know my face.
One of the small boys, one of the briefly green,
I prowled with the others along the Ohio,
Raised hell in the B&O boxcars after dark,
And sometimes in the evening
Chawed the knots out of my trousers
On the river bank, while the other
Children of blast furnace and mine

Fought and sang in the channel-current,
Daring the Ohio.

Shepherd of the dead, one of the tall men,
I did not know your face.
One summer dog day after another,
You rose and gathered your gear
And slogged downhill of the river ditch to dive
Into the blind channel. You dragged your hooks
All over the rubble sludge and lifted
The twelve-year bones.

Now you are dead and turned over
To the appropriate authorities, Christ
Have mercy on me, I would come to the funeral home
If I were home
In Martins Ferry, Ohio.
I would bring to your still face a dozen
Modest and gaudy carnations.

But I am not home in my place
Where I was born and my friends drowned.
So I dream of you, mourning.
I walk down the B&O track
Near the sewer main.
And there I gather, and here I gather
The flowers I only know best.
The spring leaves of the sumac
Stink only a little less worse
Than the sewer main, and up above that gouged hill
Where somebody half-crazy tossed a cigarette
Straight down into a pile of sawdust
In the heart of the LaBelle Lumber Company,
There, on the blank mill field, it is the blind and tough
Fireweeds I gather and bring home.
To you, for my drowned friends, I offer
The true sumac, and the foul trillium
Whose varicose bloom swells the soil with its bruise;
And a little later, I bring
The still totally unbelievable spring beauty
That for some hidden reason nobody raped
To death in Ohio.

Your Name in Arezzo

Five years ago I gouged it after dark
Against a little crippled olive's bark.
Somebody there, four, three, two years since then
Scattered the olives back to earth again.
Last summer in the afternoon I took
One tine, and hollowed out your name in rock,
A little one someone had left behind
The Duomo at the mercy of the wind.
The wind, as always sensitive to prayer,
Listened to mine, and left my pebble there,
Lifted your glistening name to some great height
And polished it to nothing overnight.
If the old olive wind will not receive
A name from me, even a name I love,
Fragile among Italian silences,
Your name, your pilgrim following cypresses,
I leave it to the sunlight, like the one
Landor the master left his voice upon.

Dawn near an Old Battlefield, in a Time of Peace

Along the water the small invisible owls
Have fallen asleep in the poplars.
Standing alone here downshore on the river Yonne,
I can see only one young man pausing
Halfway over the stone bridge,
At peace with Auxerre.

How can he call to mind now
The thing he has never known:
One owl wing
Splayed in the morning wheat?
This young man
Sees only ripples on the Yonne.

How can he call to mind now,
And how can I,

His fathers, my fathers, crawling
Blind into the grain,
Scrambling among the scorched owls
And rats' wings for food?

All the young fathers
Are gone now. Mercy
On the young man
Who cannot call to mind now
The torn faces in the field.

Mercy on the pure Yonne washing his face in the water.

Mercy on me.

A Fishing Song

I have never killed anybody
Except a gopher, and some fish.
I blatted fine gold hair all over hell's half acre
With a shotgun beside a road.
And one fish among many, a sunfish, I liked.
I cut his throat, and I ate him.
Whatever is left of the gopher's little ratface,
So far more sensitive than a song-thrush's face
When you see it up close,
Blows on a prairie somewhere.
Minnesota's dead animals are too many
For me to remember.
Yet I live with and caress the body
Of the sunfish. One out of many,
I caught him out of sheer accidental daring
As he tried to hide in the sunlight.
Leaping toward the Marsh Lake Dam,
He pretended he was merely a little splinter
In the general noon.
I knew better about his life.
Sweet plum, little shadow, he feeds my brother,
My own shadow.

On Having My Pocket Picked in Rome

These hands are desperate for me to stay alive. They do not want to lose me to the crowd. They know the slightest nudge on the wrong bone will cause me to look around and cry aloud. Therefore the hands grow cool and touch me lightly, lightly and accurately as a gypsy moth laying her larvae down in that foregone place where the tree is naked. It is only when the hands are gone, I will step out of this crowd and walk down the street, dimly aware of the dark infant strangers I carry in my body. They spin their nests and live on me in their sleep.

A Finch Sitting Out a Windstorm

Solemnly irritated by the turn
The cold air steals,
He puffs out his most fragile feathers,
His breast down,
And refuses to move.
If I were he,
I would not clamp my claws so stubbornly around
The skinny branch.
I would not keep my tiny glitter
Fixed over my beak, or return
The glare of the wind.
Too many Maytime snowfalls have taught me
The wisdom of hopelessness.

But the damned fool
Squats there as if he owned
The earth, bought and paid for.
Oh, I could advise him plenty
About his wings. Give up, drift,
Get out.

But his face is as battered
As Carmen Basilio's.
He never listens
To me.

Caprice

Whenever I get tired
Of human faces,
I look for trees.
I know there must be something
Wrong, either with me or Italy,
The south of the angels.
Nevertheless, I get away
Among good trees, there are
So many. The trouble is
They keep turning faces toward me
That I recognize:

Just north of Rome
An ilex and an olive tangled
Their roots together and stood one afternoon,
Caught in a ring of judas
And double cherry.
They glared at me, so bitter
With something they knew,
I shivered. They knew
What I knew:
One of those brilliant skeletons
Was going to shed her garlands
One of these days and turn back
Into a girl
Again.

Then we were all going to be
Sorry together.

A Rainbow on Garda

The storm crawls down,
Dissolving the distances
Of the mountain as though
They were nothing.

The rain already
Hangs a gray shawl
In front of Bardolino.

The town is gone:

In the darkness of evening,
The darkness of high stone,
And a black swallow folding
Its face in one wing.

I too am ready
To fold my face.
I am used to night, the gray wall
Where swallows lie still.

But I am not ready for light
Where no light was,
Bardolino risen from the dead, blazing
A scarlet feather inside a wing.

Every fool in the world can see this thing,
And make no more
Of it than of Christ, frightened and dying
In the air, one wing broken, all alone.

My Notebook

This friendly shadow of pine leaves
Goes by my side.
Its hands lie open to me on tables
When doors close.

Whenever I grow tired of speaking
And my dry lungs
Want only to hover still in my body,
It nods like rain.

The kindest moment it gave me came
One white afternoon:
The sun blanched all the walls in Grottaglie,
That southernmost olive.

Some nervous splinter
Worked under my skin.
I skinned my lips back to say something murderous,
Some savage thing.

It opened its pages
And showed me what it had:
Half of my name clear, the rest
Almost gone.

Streaked in a green stain,
An insect had flown in,
Quiet on the white leaf, paying
My name no mind.

Leave Him Alone

The trouble with me is
I worry too much about things that should be
Left alone.
The rain-washed stone beside the Adige where
The lizard used to lie in the sun
Will warm him again
In its own time, whether time itself
Be good or bad.
I sit on a hill
Far from Verona, knowing the vanity
Of trying to steal unaware on the lizards in the evening.
No matter how quickly
I pounce
Or slowly creep among the low evergreens
At the bend of the water,
He will be there
Or not there, just as

The sunlight pleases him.
The last feather of light fallen lazily down
Floats across the Adige and rests a long moment
On his lifted face.

Regret for a Spider Web

Laying the foundations of community, she labors all alone. Whether or not God made a creature as deliberately green as this spider, I am not the one to say. If not, then He tossed a star of green dust into one of my lashes. A moment ago, there was no spider there. I must have been thinking about something else, maybe the twenty-mile meadows along the slopes of the far-off mountain I was trying to name, or the huge snows clinging up there in summer, with their rivulets exploding into roots of ice when the night comes down. But now all the long distances are gone. Not quite three inches from my left eyelash, the air is forming itself into avenues, back alleys, boulevards, paths, gardens, fields, and one frail towpath shimmering as it leads away into the sky.

Where is she?

I can't find her.

Oh: resting beneath my thumbnail, pausing, wondering how long she can make use of me, how long I will have sense enough to hold still.

She will never know or care how sorry I am that my lungs are not huge magnificent frozen snows, and that my fingers are not firmly rooted in earth like the tall cypresses. But I have been holding my breath now for one minute and sixteen seconds. I wish I could tower beside her forever, and be one mountain she can depend upon. But my lungs have their own cities to build. I have to move, or die.

In Memory of the Ottomans

This man, mending his nets as the sun goes down, tells me religiously something I find dark: fog in the countryside of Otranto is unknown. As the starfish in the evening condense deep in the water, the light does not know what to do with itself. So the brown ridges down one side of the man's face turn green as spring rocks. Fog is unknown in Otranto, offshore from Otranto, behind Otranto. I can't believe he has never gone there. He won't say anything more about it, land or sea. What language do the hawks' tongues cry in for prayer, in that wilderness where the sea loses its way? I find this man dark. We both peer toward Greece, toward the horizon. The moon sways like a blunted scimitar.

Time

Once, with a weak ankle, I tried to walk. All I could do was spin slowly a step or two, and then sit down. There has to be some balance of things that move on the earth. But this morning a small tern is flying full of his strength over the Ionian Sea. From where I stand, he seems to have only one wing. There is either something wrong with my eyes in the sunlight or something unknown to me about the shadow that hangs broken from his left shoulder. But the shadow is no good to me now. He has dropped it into the sea. There has to be some balance of things that move on the earth. But he is not moving on the earth. Both of my ankles are strong. My hair is gray.

Taranto

Most of the walls
In what the Italians call
The old city
Are stained with suffering.

The dull yellow scars
Of whooping cough and catarrh
Hang trembling in the sea air, filaments
In an old man's lung.

American and German
Machine-gun bullets

Still pit the solitary hollows
Of shrines and arches.

To talk through is to become
Blood in a young man's lung,
Still living, still wondering
What in hell is going on.

But long before the city grew old, long
Before the Saracens fluttered like ospreys
Over the waters and sang
The ruin song,

Pythagoras walked here leisurely
Among the illegal generation
From Sparta, and Praxiteles
Left an astonished girl's face on a hillside

Where no hills were,
But the sea's.

A Mouse Taking a Nap

I look all alike to him, one blur of nervous mountains after an-
other. I doubt if he loses any sleep in brooding and puzzling out
why it is I don't like him. The huge slopes and valleys, golden as
wild mustard flowers in midsummer, that he leaves lying open and
naked down the sides of a Gorgonzola, seem to him only a discovery,
one of the lonely paradises: nothing like the gray wound of a slag
heap, nothing like the streams of copperous water that ooze out of
the mine-mouths in southern Ohio. I wonder what it seems to him,
his moment that he has now, alone with his own sunlight in this
locked house, where all the cats are gone for a little while, hunting
somebody else for a little while.

Jerome in Solitude

To see the lizard there,
I was amazed I did not have to beat
My breast with a stone.

If a lion lounged nearby,
He must have curled in a shadow of cypress,
For nobody shook a snarled mane and stretched out
To lie at my feet.

And, for a moment,
I did not see Christ retching in pain, longing
To clutch his cold abdomen,
Sagging, unable to rise or fall, the human
Flesh torn between air and air.

I was not even
Praying, unless: no,
I was not praying.

A rust branch fell suddenly
Down from a dead cypress
And blazed gold. I leaned close.
The deep place in the lizard's eye
Looked back into me.

Delicate green sheaths
Folded into one another.
The lizard was alive,
Happy to move.

But he did not move.
Neither did I.
I did not dare to.

At the End of Sirmione

Conventional melancholy leaves me
Cold in this rain.
Across the lake water
The towns are not going to die.

They are folding, opening,
And folding in the mist.
Like a blind man, trusting
His garden, I can name them:

Bardolino thin on the longest shore.
Garda with two plateaus.
San Vigilio alone and half under water.
Maderno where travelers get drunk on lake water.

And Gargnano, Gargnano,
Where D. H. Lawrence and his donkey
Got lost on the mountain
On their way to church.

And Sirmione, here, the lizard of cisterns, turning
Silver as olive in the underside of rain
That leaves me alone on the cliff's grotto, anything
But cold.

Venice

Crumbling into this world,
Into this world's sea, the green
Sea city decays.
The cats of the early evening,
Scrawny and sly,
Gloat among lengthening shadows of lions,
As the great Palladian wings lean toward the water and slowly
Fall and fall.
The city of shifting slime ought not to be
In this world.

It ought to drift only
In the mind of someone so desperately
Sick of this world,
That he dreams of himself walking
Under crystal trees,
Feeding the glass
Swans there, swans born
Not in the fragile calcium spun among feathers
But out of the horrifying fire that
A sullen laborer spins
In his frigid hands, just barely, just just barely not wringing
The swan's neck.

Between Wars

Flocks of green midges and the frail
Skeletons of mosquitoes hang
Hidden and calm beside some wall.
No matter why the swallows sang,
Last evening, and no matter now
Why they cavort, flutter, and soar.
They are not hungry anyhow.
There are no insects any more.

Far down the hill the Tuscan hawks
Fly wide awake. They surely see
Swallows scattering above blind rocks,
Daring the dreadful risk of joy.
A little while, the hawks will come
And shatter two or three or four,
The rest die where they started from.
There are no swallows any more:

Only a hundred fluttering by,
A million midges green and gone,
Two hawks amazing the blind sky,
And earth leaving itself alone.

Among Sunflowers

You can stand in among them without
Being afraid.
Many of these faces
Look friendly enough,
Small ones will lean their damp golden foreheads
Against your body.
You can even lift your hands
And take some faces between them,
And draw them down
Near your own,
Gently.
Here,
And there,
A tall one, the stalk brittle and scarred,
Offers a haggard and defeated glance
With what would be good will in an old man,
And a shrug of forgiveness. There are old women
Among them who had no hope, dead,
Sprawled weightless in root-troughs.
So I can blame the faces for looking
Alike as they turn
Helplessly toward noon.
Any creature would be a fool to take the sun lightly,
The indifferent god of brief life, the
Small mercy.

In a Field near Metaponto

The huge columns, the temple of Apollo,
Have blown over in the nights.
I am tempted to say
It doesn't matter. The frightened men who crept forward
And cowered here, and turned back, are dead,
Of no account now.
But now
A great block of cloud falls over
In an instant, the sun

Lashes its flames on the sea's shivering spine
And glares straight down among the glittering hordes
Of poppies where I stand. They can do nothing.
They lean upward and lay
The secrets of their bodies bare to this light,
Till they die. I lean down,
Pluck one poppy, tuck it
Beside my ear like a Greek and stare for an instant
And then turn away.

Camomilla

Summer is not yet gone, but long ago the leaves have fallen. They never appeared to gather much sunlight or threw a measurable shade, even when they were most alive. They hid as long as they could beneath the white flowers and seemed to turn their faces away. They were like the faces of frightened people in a war. They silently wish they were anonymous, but they know that sooner or later someone will find them out. Everything secret to them will become commonplace to an army of invading strangers. Every stranger will know that each native of the defeated place was given at his birth, like a burden, the names of both his parents and his grandparents and great-grandparents, until there is scarcely enough room on a police form for all the names he carries around with him. Just like such brutally ransacked people, the camomilla leaves turn their faces away. If I could look toward them long enough in this field, I think I would find them trying to hide their birthmarks and scars from me, pretending they had no beards or ribbons or long braids of half-legible letters from home hidden uselessly beneath their clothes. The faces of camomilla leaves would wish me away again, wish me back into the sea again, wish me to leave them alone in peace.

Yes, But

Even if it were true,
Even if I were dead and buried in Verona,

I believe I would come out and wash my face
In the chill spring.
I believe I would appear
Between noon and four, when nearly
Everybody else is asleep or making love,
And all the Germans turned down, the motorcycles
Muffled, chained, still.

Then the plump lizards along the Adige by San Giorgio
Come out and gaze,
Unpestered by temptation, across the water.
I would sit among them and join them in leaving
The golden mosquitoes alone.
Why should we sit by the Adige and destroy
Anything, even our enemies, even the prey
God caused to glitter for us
Defenseless in the sun?
We are not exhausted. We are not angry, or lonely,
Or sick at heart.
We are in love lightly, lightly. We know we are shining,
Though we cannot see one another.
The wind doesn't scatter us,
Because our very lungs have fallen and drifted
Away like leaves down the Adige,
Long ago.

We breathe light.

To the Adriatic Wind, Becalmed

Come on.
Shift your wings a little.
You have plenty of strength left in your shoulders,
Your hawk mouth that does not care,
Your pure beak glittering like a scimitar
Proud of moonlight.
Come back to Venice.
Come back.
It's no skin off you.

The city is sagging.
One mere whir of one of your minor plumes
Could blow it down,
All the way into the water
Where the towers belong.
Already the golden horses of San Marco
Have stepped carefully down in the darkness,
Placed their frail ankles one after another
Over the damp cobbles, whickering lightly,
And gone. Come on.

There is no saving the horses now, they are lost
Inland somewhere, stumbling and shying
In the strange grass.
Now, in fresh dawn,
The opening morning glory of the sea,
Now is the time
To do beloved Venice a kindness.
Come, blow it the rest of the way.
Come on.

Snowfall: A Poem about Spring

The field mouse follows its own shadow
Up out of the twelve-inch fall
From a thin surface on one side of the path
Into a dark laurel some
Five feet away.

I take my little walk
Five feet beyond you and, all alone,
I follow the field mouse.
He and I track
The skeleton of an acorn, over
To the other side of the path.

He and I
Are gone a little,
But you

Somehow go over there at the other end of the snow tunnel,
    your throat

Bundled with laurel.

Ah, we breathe, we two,
We are not afraid of you, we will come out

And gather with you.

Honey

My father died at the age of eighty. One of the last things he did
in his life was to call his fifty-eight-year-old son-in-law "honey." One
afternoon in the early 1930's, when I bloodied my head by pitching
over a wall at the bottom of a hill and believed that the mere sight
of my own blood was the tragic meaning of life, I heard my father
offer to murder his future son-in-law. His son-in-law is my brother-
in-law, whose name is Paul. These two grown men rose above me
and knew that a human life is murder. They weren't fighting about
Paul's love for my sister. They were fighting with each other because
one strong man, a factory worker, was laid off from his work, and
the other strong man, the driver of a coal truck, was laid off from
his work. They were both determined to live their lives, and so they
glared at each other and said they were going to live, come hell or
high water. High water is not trite in southern Ohio. Nothing is trite
along a river. My father died a good death. To die a good death
means to live one's life. I don't say a good life.
    I say a life.

With the Gift of a Fresh New Notebook
I Found in Florence

On the other side of the bridge,
Over the Arno,
Across the Ponte Vecchio, across
The street from the Pitti Palace, below the garden,

Under the shadow of the fortress,
I found this book,
This secret field of the city down over the hill
From Fiesole.

Nobody yet has walked across and sat down
At the edge under a pear tree
To savor the air of the natural blossoms and leave them
Alone, and leave the heavy place alone.

The pages have a light spirit
That will rise into blossom and harvest only
After your hand touches them.
Then the book will grow
Lighter and lighter as the seasons pass.
But, so far, this field is only
A secret of snow.

Now this slender field lies only a little uphill
From the river, and the pale water
Seems to be turning everything
It mirrors into snow.
It is that snow before anyone
Has walked across it
Slowly as children walk on their way to school
In the glittering Ohio morning,
Or quickly as the breathless
Ermine scamper upward through the light crust
In one indeterminate spot and then stitch
A threadwork across the whiteness and suddenly
Vanish as though blown like flakes back upward.

Red and white flowers lie quietly all around
The edges of the field,
And it doesn't matter that they don't grow there now.
For one time they grew there
Long enough to make the air
Vivid when they vanished.

I suppose I could imagine
The trees that haven't yet grown here.
But I would rather leave them to find their way

Alone, like seedlings lost in a cloud of snowflakes.
I would rather leave them alone, even
In my imagination, or, better still,
Leave them to you.

Leaving the Temple in Nîmes

And, sure enough,
I came face to face with the spring.
Down in the wet darkness of the winter moss
Still gathering in the Temple of Diana,
I came to the trunk of a huge umbrella pine
Vivid and ancient as always,
Among the shaped stones.
I couldn't see the top of the branches,
I stood down there in the pathway so deep.
But a vine held its living leaves all the way down
To my hands. So I carry away with me
Four ivy leaves:

In gratitude to the tall pale girl
Who still walks somewhere behind the pine tree,
Slender as her hounds.
In honor of the solitary poet,
Ausonius, adorer of the southern hillsides
Who drank of the sacred spring
Before he entered this very holy place
And slowly tuned the passionate silver
Of his Latin along the waters.

And I will send one ivy leaf, green in winter,
Home to an American girl I know.
I caught a glimpse of her once in a dream,
Shaking out her dark and adventurous hair.
She revealed only a little of her face
Through the armful of pussy willow she gathered
Alive in spring,
Alive along the Schuylkill in Philadelphia.

She will carry this ivy leaf from Diana's pine
As she looks toward Camden, across the river,
Where Walt Whitman, the chaste wanderer
Among the live-oaks, the rain, railyards and battlefields,
Lifts up his lovely face
To the moon and allows it to become
A friendly ruin.
The innocent huntress will come down after dark,
Brush the train smoke aside, and leave alone together
The old man rooted in an ugly place
Pure with his lovingkindness,
And a girl with an ivy leaf revealing her face
Among fallen pussy willow.

A Winter Daybreak above Vence

The night's drifts
Pile up below me and behind my back,
Slide down the hill, rise again, and build
Eerie little dunes on the roof of the house.
In the valley below me,
Miles between me and the town of St.-Jeannet,
The road lamps glow.
They are so cold, they might as well be dark.
Trucks and cars
Cough and drone down there between the golden
Coffins of greenhouses, the startled squawk
Of a rooster claws heavily across
A grove, and drowns.
The gumming snarl of some grouchy dog sounds,
And a man bitterly shifts his broken gears.
True night still hangs on,
Mist cluttered with a racket of its own.

Now on the mountainside,
A little way downhill among turning rocks,
A square takes form in the side of a dim wall.
I hear a bucket rattle or something, tinny,
No other stirring behind the dim face

Of the goatherd's house. I imagine
His goats are still sleeping, dreaming
Of the fresh roses
Beyond the walls of the greenhouse below them
And of lettuce leaves opening in Tunisia.

I turn, and somehow
Impossibly hovering in the air over everything,
The Mediterranean, nearer to the moon
Than this mountain is,
Shines. A voice clearly
Tells me to snap out of it. Galway
Mutters out of the house and up the stone stairs
To start the motor. The moon and the stars
Suddenly flicker out, and the whole mountain
Appears, pale as a shell.

Look, the sea has not fallen and broken
Our heads. How can I feel so warm
Here in the dead center of January? I can
Scarcely believe it, and yet I have to, this is
The only life I have. I get up from the stone.
My body mumbles something unseemly
And follows me. Now we are all sitting here strangely
On top of the sunlight.

Index of Titles

Index of First Lines